DITCH & SWITCH!

50 Value-Based Pricing Examples for Law Professionals

Shaun Jardine

BENNION
KEARNY

First published in 2025 by Bennion Kearny Ltd
Woodside, Oakamoor, ST10 3AE, UK
www.BennionKearny.com
ISBN: 978-1-915855-42-8

Cover design by Hannah Powell.

ABOUT THE AUTHOR

Shaun Jardine is the UK's leading champion of Value-Based Pricing in the legal sector and author of the game-changing "Ditch the Billable Hour!" - the book that's revolutionizing how law firms think about pricing.

A former practicing lawyer, Shaun now leads Big Yellow Penguin Ltd, as he continues his mission to liberate law firms from billable hour tyranny, consulting on pricing innovation and strategic change that delivers genuine competitive advantage.

This book is dedicated to Team Jardine.

ACKNOWLEDGEMENTS

Writing a second book has been less stressful than the first time, and exhilarating in equal measure, and I am grateful to many people who have made this possible.

To Ron Baker, who very kindly agreed to write the foreword for this book. It was after meeting Ron in the USA in 2017 that I caught the bug for value-based pricing. Little did I know then that it would become a calling!

To the "Wise" people who feature in Part 3 of the book, and who gave up their time to contribute their thoughts on the future of pricing. Thank you all.

To John Hocker of E Learning Group, whose technical skill and patience helped bring the Value Voyage™ platform to life. Your ability to transform my sometimes-chaotic vision into user-friendly technology has been nothing short of remarkable. The lawyers now benefiting from Value Voyage owe you an enormous debt of gratitude.

To Andy Vernon and Suj Legha of CommCoreAI - quite literally the brains behind Declan AI. When they first suggested creating an AI-powered penguin to help lawyers with value-based pricing, I didn't question their sanity (at least not out loud!). CommCoreAI's technical expertise and creative problem-solving have brought Declan to life in ways I never imagined possible. You've made legal technology both intelligent and entertaining - no mean feat!

To James Lumsden Cook of Bennion Kearny, who took yet another punt on a second book from this penguin-obsessed lawyer. Your faith in my work and your publishing expertise continue to astound me. Thank you for believing that the legal world needs more disruption, even when it comes packaged in penguin suits.

To all those inquisitive lawyers who have attended training events, asked challenging questions, and pushed back when necessary. Your intellectual curiosity and willingness to explore new approaches have sharpened my thinking and improved my teaching. You've made me a better consultant and, dare I say, a better penguin.

To the podcast hosts who invited me onto their shows, often with no idea what they were letting themselves in for. Your platforms have allowed these ideas to reach lawyers across the globe, and your thoughtful questions have helped refine the message along the way.

To the conference organizers who have invited me to speak at their events - sometimes even after discovering I occasionally dress as a penguin. Your courage in booking unconventional speakers helps keep our profession vibrant and forward-thinking.

And finally, to everyone who purchased "Ditch the Billable Hour!" - including that particular USA-based lawyer who bought a second-hand copy that appeared to have been stolen from a library. You know who you are, and whilst I question your acquisition methods, I deeply appreciate your commitment to learning about value-based pricing!

Your collective support, wisdom, and occasional madness have made this work possible.

Thank you all.

Foreword By Ron Baker

It was the legal profession that first adopted hourly billing and time tracking in 1919. Over a century later, we are still shackled to the clock. Has the world changed since then? Only in every conceivable way. Yet this profession clings to a business model conceived in the horse-and-buggy era, as if time were the true measure of value. The billable hour is dead – we simply haven't held the funeral yet.

This is no small matter of "efficiency" or "alternatives." A business model is never neutral; it reveals what you revere. And the legal profession must ask itself: do we really revere billable hours over guiding clients toward justice, peace of mind, and a better future? If so, we have consecrated the very conditions of moral injury. Burnout is the wrong diagnosis. The wound goes deeper: it is a betrayal of what it means to be a professional.

AI now exposes the absurdity for all to see. When a machine can do in seconds what once took hours, billing by the hour becomes not only obsolete but obscene. Those who cling to it will find themselves in a race to the bottom: faster machines, fewer hours, shrinking relevance. But those who embrace AI as a lever for transformation will be liberated. AI is not a threat to value-based pricing; it is its greatest ally, unleashing human capacity for wisdom, counsel, and creativity – the things only professionals can profess.

Here is the deeper truth: products and services say, *"Look what we can do."* Transformations reveal, *"Look at who you can become."* Fee-for-service models can only sell outputs; they are blind to outcomes. They commodify expertise instead of magnifying impact. Lawyers need to learn how to calculate prices for their services which are not based on time but value and – importantly – give clients choice. *Ditch & Switch* seeks to dispel myths that choices cannot be created by lawyers, and Shaun ably demonstrates how different price points and service levels can be generated. Value-based pricing is a business model that is fit for the AI age.

Law is not about transactions. A will is not a document; it is peace of mind for a family. A merger is not paperwork; it is the birth of a new enterprise. A defense is not hours in court; it is the preservation of reputation, livelihood, or even life. These are transformations – and transformations cannot be priced by the hour. They must be priced by value, and stewarded by courage.

The next two to three years will test the mettle of the profession. Will lawyers tinker around the edges with hourly billing "alternatives" or will they embrace models that align with what they profess to stand for?

Lawyers need to move to a model which embraces loyalty over leverage, long-term guidance over short-term gain, transformations over transactions.

Value-based pricing, giving clients price certainty and a choice of service levels and options, is not radical. But, sadly, many professionals (and not just lawyers) believe it is.

The choice is stark. Remain a guild that reveres the clock, or rise as a calling that reveres the client. One path leads to moral injury and irrelevance. The other, to moral courage and reinvention. The billable hour is already a relic. The only question is whether we will bury it – and step boldly into the future of the Transformation Economy.

Ronald J. Baker is a recovering CPA (Inactive) by education, a writer by conviction, and a reformer by necessity. Author of eight books – among them *Implementing Value Pricing* and *Time's Up!* – he co-founded **THRESHOLD** and co-hosts the podcast, *The Soul of Enterprise: Business in the Transformation Economy.* Named in *Accounting Today's* Top 100 and Top 10 Most Influential People lists, inducted into the CPA Practice Advisor Hall of Fame, and a faculty member of the Professional Pricing Society, Ron calls the professions to profess again: not hours, but meaning; not transactions, but transformations; not survival, but human flourishing.

Contents

PART 1: WHY ARE YOU READING THIS BOOK?

In 2023, I wrote my 400-page magnum opus (my description, certainly!) – *Ditch The Billable Hour!*

*Ditch the Billable Hou*r! offers a clear, no-nonsense guide to transforming how lawyers think about pricing. It challenges the outdated reliance on time-based billing and provides a practical roadmap for implementing Value-Based Pricing (VBP) in law firms of all sizes – particularly those outside the global Top 50.

Most clients hate paying by the hour. They want certainty, transparency, and value – not six-minute units. Meanwhile, most law firms continue using the billable hour because "It's how we've always done it." *Ditch The Billable Hour!* shows why that mindset is not just outdated, it's costing firms money, talent, and client trust.

I argue that legal services are not commodities and shouldn't be priced like ones. Instead, lawyers should be paid, based on the **value they create**, not the time it takes to deliver.

I define value-based pricing simply: "A price that is fair to both the client and the law firm." In my case, as a lawyer, it's not the 6-minute unit that clients are paying for, it's 6 minutes plus 36 years of experience.

Ditch The Billable Hour! worked to a comprehensive "8P Point Plan" for companies and lawyers embracing VBP and provided a top-to-toe exploration of VBP and how to implement it across organizations of all sizes, and all the people in said organizations. Indeed, the people are key. The book assigns different titles and roles to members of a firm looking to implement VBP. (At the end of Part 1, you'll see an example of a Pioneer Penguin, who is someone who is part of a pilot group that will support, deliver, and champion the change that needs to happen in a firm. They are key influencers and proactive members of staff who can help you plan and execute change.)

SO WHY DID I WRITE THIS BOOK?

Let's be brutally honest: not every busy legal professional has the luxury of sitting down with a 400-page book, absorbing all its QR code-linked resources, and then finding additional time to truly think – really think – about how those learnings apply to their specific business. Let alone actually creating the tools required to implement change.

Sometimes, you just want to see something in action, to get a feel for how it really works before going deeper into the process.

That's precisely why *Ditch and Switch* came into being.

So, here you are, reading this deliberately shorter, more focused book, packed with practical examples: what questions to ask, what value gets created, and how to present compelling service options to clients.

Ditch the Billable Hour! and *Ditch & Switch* go hand in hand.

VALUE-BASED PRICING: WHY NOW?

The legal landscape has shifted dramatically, and here's why VBP isn't just nice to have – it's essential:

- Technology, particularly GenAI, has revolutionized the game. Clients now have access to AI tools that can draft contracts, review documents, and provide legal guidance in seconds.

- Starting a law firm has never been easier. Disruptors are entering the market daily, unencumbered by traditional billing practices.

- Relentless pressure on fees from increasingly sophisticated clients.

- Mounting pressure on operational costs whilst maintaining service quality.

- The battle for top talent is fiercer than ever.

- Clients simply don't believe the billable hour delivers good value for their investment.

- Geography no longer matters. Clients can instruct lawyers anywhere, and agile working has permanently changed how legal services are delivered.

Meanwhile, many legal professionals continue making costly assumptions:

- We don't know how to charge, based on value.

- Our clients know exactly what our competitors charge.

- Our competitors' pricing reflects what clients actually want to pay.

- Our clients regularly undertake detailed price comparisons.

- Our clients won't pay premium rates.

WHAT DO CLIENTS ACTUALLY WANT WHEN BUYING LEGAL SERVICES?

Countless studies have explored this question, and the answer is remarkably consistent. Clients want:

- Lawyers who truly understand their situation.

- Tangible results.

- Pricing certainty.

- Complete transparency.

- Zero nasty surprises.

- Ready availability when needed.

- That crucial 'got my back' reassurance.

- Crystal-clear communication.

- Peace of mind.

- No hidden extras.

- Value for money.

WHAT IS VALUE?

Here's where things become fascinating.

1. Value Is Entirely Subjective

People define value based on personal preferences, needs, and experiences. What one person treasures, another dismisses entirely. Lawyers must grasp that value is determined by the client's perception, never by the lawyer's effort or time invested.

If you watch BBC television's "The Repair Shop" (where experts repair/renew/refurbish personally meaningful items for the general public) you'll see guests become emotional over what appears to be worthless old tat. Why? Because they love it, and we don't. It's the same with "Antiques Roadshow"... families clutch some old jewelry claiming they'll "treasure it forever" while you're shouting at the screen, "Bet they sell that at the next auction!" (Or is that just me?)

Our feelings about value can differ completely.

2. Value Isn't Rational

Because we're all different, what seems rational varies enormously. Buyers often behave irrationally – choosing brands, paying premiums, or sticking with familiar products for emotional or habitual reasons. Whether it's my mate Dave spending £23,000 servicing his McLaren, or people queuing at midnight for the latest iPhone, people pay for convenience, trust, and emotional connection – not just utility.

3. Value Is Contextual

The same product can have vastly different values depending on the setting. Water costs pennies at home but pounds in a restaurant – or hundreds during a crisis. Context changes everything. Legal services are identical: urgency, timing, and circumstances dramatically affect perceived value.

4. Value Is A Feeling

Look again at those "Repair Shop" clients. Clients often equate value with how your service makes them feel – safe, empowered, heard, respected.

I often mention the emotional attachment I have to a cheap watch my late father gave me. It's worth virtually nothing. But to me, it's incredibly valuable.

We know people willingly pay more when they believe they're contributing to a good cause – Fairtrade bananas, for instance. We feel we're helping someone in a distant land.

Lawyers must learn to recognize these emotional drivers when advising and pricing. As humans, these drivers affect our buying decisions daily. Let's acknowledge that our clients experience the same when buying from us.

5. Value Is In The Outcome, Not The Input

Clients don't care how long something takes; they care about the result. A lawyer who solves a complex problem in 20 minutes using expertise and precedent creates significant value, far beyond the actual time spent.

6. Value Requires Empathy And Enquiry

Most lawyers assume clients only care about cost. They're wrong. Clients care about trust, certainty, outcomes, and reassurance. These are fundamentally emotional needs that must be acknowledged and addressed.

To uncover real value, lawyers must learn to ask better questions, listen empathetically, and genuinely understand client motivations. Unfortunately, many lawyers feel they're too busy to invest time in this crucial area, often thinking, "We must just get on with the work."

This mindset is precisely what's holding the profession back.

THE KEY BENEFITS OF EMBRACING VALUE-BASED PRICING

Let's be crystal clear about why you should choose to embrace VBP.

1. Client-Centric Value Delivery

VBP aligns pricing with client outcomes, not internal costs or time spent, because clients want results, not invoices itemizing every six-minute increment. This approach builds stronger, more transparent relationships by focusing on what the client actually values most. It eliminates billing surprises entirely as clients know exactly what they're getting and what it will cost from the outset.

2. Increased Profitability

Firms can capture genuine value for the results they deliver, not just the hours they've logged, which stops the destructive "discount by default" mindset that steadily erodes margins. This allows pricing to reflect expertise, speed, workload pressures, and client urgency rather than arbitrary inputs that bear no relation to the actual value created.

3. Better Cash Flow And Financial Predictability

VBP shifts firms towards upfront pricing and payment models, dramatically improving cash flow whilst enabling clients to budget legal spend confidently with fixed or option-based pricing. This approach significantly reduces write-offs and billing disputes, creating a win-win scenario for both firm and client.

4. Competitive Differentiation

Value-based pricing sets your firm apart from competitors still clinging to outdated hourly models and demonstrates innovation, empathy, and a modern understanding of client needs. This transforms pricing from a necessary evil into a strategic advantage that clients actively seek out.

5. Higher Client Satisfaction And Loyalty

Clients appreciate clarity, certainty, and control over their pricing choices, and positive pricing experiences increase trust and lead to more referrals and repeat business. This approach creates advocates rather than merely satisfied customers, turning your pricing strategy into your most powerful marketing tool.

6. Enhanced Team Morale And Efficiency

VBP removes the soul-crushing pressure to "churn hours" or justify time sheets, shifting focus to genuine problem-solving and client service rather than clock-watching. Lawyers feel significantly more confident discussing fees when they're based on value rather than time, creating a more positive and productive working environment.

7. Strategic Business Alignment

This approach forces firms to properly define their pricing strategy, pricing policies, value proposition, and client experience whilst encouraging clearer scoping, thoughtful service design, and process efficiency. It supports better client segmentation and gives firms the courage to deselect low-value work that drains resources.

8. Creates A Culture Of Learning And Improvement

VBP encourages firms to capture valuable lessons learned from both pricing successes and failures, promoting better internal communication about how value is actually created and delivered. This supports the development of essential pricing tools like Big Books of Usefulness (BBU) that become invaluable institutional knowledge assets.

THE COMMON PITFALLS OF VALUE-BASED PRICING

1. Lack Of Confidence In Pricing Conversations

Lawyers often lack the confidence to discuss value or quote fixed fees, and this fear of rejection leads to chronic under-pricing or defaulting to familiar hourly rates. Without genuine confidence, the firm inevitably reverts to time-based thinking, and VBP becomes nothing more than hollow marketing speak that fools no one.

2. Failure To Discuss (Let Alone Define) Value With The Client

If you don't ask the client what success looks like, you simply cannot price for value, and making assumptions leads to misaligned expectations and inevitable dissatisfaction. Firms must develop essential skills and create value-based questions which lead to meaningful value-based conversations. Crucially, these questions should be documented in your Big Book of Usefulness (BBU) so they become part of your standard practice rather than left to chance.

3. Pricing Based On Time In Drag

Many firms create "fixed fees" based on estimated hours multiplied by hourly rate, but this is not true VBP – it's merely a repackaged time model, prone to exactly the same problems. This approach restricts profitability and completely misses the point that value lies in the outcome, not the input.

4. Inconsistency And Lack Of Policy

Without a documented pricing policy or process, lawyers price ad hoc and simply do what they've always done. At one firm, I asked 15 lawyers in the same department to price the same residential property sale scenario without consulting each other, and I received 13 different prices! Inconsistent pricing confuses clients and fundamentally undermines trust, which is why firms must build repeatable systems and tools, including Fixed Price Agreement templates, BBU books, and structured processes.

5. Discounting Without Strategy

Discounts on quoted prices are often applied too early or unnecessarily, and crucially, when a discount is offered, the service level isn't reduced, leaving clients feeling the higher initial price was an attempt to rip them off. Giving discounts freely trains clients to expect lower prices as standard, and most lawyers can't even calculate the impact of a discount on profit.

6. Insufficient Training Or Buy-In

VBP fails spectacularly when it's seen as "just another initiative". Without genuine management buy-in and comprehensive training across the firm, it simply won't stick.

Lawyers need proper education, training, and then the opportunity to practice what they've learned. Without essential tools, like a Big Book of Usefulness, valuable learnings are lost and costly mistakes get repeated endlessly.

Pricing must become embedded in your firm's culture – not treated as a one-time project that gets forgotten after the initial enthusiasm wanes.

7. Fear Of Losing The Work

Lawyers often worry that quoting a value-based fee will frighten off potential clients. But trying to please everyone leads to undervalued, overworked practices that satisfy nobody.

VBP requires client deselection and the genuine courage to walk away from bad-fit work. Sometimes the bravest thing you can do is say "no."

8. Misunderstanding What VBP Actually Is

Some lawyers think VBP is simply charging more or plucking a number out of thin air. Others believe it's unethical to charge different clients different prices for similar work.

Let's face facts: all clients are different. Their problems are different. The resources required to solve their problems will be different. The way they engage with their lawyers will be different. Their urgency levels, risk tolerance, and desired outcomes vary enormously.

VBP isn't about arbitrary pricing, it's about intelligently aligning your price with client-defined value. That's the difference between pricing strategically and pricing desperately.

WHY OPTIONS ARE ESSENTIAL

In Part 2 of this book, you will see a variety of templates which aim to give clients options and a choice of service levels.

Offering clients pricing options isn't just a smart strategy; it's absolutely essential to delivering value-based pricing effectively. Here's why:

1. Clients Want Choice, Not Dictation

Clients don't want to be told, "This is the price – take it or leave it." That's essentially a 50/50 gamble.

Presenting options empowers clients to decide what they want to pay, and it removes sales pressure. If you give a client three options plus a fourth "don't buy" option, you have a 75% chance of making a sale.

It shifts the mindset from "Do I want to work with this lawyer?" to "How do I want to work with this lawyer?"

2. Options Demonstrate Flexibility And Value

By offering a range of prices with corresponding benefits, clients can align their choice with their budget, risk appetite, and desired outcomes.

It reinforces transparency and signals that the lawyer understands different clients have different needs.

3. Options Increase Uptake And Spending

This "Good, Better, Best" or "Gold, Silver, Bronze" model improves conversion rates and average transaction value.

By creating a gold option, your clients become aware of the extra services you and your colleagues can offer. *They don't know what these are until you tell them!*

Clients see the value in higher tiers when they compare them side-by-side.

4. Options Encourage Better Conversations

Options open the door to meaningful value discussions.

Instead of debating hourly rates or vague estimates, you can talk about outcomes, scope, and service guarantees.

5. Options Clarify What Is (And Isn't) Included

They make scope creep far less likely. Each option clearly defines what the client gets, reducing ambiguity and disputes.

If a client wants to move up a level, that's fine. As long as you charge them appropriately for doing so.

6. Options Build Trust

Clients feel in control, because they are actually in control. You've given them genuine choice. They appreciate being treated like informed buyers, not passive recipients of an unquantified, open-ended billable hour nightmare.

I often ask lawyers I train how many of them would engage a builder and all subcontractors to build an extension to their home and agree to pay all the trades on a day work basis. Not one lawyer has said they would do that, yet. Why? Because we want price certainty. Our clients are no different.

7. Options Are Professional

They show that the firm is prepared, client-focused, and commercially aware. They demonstrate that we're genuine experts. Isn't it odd that many law firms profess to be experts in areas of law, yet – despite their expertise – they cannot price what they do?

Templates and structured models make options easier to present and replicate consistently across the business.

WHY CONFIDENCE IS CRUCIAL IN VALUE-BASED PRICING

If you've been paying attention, you'll have noticed I keep banging on about confidence. Why? Because it's absolutely fundamental to your success.

Confidence is the often-overlooked cornerstone of successful value-based pricing. Here's the uncomfortable truth: no matter how well-trained a lawyer is in pricing theory, without the genuine self-assurance to hold pricing conversations, communicate value effectively, create options they're prepared to defend, and resist the urge to discount at the first hint of resistance, the entire implementation will fail spectacularly.

Think about it this way: if you don't believe you're worth the price you're quoting, why on earth would your client?

Confidence manifests in several crucial ways:

- The ability to present options without apologizing or immediately offering discounts.

- Standing firm when clients push back on pricing (and they will).

- Having meaningful conversations about value rather than rushing to justify costs.

- Walking away from clients who don't value what you offer.

- Believing that your expertise, speed, and results justify premium pricing.

Without confidence, lawyers default to what feels "safe" – hourly billing, discounting, and competing on price rather than value. They become order-takers rather than trusted advisors.

The irony? Clients actually prefer confident lawyers. They want someone who knows their worth and who can guide them with authority. A lawyer who fumbles through pricing conversations or immediately drops their fees signals uncertainty about their own capabilities.

Building pricing confidence takes time, practice, and – yes – sometimes a few bruised egos along the way. But it's non-negotiable if you want VBP to work.

Lack Of Confidence Leads To Discounting

When lawyers lack confidence in their pricing or their own value, discounting becomes their default escape route. This is especially true in competitive situations, when lawyers panic about losing work. That treacherous internal voice whispers: "Maybe this is too expensive," or "What if they say no?"

Your thinking time, your expertise, your ability to explore options and find solutions – that's precisely what clients are paying for. Stop giving it away because you lack the confidence to charge what you're worth.

The cruel irony? Clients often value the work you don't charge for more than the work you do.

Confidence Enables Value Conversations

Confident lawyers ask fundamentally better questions. They focus on uncovering the client's genuine definition of success and tailor pricing accordingly. They don't hide behind hourly rates or vague estimates – they talk outcomes, results, and value.

This is precisely why I preach that questions should be collated in your Practice Area Big Book of Usefulness. Capture the knowledge and share it across your team.

Confidence gives lawyers the courage to say, "Let's explore what success looks like to you," and then build pricing that genuinely reflects that vision. Without confidence, these crucial conversations simply don't happen. Lawyers retreat into transactional, time-based thinking – not because they want to, but because it feels safer.

Here's the reality check: if AI is going to take over routine legal work (and it absolutely will), what lawyers can charge premium fees for is our expertise, judgement, and ability to add genuine value. We have to start believing we can add that value and demonstrate it clearly to our clients.

The Client Feels Your Confidence (Or Lack Of It)

Clients are remarkably perceptive. If a lawyer is hesitant, fidgety, or unclear when discussing fees, the client will immediately sense that uncertainty. This creates doubt – not just about the price, but about the lawyer's competence and the entire service itself.

Conversely, a confident lawyer inspires trust. They signal that they know exactly what they're doing, they understand what the client needs, and they can deliver results.

Confidence Can Be Trained

Here's the encouraging news: pricing confidence isn't an innate trait – it's a skill that can be learned and developed. That's one of the reasons you've invested your hard-earned cash in this book!

Through role play, coaching, creating robust systems, and deliberate practice, lawyers can become genuinely comfortable with pricing conversations.

Don't get me wrong – I know lawyers are supremely confident when fighting their client's corner on the merits of a case. We're legal superheroes! But when it comes to asking for a fee for our work, we crumple like a cheap suit.

Even worse (and don't get me started), some lawyers – I'm looking at you, residential conveyancers – actually agree not to charge anything at all for work undertaken if a transaction goes abortive. That's not client service; that's commercial suicide.

Confidence Builds Sustainable Profitability

Ultimately, confident pricing creates a virtuous cycle that transforms your entire practice. It builds stronger client relationships because clients respect lawyers who know their worth and who can articulate their value clearly. No one wants to work with someone who seems uncertain about their own capabilities.

Higher margins naturally follow because confident lawyers don't race to the bottom on price. They understand that competing on price alone is a mug's game – there's always someone willing to work for less. Instead, they compete on value, expertise, and results.

Less stress becomes inevitable when you're not constantly worried about write-offs, fee disputes, or whether you've charged enough to cover your costs. When pricing is aligned with value rather than arbitrary time calculations, both lawyer and client know exactly what they're getting into.

But here's the real magic: confident pricing attracts better clients. The clients who argue about every penny, demand detailed time breakdowns, and treat you like a commodity? They disappear. Instead, you attract clients who value expertise, want results, and understand that quality costs more than mediocrity.

This isn't just about making more money (though that's rather nice), it's about creating a sustainable practice where you can focus on doing brilliant legal work instead of constantly justifying your existence through timesheets.

The lawyers who master confident pricing don't just survive – they thrive. They work with clients they actually enjoy, on matters that challenge them, for fees that reflect their true worth.

That's not just better business... that's a better life.

MY SURVEY FINDINGS

I've conducted *many* surveys of firms (more than 165 to date). I absolutely love doing them and then feeding back the results to a room full of partners or pioneer penguins. The surveys are always anonymous so staff can answer safely, knowing it won't be career-limiting to give honest feedback about how they feel about their firm's pricing.

The surveys have many common traits. These are the edited highlights – brace yourself for some uncomfortable truths!

Q: I am confident that the work we do helps and benefits our clients.

Always/Yes: ranges from 80-94%

> My Take: This is brilliant! Lawyers know they add value, they just can't price it properly. If you're 90% confident you help clients, why are you so terrible at charging for that help?

Q: Which of these are issues within your firm?

Work-life balance challenges: 63%

Risk of burnout for some individuals: 61%

Significant resources spent on time recording: 15%

Significant resources spent on chasing unpaid bills: 30%

Lack of confidence in negotiating fees at the outset of a matter: 40%

Lack of confidence when asking for an increased fee when a matter is progressing: 62%

> My Take: Houston, we have a problem! Two-thirds of lawyers struggle with work-life balance, yet 62% lack confidence asking for fee increases when work gets complex. You're working yourselves into the ground whilst undercharging. That's not noble – that's barmy!

Q: I believe my firm tends to reduce prices based on what our competitors may charge.

Not at all: 35%

To some extent: 44%

Always/Yes: 21%

> My Take: So, 65% of firms let competitors dictate their pricing? That's not strategy – that's surrendering control of your business to people you're supposedly competing against!

Q: My colleagues and I know how to confidently deal with price objections from clients when we receive them.

Not at all: 15%

To some extent: 65%

Always: 20%

> My Take: Only 20% can confidently handle price objections? No wonder lawyers discount so quickly! You can't win a game you don't know how to play.

Q: Would you be happy for someone else to price work initially at the outset, and then leave you to get on and deliver the service to the client?

Not at all: 37%

To some extent: 43%

Always: 20%

> My Take: This is fascinating, 63% would welcome help with pricing, yet most firms don't provide it. There's a massive opportunity here for centralized pricing expertise.

Q: What prevents your firm from charging more for your services?

'Nothing'

'The local market/competition'

'Quality of service for clients'

'Concern about profitability, losing clients/fear'

'Referrers' fee scales'

'The customers we service can ill afford higher fees'

'Management decisions'

'Clients will leave'

'We will be too expensive'

'They will think we are ripping them off'

> My Take: Look at all that fear! Most of these are assumptions, not facts. When did lawyers become mind-readers who know exactly what clients think about pricing? The real barrier isn't external – it's internal confidence.

Q: I believe that some of the clients my firm acts for should be dismissed as they are too painful and/or unprofitable to act for.

A: I have had a range of answers, here, between 50 and 100%

> My Take: Your own staff are telling you which clients to sack, yet most firms ignore this wisdom. If your team knows who the problem clients are, why are you still acting for them?

Q: What prevents your firm from deselecting clients?

A: Included 'Worry about our reputation', 'Inertia', and 'Partners'

> My Take: "Partners" preventing client deselection, now that's revealing! And "worry about reputation" – your reputation suffers more from keeping terrible clients than from professionally parting ways with them.

Q: When someone joins your team, how is pricing training undertaken?

A: The answers that come back are usually mixed:

'A Partner tells them what to do'

'They are told their hourly rate'

And the vast majority of people respond, 'It isn't'

> My Take: This is negligence! You wouldn't let someone practice law without legal training, yet you let them price services without pricing training. No wonder confidence is so low.

Q: How are your pricing policies currently documented?

A: Predominantly, the answers are 'They are not'

> My Take: So, you have detailed procedures for everything else, but wing it on the thing that determines your profitability? Brilliant strategy!

Q: How is pricing set and reviewed at your firm?

A: Answers are usually negative, with many respondents confirming 'I have no idea'

> My Take: "I have no idea" about pricing in a business where pricing determines survival? That's like saying "I have no idea" how we breathe.

Q: What currently stops you from setting fees based on value to the client?

Answers include: 'We don't know the value of our work to clients.'

'Partners are uncomfortable with it.'

'We don't have the skill sets.'

'Our IT systems don't allow us to do it.'

> My Take: Finally, some honest answers! These are all solvable problems, but only if you're willing to solve them. Most firms complain about these barriers instead of removing them.

How would your firm answer similar questions to these?

I have news for you; most firms answer the same way.

These survey results paint a clear picture: lawyers know they add value, they know they should charge more, they know which clients to sack, yet they lack the confidence, training, and systems to act on this knowledge. The gap between knowing and doing is where profitability goes to die!

AND FINALLY.... A PIONEER PENGUIN SUCCESS STORY

One of my most memorable success stories concerned a lawyer who attended her firm's first VBP pricing meeting with me. During that session, she heard her CEO clearly state that it was OK to price clients differently, that lawyers did not have to take on every bit of work because the firm needed more than their fair share of the good stuff, that all clients were not the same, and that it was perfectly acceptable to charge more for different service levels. The CEO also emphasized that if you're busy, it's absolutely OK to charge more.

This lawyer heard what the CEO said and immediately applied it. Later, that same week, she successfully increased her price for a piece of work by £2,000 – a whopping 45% increase – for a client that she believed was going to be difficult to act for and manage. She asked for more because she had loads of work on, and when taking initial instructions, the client demonstrated he was going to be demanding and problematic. The lawyer didn't want to do the work at the "normal price" they would have quoted, but now she was empowered to price it differently and, if necessary, turn the work away entirely.

The client accepted the increased price without question.

What level of lawyer do you think would be brave enough to take on board what she heard on day one of a training session and apply it? Would you be surprised to know she was a first-year legal apprentice? I was! So, if a colleague or partner in a law firm tells you this can't be done, tell them they are wrong. They are just lacking confidence.

PART 2 – THE SCENARIOS

Welcome to Part 2 of the book, which presents a series of private client and commercial legal scenarios structured into tiered service offerings.

IMPORTANT NOTE

These scenarios are entirely fictitious creations, designed to demonstrate the power of Value-Based Pricing thinking. Any resemblance to real people, businesses, or legal matters is purely coincidental.

You might not fancy all the suggestions or questions that have been crafted, and that's perfectly fine! Some may seem over the top, others might feel uncomfortable, and a few could make you squirm in your ergonomic office chair. That's rather the point!

Each situation starts with a SCENARIO, followed by tiers of service defined as GOLD, SILVER, and BRONZE with associated deliverables and outcomes. There are additional key headings, including assumptions, exclusions, technical deliverables, communication structure, follow-up services (so you can keep in touch), and assumptive closing questions you could use to ask for the business.

The real magic here is showing that options can be created from virtually nothing. Each scenario started with just a few lines of basic information, yet look what blossomed! Imagine the extraordinary value propositions you could craft with the full details of a real-life case, complete with all the nuances, client emotions, and specific circumstances that make each matter unique. All of the scenarios are just examples. I am not saying they will work in your jurisdiction where you practice law, or apply in every case. They are examples to get you thinking about what YOU could offer your clients. Many lawyers genuinely struggle to articulate the tremendous value they create through their work; that's precisely why I've laid it out so explicitly in these examples.

Possibility Thinking... here's your challenge: when tackling your next real case, gather your team and ask the transformational question: "What could we POSSIBLY include in a Gold service option?" Focus intensely on that word "POSSIBLY"; don't self-censor, don't worry about practicalities initially, just let the ideas flow. You'll be amazed at how creativity flourishes when you remove the mental barriers. Later, you can disregard the truly unworkable suggestions and focus your energy on developing the brilliant, viable options that will revolutionize how your clients see value.

Penguin logic... Remember, every Gold-standard service started as someone's "impossible" idea!

THE POWER OF SERVICE GUARANTEES - BACKING YOURSELF

Can I raise one more topic before you delve into the options? It's an area where many lawyers get their feathers ruffled unnecessarily! Service Guarantees!

Service Guarantees aren't about promising to win every case or guaranteeing specific outcomes. Instead, you're guaranteeing HOW you'll deliver your service, not WHAT the result will be. It's about backing yourself on the things you can absolutely control: your responsiveness, your communication, your professionalism, and your client care standards.

Think about it. You're already implicitly guaranteeing your service every time you take on a client! The difference is that most firms never explicitly state what clients can expect, leaving everyone in a frustrating guessing game. Service Guarantees transform vague promises into concrete commitments that clients can rely upon. When you guarantee a two-hour response to emergency calls or promise weekly progress reports, you're not being reckless, you're being professional and accountable.

"But what if we can't deliver?" I hear you say! Here's the beautiful truth: these guarantees force you to examine your systems and actually improve how you work. If you can't guarantee a 24-hour turnaround on critical documents, perhaps that reveals a workflow problem that needs fixing anyway! Start by having an honest team conversation about what you can genuinely "back yourself" to deliver. You'll be surprised how much you already do well that could become a powerful Service Guarantee.

The examples are endless and often industry-specific:

• Senior lawyer involvement guarantees for complex matters

• Daily progress reports during critical litigation phases

• Same-day responses to urgent property matters

- That you will notify clients in advance when you go on holiday

- That lawyers providing Gold-service level work will have smaller-than-average caseloads

- That you will ensure you avoid legalese when communicating with clients

- That you will take the time to ensure you fully understand the client's case

Some firms even offer service satisfaction guarantees where clients can adjust fees up or down based on service quality. Now, that takes some serious confidence!

Penguin logic… Start small, start somewhere. Challenge your team: "What would we be comfortable guaranteeing to every client?" You might discover you're already delivering Gold-standard service, you're just not telling anyone about it!

PRIVATE CLIENT SCENARIOS

SCENARIO 1: ESTATE PLANNING & BUSINESS PROTECTION

Sarah Willis (42), tech entrepreneur. Recently divorced with two children, Sarah's business has just received major investment. After reading about a business owner who died suddenly, leaving chaos, she wants to protect her £2.5M business, ensure her children's future, and minimize tax exposure. Her elderly parents might also need future care.

GOLD - COMPLETE WEALTH PROTECTION & LEGACY MASTERY SERVICE (£££)

• Total Estate Architecture: Comprehensive estate planning protecting £2.5M business value and ensuring children's financial security
• Business Succession: Advanced business protection strategies maintaining company value and operational continuity
• Tax Optimization: Sophisticated structuring minimizing inheritance tax, capital gains tax, and maximizing business property relief
• Family Wealth Protection: Multi-generational planning ensuring children's education, housing, and future prosperity
• Divorce-Proof Asset Strategy: Advanced asset protection preventing future relationship risks affecting family wealth
• Elder Care Financial Planning: Comprehensive care cost planning and funding strategies for ageing parents
• Investment Protection Framework: Safeguarding recent business investment and future funding opportunities
• Crisis Management Architecture: Complete contingency planning for death, incapacity, or business emergencies

ASSUMPTIONS:

• Full access to business records, investment documentation, divorce settlement details, and family financial information
• Authority to implement sophisticated trust structures and business reorganization strategies
• Sarah participates actively in family financial planning discussions and decision-making processes

• Business continues growth trajectory and maintains investment appeal during planning implementation
• Family relationships remain stable, enabling effective wealth transfer and protection strategies

EXCLUSIONS:

• Independent business valuations and investment portfolio reviews (coordinated but separately instructed)
• Ongoing business management and operational consultancy beyond succession planning requirements
• Elder care service provision and nursing home selection (financial planning provided)

TECHNICAL DELIVERABLES:

• Comprehensive will and estate planning with advanced tax optimization and business protection
• Sophisticated trust structures protecting business assets and providing children's long-term security
• Business succession plan maintaining operational continuity and investment attractiveness
• Divorce-proof asset protection strategies preventing future relationship risks
• Elder care financial planning, including care cost funding and inheritance protection
• Tax-efficient wealth transfer structures maximizing family wealth preservation
• Crisis management protocols for business and family emergencies

COMMUNICATION STRUCTURE:

• Immediate: Partner direct access for urgent estate, business, and family decisions (24/7)
• Fortnightly: Strategic wealth planning meetings with comprehensive progress reviews
• Monthly: Family financial planning sessions, including children's future planning discussions
• Annual: Complete estate and business protection reviews with strategy updates

FOLLOW-UP SERVICES:

• Lifetime estate planning maintenance with annual reviews and strategy optimization
• Priority access for all future Willis family legal and business protection matters
• Children's future legal needs support, including education funding
• Preferred rates for ongoing business succession and family wealth management

SILVER - ENHANCED ESTATE PLANNING & BUSINESS PROTECTION SERVICE (££)

• Estate Planning Framework: Comprehensive will and inheritance planning protecting business and family assets
• Business Protection Strategy: Succession planning, maintaining business value and operational stability
• Tax Planning Optimization: Advanced structuring, minimizing inheritance tax and preserving family wealth
• Children's Future Security: Trust structures and financial planning ensuring long-term prosperity
• Asset Protection Planning: Strategies protecting wealth from future relationship and business risks
• Elder Care Planning: Financial planning for parents' care costs and inheritance implications

ASSUMPTIONS:

• Standard business hours availability with priority support during estate planning implementation
• Sarah coordinates family discussions with professional estate planning guidance
• Moderate complexity estate planning is sufficient for business protection and family security objectives
• Estate planning achieved through established structures without complex reorganization

EXCLUSIONS:

• 24/7 availability for family crises and urgent business decisions
• Comprehensive business restructuring and advanced tax planning
• Ongoing lifetime estate maintenance and annual reviews

• Complex divorce-proof asset protection strategies

COMMUNICATION STRUCTURE:

• Business hours: Direct senior lawyer contact for estate and business matters
• Monthly: Progress calls and estate planning implementation updates
• Quarterly: Written estate planning reports and tax strategy reviews

BRONZE - ESSENTIAL ESTATE GUIDANCE SERVICE (£)

• Estate Planning Assessment: Analysis of will requirements and basic inheritance tax planning
• Business Protection Basics: Fundamental succession planning and business continuity advice
• Tax Planning Framework: Essential guidance on inheritance tax implications and basic mitigation strategies
• Children's Security Planning: Basic trust advice and financial planning for children's future needs
• Implementation Roadmap: Clear action plan for estate planning execution and professional coordination

ASSUMPTIONS:

• Single comprehensive consultation covering essential estate planning requirements
• Standard office hours availability only
• Sarah manages family discussions and business matters directly with legal guidance
• Template estate planning structures sufficient for basic business and family protection

EXCLUSIONS:

• Complex business succession planning and restructuring
• Advanced tax optimization and sophisticated trust structures
• Elder care financial planning and ongoing family support
• Crisis management and emergency planning protocols

COMMUNICATION STRUCTURE:

• Email and telephone during business hours only
• 48-hour response commitment for estate planning queries

• Single follow-up consultation included for implementation guidance

ASSUMPTIVE CLOSING QUESTIONS:

• "Given your £2.5M business value and responsibility for your children's futures, shall we implement the complete Gold service to protect everything you've built?"
• "When should I begin establishing the trust structures to ensure your children's financial security regardless of what happens?"
• "Shall I commence advanced tax planning immediately to preserve maximum wealth for your family?"
• "Should we start implementing business succession measures this week to protect your recent investment and operational continuity?"

VALUE-BASED QUESTIONS TO ASK:

• "What would losing the £2.5M business value to unnecessary inheritance tax cost your children's futures?"
• "How much would business chaos cost if something happened to you without proper succession planning?"
• "What's the financial impact if your recent major investment is lost due to inadequate business protection?"
• "If your parents need expensive care, how much would that cost without proper financial planning?"
• "What would your children lose if business assets became tied up in legal complications?"
• "How much could future relationship complications cost without proper asset protection strategies?"

VALUE CREATED:

• Business Preservation: Protects £2.5M business value through comprehensive succession planning and operational continuity
• Children's Security: Ensures long-term financial prosperity through sophisticated trust structures and education funding
• Tax Efficiency: Minimizes inheritance tax exposure, potentially saving significant tax liabilities
• Investment Protection: Safeguards recent business investment and maintains attractiveness for future funding opportunities

- Family Stability: Provides complete financial security, enabling focus on business growth and family wellbeing
- Asset Protection: Prevents future relationship risks affecting family wealth and business assets
- Elder Care Security: Ensures parents receive quality care without depleting children's inheritance
- Peace of Mind: Eliminates anxiety about business and family security, enabling confident entrepreneurial focus
- Legacy Preservation: Creates multi-generational wealth transfer, ensuring Willis family prosperity for decades
- Crisis Preparedness: Provides complete contingency planning protecting family and business through any emergency

SCENARIO 2: DIVORCE

James Patterson (38), secondary school teacher. After discovering his wife's affair with a colleague, James wants to end his 12-year marriage. He's worried about maintaining relationships with his three children, keeping the family home where he's created a teaching studio, and protecting his pension. He's never handled legal matters before and feels overwhelmed.

GOLD - COMPLETE FAMILY PROTECTION & EMOTIONAL SUPPORT SERVICE (£££)

- Children-First Strategy: Comprehensive parenting plan ensuring maximum contact time and protecting father-child relationships through transition
- Home Protection: Strategic approach seeking to secure the family home and teaching studio, preserving James's livelihood and stability
- Pension: Pension protection and optimal division ensuring retirement security remains intact
- Emotional Resilience Support: Integrated counselling liaison and wellbeing program helping James navigate divorce trauma professionally
- Affair Evidence Management: Strategic handling of infidelity evidence to maximize divorce outcome whilst protecting children from details

• New Client Confidence Building: Comprehensive legal education and hand-holding through every process step for complete peace of mind
• Financial Future Security: Complete financial settlement strategy ensuring fair division whilst protecting teaching career income
• Communication Management: Professional handling of all spouse interactions, protecting James from direct conflict and emotional manipulation

ASSUMPTIONS:

• Full access to all financial records, property documentation, and pension arrangements
• James's wife engages constructively in settlement discussions without prolonging proceedings unnecessarily
• Children's welfare remains a paramount priority for both parents throughout the process
• Teaching profession income remains stable during divorce proceedings
• Property valuations and pension assessments can be obtained within standard timeframes

EXCLUSIONS:

• Individual counselling services for James (arranged and coordinated but separately charged)
• Independent financial advice beyond legal settlement requirements (coordinated but separately instructed)
• Private investigation services regarding the affair (arranged if required but separately charged)
• Children's support if welfare disputes arise

TECHNICAL DELIVERABLES:

• Comprehensive parenting plan maximizing James's contact time and protecting father-child relationships
• Property settlement strategy securing family home and teaching studio for continued professional use
• Complete pension analysis and protection, ensuring optimal division and retirement security
• Financial disclosure and settlement framework, achieving fair division whilst protecting future income
• Strategic use of affair evidence

• Divorce petition and all court documentation prepared with comprehensive legal representation
• Settlement negotiation and court representation, ensuring optimal outcome through all proceedings

COMMUNICATION STRUCTURE:

• Immediate: Partner direct access for urgent child welfare and emotional crisis support (24/7)
• Daily: Text/WhatsApp updates during critical negotiation periods and court proceedings
• Weekly: Strategic planning calls with comprehensive progress reviews and emotional support
• Emergency availability: Crisis support during difficult spouse interactions or child access issues

FOLLOW-UP SERVICES:

• 24-month post-divorce monitoring for settlement enforcement and child arrangement modifications
• Annual financial review ensuring ongoing compliance and arrangement optimization
• Priority access for future family law matters, including child arrangement variations
• Continued emotional support liaison with counselling services and wellbeing programs

---

SILVER - ENHANCED DIVORCE GUIDANCE & ASSET PROTECTION SERVICE (££)

• Parenting Plan Development: Structured approach to securing good contact arrangements and protecting parent-child relationships
• Home Security Strategy: Professional guidance on retaining the family home and teaching studio through settlement negotiations
• Pension Protection: Comprehensive analysis and protection of pension rights and retirement planning
• Settlement Negotiation: Strategic approach to achieving fair financial division whilst protecting teaching income
• Emotional Support Coordination: Professional referrals and guidance through divorce emotional challenges
• Legal Process Management: Complete handling of divorce proceedings with clear explanation throughout

ASSUMPTIONS:

- Standard business hours availability with extended support during court proceedings
- James manages some direct communication with his spouse under professional guidance
- Settlement achieved through negotiation without complex court proceedings
- Basic emotional support is sufficient alongside professional referrals to counselling services

EXCLUSIONS:

- 24/7 crisis support availability
- Extensive ongoing post-divorce monitoring
- Complex financial restructuring beyond standard settlement

COMMUNICATION STRUCTURE:

- Business hours: Direct lawyer contact for divorce and child arrangement matters
- Bi-weekly: Progress calls with settlement and parenting plan updates
- Monthly: Written progress reports and legal proceedings status

BRONZE - ESSENTIAL DIVORCE GUIDANCE SERVICE (£)

- Divorce Process Guidance: Clear explanation of divorce procedures and legal requirements
- Parenting Arrangement Advice: Basic guidance on contact arrangements and children's welfare priorities
- Financial Settlement Framework: Essential advice on asset division, including home and pension considerations
- Legal Documentation: Preparation of essential divorce papers and court submissions
- Settlement Support: Guidance on negotiating fair financial arrangements

ASSUMPTIONS:

- Single comprehensive consultation covering essential divorce requirements and legal process
- Standard office hours availability only

• James manages direct spouse communication and negotiation with a legal guidance framework
• Template approaches are sufficient for straightforward divorce and settlement

EXCLUSIONS:

• Ongoing emotional support and crisis management
• Complex asset protection strategies
• Extensive court representation
• Post-divorce enforcement and monitoring

COMMUNICATION STRUCTURE:

• Email and telephone during business hours only
• 48-hour response commitment for urgent divorce queries
• Single follow-up consultation included for settlement clarification

ASSUMPTIVE CLOSING QUESTIONS:

• "Given the importance of protecting your relationship with your three children and securing your teaching studio, shall we implement the comprehensive Gold service immediately?"
• "Shall I start the home protection strategy today to secure your teaching studio and family stability?"
• "Should we commence the pension protection analysis immediately to safeguard your retirement security?"

VALUE-BASED QUESTIONS TO ASK:

• "How much would losing your family home and teaching studio cost in relocation expenses and lost income?"
• "What would an unfair pension division cost your retirement security and future financial stability?"
• "If this divorce process drags on for years, what would the emotional toll cost your mental health and teaching career?"

VALUE CREATED:

• Father-Child Protection: Secures maximum contact time, ensuring James maintains strong relationships with his three children throughout their development
• Home Security: Preserves family home and teaching studio, enabling continued professional practice and financial stability

• Pension Protection: Safeguards retirement security, ensuring fair division without devastating long-term financial consequences
• Emotional Stability: Provides professional support and guidance through divorce trauma, protecting mental health and teaching career
• Fair Settlement: Achieves optimal financial outcome considering affair circumstances whilst protecting future income

SCENARIO 3: LASTING POWER OF ATTORNEY

William Laing (71), retired accountant. Recently diagnosed with early-stage dementia, William wants to ensure his wife can manage their affairs and make healthcare decisions. He's worried about his extensive investment portfolio and wants to protect his wife from future stress.

GOLD - COMPLETE CAPACITY PROTECTION & FAMILY SECURITY SERVICE (£££)

• Comprehensive LPA Architecture: Both Property & Financial Affairs and Health & Welfare LPAs with sophisticated decision-making frameworks protecting William's interests
• Investment Portfolio Protection: Advanced financial management instructions ensuring investment portfolio security and growth strategies
• Family Stress Elimination: Complete guidance package for William's wife, including training, support systems, and professional backup
• Capacity Window Maximization: Urgent processing ensuring LPAs executed whilst William retains full legal capacity
• Healthcare Decision Framework: Detailed medical treatment preferences and care instructions protecting William's dignity and wishes
• Financial Safeguarding System: Anti-fraud protection, spending guidelines, and asset preservation strategies
• Professional Support Network: Coordinated team including financial advisors, healthcare specialists, and dementia support services

• Future Care Planning: Comprehensive care pathway planning, including residential care funding and family support strategies

ASSUMPTIONS:

• William currently retains full mental capacity for LPA execution and decision-making
• Access to complete financial records, investment portfolios, and healthcare preferences
• William's wife is willing to accept attorney responsibilities with appropriate training and support
• Medical professionals available for capacity assessments and healthcare preference discussions
• Financial advisors and investment managers cooperate with LPA implementation requirements

EXCLUSIONS:

• Independent medical capacity assessments (arranged but separately charged)
• Financial advisor fees and investment management charges (coordinated but separately billed)
• Ongoing care service provisions and residential care costs (planning provided)
• Family therapy or counselling services beyond legal guidance and support

TECHNICAL DELIVERABLES:

• Comprehensive Property & Financial Affairs LPA with detailed investment and spending guidance
• Health & Welfare LPA with sophisticated medical treatment and care preferences
• Complete attorney guidance package with training materials and ongoing support protocols
• Financial safeguarding framework, including fraud protection and spending oversight systems
• Healthcare decision-making guide with treatment preferences and dignity protection measures
• Professional coordination system linking legal, financial, and healthcare services
• Future care planning documentation, including funding strategies and family support systems

COMMUNICATION STRUCTURE:

- Immediate: Partner direct access for urgent capacity and healthcare decisions (priority response)
- Weekly: Progress meetings with William and his wife, ensuring comprehensive understanding and comfort
- Monthly: Professional coordination meetings with financial advisors and healthcare teams
- Ongoing: Quarterly check-ins post-registration, ensuring LPA effectiveness and family confidence

FOLLOW-UP SERVICES:

- 12-month post-registration support ensuring LPA effectiveness and family confidence
- Annual reviews of financial arrangements and healthcare preferences with adjustment options
- Priority access for future capacity-related matters and family support needs
- Preferred rates for ongoing dementia-related legal support and family guidance

---

SILVER - ENHANCED LPA PROTECTION & FAMILY SUPPORT SERVICE (££)

- Dual LPA Creation: Property & Financial Affairs and Health & Welfare LPAs with essential decision-making guidance
- Investment Portfolio Guidance: Financial management instructions protecting investment assets and providing the wife with confidence
- Attorney Training Program: Comprehensive guidance for William's wife on attorney responsibilities and decision-making
- Healthcare Preferences: Medical treatment wishes and care preferences documentation
- Financial Protection: Basic safeguarding measures and spending guidance for asset protection
- Professional Coordination: Liaison with financial advisors and healthcare providers for seamless implementation

ASSUMPTIONS:

- Standard business hours availability with priority support during capacity assessment periods

• William coordinates medical appointments and financial advisor meetings with legal guidance
• Basic attorney training sufficient for wife's confidence and LPA implementation
• Registration achieved through standard OPG processes without complex requirements

EXCLUSIONS:

• 24/7 availability for urgent capacity or healthcare decisions
• Comprehensive future care planning and residential care funding strategies
• Extended family support and dementia-specific guidance programs
• Ongoing post-registration monitoring and adjustment services

COMMUNICATION STRUCTURE:

• Business hours: Direct senior lawyer contact for LPA and capacity matters
• Bi-weekly: Progress calls ensuring LPA completion whilst capacity remains
• Monthly: Written updates on registration progress and family support requirements

BRONZE - ESSENTIAL LPA GUIDANCE SERVICE (£)

• Standard LPA Preparation: Property & Financial Affairs and Health & Welfare LPAs with basic decision-making guidance
• Attorney Guidance: Essential advice for William's wife on attorney responsibilities and basic decision-making
• Healthcare Preferences: Fundamental medical treatment wishes and care preferences documentation
• Financial Instructions: Basic guidance on investment portfolio management and spending decisions
• Registration Support: Standard OPG registration process management and basic guidance

ASSUMPTIONS:

• Single comprehensive consultation covering essential LPA requirements and attorney guidance
• Standard office hours availability only

- William manages capacity assessments and professional coordination directly with basic legal guidance
- Template LPA structures are sufficient for basic protection and decision-making requirements

EXCLUSIONS:

- Complex financial planning and investment portfolio protection strategies
- Comprehensive attorney training and ongoing family support services
- Professional coordination with financial advisors and healthcare providers
- Post-registration monitoring and LPA effectiveness reviews

COMMUNICATION STRUCTURE:

- Email and telephone during business hours only
- 48-hour response commitment for LPA and capacity queries
- Single follow-up consultation included for registration completion

ASSUMPTIVE CLOSING QUESTIONS:

- "Given William's dementia diagnosis and extensive investment portfolio, shall we implement the complete Gold service to protect both his assets and his wife's peace of mind?"
- "When should I begin the urgent LPA preparation to ensure registration whilst William retains full capacity?"
- "Shall I commence comprehensive attorney training for your wife immediately to build her confidence in managing your affairs?"
- "Should we start coordinating with your financial advisors this week to ensure seamless portfolio protection?"

VALUE-BASED QUESTIONS TO ASK:

- "What would losing control of your extensive investment portfolio due to inadequate LPA planning cost your family financially?"
- "How much stress and anxiety would your wife experience trying to manage complex financial affairs without proper guidance and protection?"

• "What's the emotional cost to your family if healthcare decisions can't be made according to your wishes?"
• "If your capacity window closes before LPAs are registered, what would Court of Protection applications cost in time, money, and family stress?"
• "How much would financial fraud or poor investment decisions cost if adequate safeguards aren't in place?"
• "What would the impact be on your wife's health and wellbeing if she's overwhelmed by complex financial and healthcare responsibilities?"

VALUE CREATED:

• Capacity Window Protection: Ensures LPAs executed whilst William retains full legal capacity, preventing future Court of Protection complications
• Investment Portfolio Security: Protects extensive financial assets through sophisticated management instructions and safeguarding measures
• Family Stress Elimination: Provides William's wife with confidence, training, and support systems, reducing anxiety and overwhelm
• Healthcare Dignity: Preserves William's medical treatment preferences and care wishes, ensuring dignified healthcare decisions
• Financial Safeguarding: Prevents fraud, poor decisions, and asset loss through comprehensive protection frameworks
• Professional Coordination: Creates a seamless support network linking legal, financial, and healthcare services for family benefit
• Future Care Planning: Establishes comprehensive care pathways and funding strategies, reducing future family burden and stress
• Peace of Mind: Delivers complete assurance that William's affairs will be managed according to his wishes with minimal family stress

SCENARIO 4: PRE-NUPTIAL AGREEMENT

Charlotte Hughes (45), restaurant chain owner. Planning to marry her partner of two years, Charlotte wants to protect her successful restaurant business and inherited property. Her fiancé supports the idea, but they want the agreement to feel fair and not damage their relationship.

GOLD - COMPLETE RELATIONSHIP & WEALTH PROTECTION SERVICE (£££)

• Relationship-First Approach: Sensitive pre-nuptial negotiations preserving love whilst protecting business assets and inherited wealth
• Business Empire Protection: Comprehensive restaurant chain safeguarding, ensuring operational continuity and ownership clarity
• Inheritance Preservation: Advanced property protection, maintaining family legacy whilst creating a fair partnership framework
• Couple Management: Professional relationship counselling approach ensuring both parties feel respected and valued
• Future-Proofed Agreement: Sophisticated prenup covering business growth, additional properties, and changing circumstances
• Independent Legal Coordination: Managing fiancé's separate representation, ensuring balanced, legally robust agreement
• Fairness Framework: Equitable provisions creating win-win outcomes that strengthen rather than threaten the relationship
• Post-Wedding Relationship Support: Ongoing guidance ensuring agreement implementation supports marital harmony

ASSUMPTIONS:

• Full access to restaurant business valuations, property details, and financial arrangements
• Both parties committed to achieving a fair, relationship-preserving agreement
• Fiancé obtains independent legal representation as coordinated through our process
• Current business performance and property values remain broadly stable during the negotiation period
• Wedding timeline allows adequate time for sensitive negotiation and agreement finalization

EXCLUSIONS:

• Independent business valuations and property appraisals (coordinated but separately instructed)
• Fiancé's independent legal fees (though process coordination included)
• Relationship counselling services beyond legal framework guidance
• Post-wedding estate planning services (arranged at preferred rates if required)

TECHNICAL DELIVERABLES:

• Bespoke pre-nuptial agreement protecting restaurant business and inherited property
• Relationship harmony framework ensuring agreement strengthens rather than threatens partnership
• Business protection protocols maintaining operational independence and growth potential
• Inheritance preservation structure protecting the family legacy for future generations
• Fair provision mechanisms creating equitable outcomes for both parties
• Implementation guidance ensuring smooth post-wedding agreement operation
• Future amendment framework allowing agreement evolution with changing circumstances

COMMUNICATION STRUCTURE:

• Immediate: Partner direct access for sensitive relationship and negotiation matters (priority response)
• Weekly: Progress meetings with both parties, ensuring a transparent, harmonious negotiation process
• Couple sessions: Joint meetings maintaining relationship focus whilst achieving legal protection
• Independent sessions: Private consultations with Charlotte, ensuring comprehensive business protection

FOLLOW-UP SERVICES:

• 24-month post-wedding monitoring, ensuring agreement operation supports marital harmony
• Annual review opportunities, adapting the agreement to business growth and changed circumstances

- Priority access for future family law matters and business legal requirements
- Preferred rates for estate planning and additional property protection services

SILVER - ENHANCED PRE-NUPTIAL PROTECTION & HARMONY SERVICE (££)

- Business Asset Protection: Comprehensive restaurant chain safeguarding and inheritance preservation framework
- Balanced Agreement Design: Fair pre-nuptial terms protecting Charlotte whilst respecting fiancé's interests
- Relationship-Sensitive Negotiation: Professional approach, maintaining couple harmony during agreement discussions
- Independent Legal Coordination: Managing separate representation, ensuring legally sound, balanced agreement
- Future Planning Framework: Agreement structure accommodating business growth and changing circumstances
- Implementation Guidance: Clear post-wedding operation ensuring agreement effectiveness and relationship stability

ASSUMPTIONS:

- Standard business hours availability with priority support during sensitive negotiation phases
- Charlotte manages day-to-day business operations with legal protection guidance
- Basic fairness provisions are sufficient for relationship harmony and asset protection
- Agreement achieved through standard negotiation without complex mediation/negotiation requirements

EXCLUSIONS:

- 24/7 availability for relationship crises and urgent negotiations
- Comprehensive post-wedding monitoring and support
- Advanced business growth planning and complex inheritance structures
- Couple counselling approach beyond the legal framework

COMMUNICATION STRUCTURE:

- Business hours: Direct senior lawyer contact for pre-nuptial matters

• Bi-weekly: Progress calls and negotiation updates with relationship sensitivity
• Monthly: Written progress reports ensuring transparency and confidence

BRONZE - ESSENTIAL PRE-NUPTIAL GUIDANCE SERVICE (£)

• Asset Protection Basics: Essential pre-nuptial agreement protecting restaurant business and inherited property
• Fair Agreement Framework: Balanced terms creating mutual respect whilst safeguarding Charlotte's assets
• Negotiation Guidance: Professional advice for managing discussions and maintaining relationship harmony
• Legal Requirements: Compliance with pre-nuptial agreement legal standards and enforceability requirements
• Implementation Framework: Clear guidance ensuring post-wedding agreement operation and effectiveness

ASSUMPTIONS:

• Single comprehensive consultation covering essential pre-nuptial requirements and relationship considerations
• Standard office hours availability only
• Charlotte manages fiancé discussions and separate legal representation coordination independently
• Template agreement structures are sufficient for basic asset protection and fairness objectives

EXCLUSIONS:

• Complex business valuation and inheritance planning
• Extensive relationship counselling and harmony management
• Independent legal coordination and negotiation management
• Ongoing post-wedding support and agreement monitoring

COMMUNICATION STRUCTURE:

• Email and telephone during business hours only
• 48-hour response commitment for pre-nuptial queries and guidance
• Single follow-up consultation included for agreement finalization

ASSUMPTIVE CLOSING QUESTIONS:

• "Given the importance of protecting your restaurant empire whilst preserving your relationship, shall we implement the complete Gold service to achieve both objectives?"
• "Shall I start communicating with your fiancé's independent representation?"

VALUE-BASED QUESTIONS TO ASK:

• "What would losing control of your restaurant chain in a future divorce cost your business empire?"
• "How much would family property and inheritance being at risk cost emotionally and financially?"
• "What's the relationship damage if pre-nuptial negotiations are unsuccessful?"
• "If the agreement isn't legally robust, what would a successful challenge cost in assets and legal fees?"
• "How much would business disruption during relationship breakdown cost in operational performance?"
• "What would losing family legacy property mean to future generations of the Hughes family?"

VALUE CREATED:

• Business Protection: Safeguards restaurant chain ownership and operational independence from potential future relationship breakdown
• Inheritance Preservation: Protects family legacy property, ensuring multi-generational wealth preservation for the Hughes family
• Relationship Harmony: Creates a fair, respectful agreement that strengthens the partnership rather than creating suspicion or resentment
• Peace of Mind: Provides complete confidence, enabling Charlotte to enter marriage with both love and security
• Legal Certainty: Ensures an enforceable agreement protecting assets whilst respecting both parties' interests and contributions
• Future Security: Establishes a framework that accommodates business growth and changing circumstances throughout marriage
• Family Legacy: Preserves inherited property, maintaining a connection to family history and future generational wealth

• Operational Continuity: Protects the restaurant business from potential relationship-related disruption or interference
• Mutual Respect: Creates a balanced framework demonstrating commitment to fairness and partnership values

Penguin logic… Charlotte isn't buying legal hours - she's purchasing relationship preservation, business security, and family legacy protection.

SCENARIO 5: CHILD CUSTODY

Abdul Rahman (36), IT consultant. Recently separated, Abdul works remotely and wants to maintain strong relationships with his children despite his ex-partner moving 100 miles away. He needs help creating a custody arrangement that allows meaningful time with his kids while accommodating his flexible work schedule.

GOLD - COMPLETE FAMILY HARMONY & CUSTODY EXCELLENCE SERVICE (£££)

• Father-Child Relationship Protection: Comprehensive custody arrangement safeguarding meaningful relationships despite geographical distance
• Remote Work Strategy: Expert structuring leveraging Abdul's flexible IT career for maximum parenting time
• Distance Overcome Framework: Creative solutions transforming a 100-mile separation from an obstacle into a manageable routine
• Conflict Minimization: Professional mediation and communication strategies protecting children from parental disputes
• Future-Proof Arrangements: Adaptive custody framework accommodating career changes, children's development, and family evolution
• Technology Integration: Modern communication solutions for maintaining daily parent-child connection across distance
• Legal Protection Shield: Comprehensive documentation preventing future custody disputes and protecting parental rights
• Child Welfare Prioritization: Evidence-based arrangements demonstrating children's best interests to courts and ex-partner

ASSUMPTIONS:

• Full access to work schedules, income details, and accommodation arrangements for optimal custody planning
• Authority to negotiate directly with the ex-partner's legal representatives for collaborative arrangement development
• Children's ages, school arrangements, and current living situations remain stable during the negotiation period
• Abdul maintains current remote working flexibility and income stability throughout the process
• Ex-partner participates constructively in mediation and child-focused arrangement discussions

EXCLUSIONS:

• Independent child psychology assessments and welfare reports (coordinated but separately instructed)
• Court representation if matter proceeds to contested litigation (separate retainer required)
• Ongoing relationship counselling services beyond legal arrangement implementation
• Travel and accommodation costs for distance parenting arrangements

TECHNICAL DELIVERABLES:

• Comprehensive custody agreement optimizing father-child time whilst respecting geographical constraints
• Remote work advantage analysis and parenting schedule designed around IT consultant flexibility
• Distance management strategy including travel arrangements, communication protocols, and shared responsibilities
• Conflict resolution framework and communication guidelines protecting children from parental disputes
• Technology integration plan maintaining daily parent-child connection through digital platforms
• Legal documentation preventing future custody challenges and protecting parental rights long-term

COMMUNICATION STRUCTURE:

• Immediate: Partner direct access for urgent child welfare and custody decisions (priority response within 2 hours)
• Weekly: Strategic progress meetings during negotiation and arrangement implementation phases

• Bi-weekly: Family mediation sessions with professional facilitation and child-focused outcomes
• Emergency: 24/7 availability for custody crisis situations and urgent child welfare matters

FOLLOW-UP SERVICES:

• 24-month arrangement monitoring, ensuring effectiveness and child welfare optimization
• Annual custody review and arrangement updates accommodating children's development and changing needs
• Priority access for future family law matters and arrangement modifications
• Preferred rates for ongoing custody support and family relationship management

SILVER - ENHANCED CUSTODY PLANNING & RELATIONSHIP PROTECTION SERVICE (££)

• Custody Strategy Development: Comprehensive arrangement balancing father-child relationships with geographical realities
• Remote Work Optimization: Strategic planning leveraging IT consultant flexibility for enhanced parenting opportunities
• Distance Management: Practical solutions for maintaining meaningful relationships across the 100-mile separation
• Mediation Support: Professional guidance facilitating collaborative discussions with ex-partner
• Legal Documentation: Comprehensive custody agreement protecting parental rights and child welfare
• Communication Framework: Guidelines and protocols minimizing conflict and protecting children

ASSUMPTIONS:

• Standard business hours availability with extended support during crucial negotiation phases
• Abdul coordinates direct discussions with ex-partner using professional mediation guidance
• Basic custody arrangement sufficient for family requirements and child welfare objectives
• Arrangement achieved through collaborative discussion without complex court intervention

EXCLUSIONS:

- 24/7 emergency availability for custody crises
- Comprehensive technology integration and daily communication protocols
- Extended post-arrangement monitoring and annual reviews
- Court representation for contested proceedings

COMMUNICATION STRUCTURE:

- Business hours: Direct senior lawyer contact for custody and mediation matters
- Weekly: Progress calls and arrangement development updates during active negotiation
- Monthly: Written progress reports and strategic advice on custody implementation

---

BRONZE - ESSENTIAL CUSTODY GUIDANCE SERVICE (£)

- Custody Assessment: Analysis of parenting options balancing child welfare with geographical constraints
- Remote Work Advantages: Basic advice on leveraging IT consultant flexibility for parenting arrangements
- Distance Solutions: Fundamental guidance on maintaining father-child relationships across separation
- Legal Framework: Essential custody agreement template and parental rights protection
- Implementation Guide: Clear action plan for arrangement negotiation and family coordination

ASSUMPTIONS:

- Single comprehensive consultation covering essential custody planning requirements
- Standard office hours availability only
- Abdul manages direct negotiations with ex-partner using a legal guidance framework
- Template custody arrangements are sufficient for basic parental rights and child welfare protection

EXCLUSIONS:

- Mediation services and conflict resolution support
- Complex distance management and technology integration

- Ongoing arrangement monitoring and modification support
- Emergency custody crisis management

COMMUNICATION STRUCTURE:

- Email and telephone during business hours only
- 48-hour response commitment for custody queries and urgent guidance
- Single follow-up consultation included for arrangement clarification

ASSUMPTIVE CLOSING QUESTIONS:

- "Given the importance of protecting your relationship with your children, shall we implement the complete Gold service to ensure they remain central to your life despite the distance?"
- "When should I begin negotiations with your ex-partner's representatives to establish the optimal custody arrangement?"
- "Shall I start developing the remote work advantage strategy immediately to maximize your parenting opportunities?"
- "Should we open a file this week to start creating a child-focused arrangement that works for everyone?"

VALUE-BASED QUESTIONS TO ASK:

- "What would not having meaningful time with your children cost you emotionally and personally?"
- "How much is maintaining a strong father-child relationship worth over the next 10-15 years?"
- "What would your children lose if the custody arrangement doesn't work effectively?"
- "If conflict escalates, what would contested court proceedings cost financially and emotionally?"
- "How much would your work flexibility be worth if we can't leverage it for parenting time?"

VALUE CREATED:

- Father-Child Bond Preservation: Protects and nurtures meaningful relationships despite geographical separation and family breakdown
- Remote Work Maximization: Transforms IT consultant flexibility from a potential disadvantage into a powerful parenting advantage

• Distance Transformation: Converts 100-mile separation from relationship barrier into a manageable routine, enabling regular contact
• Conflict Prevention: Minimizes parental disputes, protecting children's emotional welfare and family stability
• Future Security: Establishes a robust legal framework preventing custody challenges and protecting parental rights long-term
• Child Welfare Priority: Ensures arrangements serve children's best interests whilst respecting both parents' rights and circumstances
• Technology Integration: Leverages modern communication, enabling daily parent-child connection across physical distance
• Emotional Protection: Shields children from parental conflict whilst maintaining loving relationships with both parents
• Life Stability: Creates predictable, secure arrangements enabling children to thrive despite family changes
• Career Integration: Harmonizes professional IT work with parenting responsibilities, creating work-life balance excellence

Penguin logic... Abdul isn't buying legal hours - he's purchasing his children's future happiness and his own peace of mind as a father.

SCENARIO 6: HOUSE PURCHASE

Tom Chen (31) and Lisa Chen (29), first-time buyers. A young professional couple looking to buy their first home in a competitive market. They've found their dream property but are nervous about the process and want to ensure they're protected, especially as the property is leasehold.

GOLD - COMPLETE DREAM HOME PROTECTION & FIRST-TIME BUYER EXCELLENCE SERVICE (£££)

• Dream Home Guarantee: Comprehensive protection ensuring successful completion of property purchase with complete peace of mind
• Leasehold Expertise Excellence: Specialist leasehold analysis protecting against hidden costs, ground rent escalations, and management company issues

• First-Time Buyer Concierge: Dedicated hand-holding service with expert guidance through every step of the purchase journey
• Competitive Market Advantage: Priority processing and rapid response to ensure you don't lose your dream property to other buyers
• Complete Legal Shield: Thorough property investigations including planning permissions, environmental risks, boundaries, and neighborly disputes
• Financial Protection Mastery: Expert mortgage liaison, deposit protection, and completion funding coordination
• Post-Purchase Support: 12-month new homeowner guidance, including warranty claims, neighbor issues, and property queries
• Technology Integration: Real-time progress tracking app, digital document access, and instant communication portal

ASSUMPTIONS:

• Full access to property information, mortgage arrangements, and survey reports when available
• Estate agents and mortgage brokers cooperate with accelerated transaction timescales
• Tom and Lisa are available for urgent decisions during competitive market situations
• Property chain complexity remains manageable with standard first-time buyer expectations
• Seller cooperation with reasonable information requests and completion timescales

EXCLUSIONS:

• Independent property surveys and mortgage arrangement fees (coordinated but separately charged)
• Additional legal costs for unusual property complications discovered during searches
• Stamp duty land tax and Land Registry fees (calculated and managed but separately charged)
• Individual mortgage advice and financial planning services beyond legal completion requirements

TECHNICAL DELIVERABLES:

• Comprehensive leasehold analysis, including ground rent, service charges, and management company review

• Complete property legal title investigation and boundary verification
• Environmental, planning, and local authority search analysis with risk assessment
• Contract negotiation and speedy exchange management
• Mortgage legal requirements and lender liaison, ensuring smooth financing
• Post-completion Land Registry registration and title deed management
• New homeowner legal guidance package with 12-month support access

COMMUNICATION STRUCTURE:

• Immediate: Partner direct access for urgent competitive market decisions (same-day response guaranteed)
• Daily: Progress updates during active transaction phases with real-time app notifications
• Weekly: Comprehensive status calls with Tom and Lisa covering all transaction elements
• Critical phases: Senior lawyer availability for exchange, completion, and any crisis management

FOLLOW-UP SERVICES:

• 12-month new homeowner legal support, including warranty, neighbor, and property issues
• Annual property legal health checks and documentation reviews
• Priority access for future property transactions and family legal matters
• Preferred rates for ongoing residential property advice and legal requirements

USE OF TECHNOLOGY:

• Dedicated client portal with real-time transaction tracking and document access
• Mobile app providing instant updates and direct communication channels
• Digital signature capabilities enabling rapid contract execution and document processing
• Automated progress reporting with milestone notifications and completion countdown

SILVER - ENHANCED FIRST-TIME BUYER CONVEYANCING SERVICE (££)

• Professional Purchase Management: Comprehensive conveyancing service with experienced first-time buyer guidance
• Leasehold Analysis: Detailed leasehold review identifying key risks and ongoing obligations
• Property Protection: Thorough legal investigations, including searches, planning, and environmental checks
• Mortgage Coordination: Professional liaison with lenders, ensuring smooth financing and completion
• Progress Communication: Regular updates and expert guidance through the purchase process
• Post-Completion Support: Basic new homeowner guidance and document management

ASSUMPTIONS:

• Standard business hours availability with priority support during exchange and completion
• Tom and Lisa manage estate agent relationships with legal guidance and support
• Property purchase achieved through standard conveyancing processes without complex negotiations

EXCLUSIONS:

• Same-day competitive market response guarantees
• Comprehensive post-purchase ongoing support
• Advanced technology integration and real-time tracking
• Extended first-time buyer concierge services

COMMUNICATION STRUCTURE:

• Business hours: Direct lawyer contact for conveyancing and completion matters
• Weekly: Progress calls and transaction status updates
• Written: Comprehensive progress reports and legal milestone confirmations

BRONZE - ESSENTIAL FIRST-TIME BUYER CONVEYANCING SERVICE (£)

• Basic Conveyancing: Standard property purchase legal process, including searches and contract review

- Leasehold Guidance: Leasehold information and basic risk identification in a Report on Title.
- Mortgage Support: Essential lender liaison and legal completion requirements
- Purchase Completion: Contract exchange and completion process management
- Document Management: Title registration.

ASSUMPTIONS:

- Single comprehensive conveyancing service covering essential property purchase requirements
- Standard office hours availability only
- Tom and Lisa manage property chain coordination and estate agent communications directly
- Basic conveyancing service sufficient for first-time buyers

EXCLUSIONS:

- Specialist first-time buyer guidance and hand-holding services
- Competitive market priority processing and rapid response
- Post-completion new homeowner guidance

COMMUNICATION STRUCTURE:

- Email and telephone during business hours only
- Bi-weekly progress updates on conveyancing milestones
- Single completion meeting with basic new homeowner documentation

ASSUMPTIVE CLOSING QUESTIONS:

- "Given this is your dream property in a competitive market, shall we implement the complete Gold service to ensure you secure it successfully?"
- "Shall I start coordinating with your mortgage broker immediately to ensure rapid processing and completion?"
- "Should we activate the real-time tracking technology so you can monitor progress on your dream home purchase daily?"

VALUE-BASED QUESTIONS TO ASK:

- "What would losing your dream property to another buyer cost you emotionally and financially?"
- "What's the financial impact if mortgage delays prevent completion within your required timescales?"

• "How much is peace of mind worth during the biggest financial decision of your lives?"
• "What would having to start the house-hunting process again cost in time, stress, and potentially higher property prices?"

VALUE CREATED:

• Dream Home Security: Guarantees successful completion of property purchase, protecting Tom and Lisa's emotional and financial investment
• First-Time Buyer Confidence: Provides expert guidance and hand-holding, ensuring a smooth transition to homeownership
• Competitive Market Advantage: Delivers speed and priority processing crucial for securing property in challenging market conditions
• Peace of Mind: Eliminates anxiety and uncertainty through comprehensive legal investigations and ongoing support

SCENARIO 7: PROPERTY SALE

Margaret Pearson (68), retired nurse. Recently widowed, Margaret needs to downsize from her family home of 40 years. The property has some structural issues she's worried about declaring, and she needs to coordinate the purchase of a retirement flat. Time is crucial as she's found her perfect new home.

GOLD - COMPLETE PROPERTY TRANSITION & PROTECTION SERVICE (£££)

• Seamless Dual Transaction Management: Complete coordination of both property sale and retirement flat purchase, ensuring perfect timing
• Structural Issue Resolution: Expert guidance on disclosure obligations protecting Margaret from future legal claims whilst maintaining sale viability
• Compassionate Client Care: Dedicated support recognizing the emotional challenges of leaving a 40-year family home
• Time-Critical Transaction: Accelerated processing ensuring Margaret secures her perfect retirement flat
• Comprehensive Legal Protection: Full indemnity and warranty management protecting Margaret's financial interests

• Stress-Free Experience: Complete transaction management allowing Margaret to focus on her new life chapter
• Expert Property Chain Management: Professional coordination, preventing chain collapse and securing both transactions
• Post-Completion Security: Extended support ensuring smooth transition to retirement living

ASSUMPTIONS:

• Full access to property documents, structural reports, and retirement flat purchase details
• Authority to liaise directly with estate agents, surveyors, and mortgage brokers on Margaret's behalf
• Margaret is available for document signing and key decisions with flexible timing arrangements
• Property structural issues are manageable through proper disclosure and pricing strategy
• Retirement flat purchase proceeds smoothly with standard mortgage/cash arrangements

EXCLUSIONS:

• Structural surveys and building reports (coordinated but separately charged)
• Estate agency fees and property marketing costs (advised on but separately contracted)
• Removal services and property clearance (organized but separately arranged)
• Independent financial advice on pension arrangements and retirement planning

TECHNICAL DELIVERABLES:

• Complete property sale management, including structural issue disclosure strategy and legal protection
• Coordinated retirement flat purchase with accelerated conveyancing and exchange timing
• Comprehensive contract negotiation protecting Margaret's interests in both transactions
• Professional liaison with all parties, ensuring smooth transaction progression
• Expert disclosure management balancing legal obligations with commercial reality

• Complete chain management, preventing delays and securing both property transactions

COMMUNICATION STRUCTURE:

• Immediate: Partner direct access for urgent decisions and emotional support (24/7 during exchange periods)
• Daily: Progress updates during critical transaction phases with compassionate communication
• Weekly: Comprehensive briefings on both transactions with clear next steps and timelines
• Flexible: Home visits or extended consultations accommodating Margaret's comfort and convenience

FOLLOW-UP SERVICES:

• 12-month post-completion support for any property-related queries or warranty claims
• Priority access for future property or legal matters affecting Margaret's retirement
• Annual check-ins ensuring Margaret's legal affairs remain well-managed in retirement
• Preferred rates for ongoing legal services and estate planning matters

SILVER - ENHANCED DUAL PROPERTY TRANSACTION SERVICE (££)

• Coordinated Transaction Management: Professional handling of both property sale and retirement flat purchase
• Structural Issue Guidance: Expert advice on disclosure requirements and legal protection strategies
• Accelerated Processing: Priority handling recognizing the time-critical nature of retirement flat purchase
• Chain Coordination: Professional liaison preventing delays and securing both transactions
• Legal Protection: Comprehensive contract review and negotiation protecting Margaret's interests
• Supportive Communication: Regular updates and guidance throughout the transaction process

ASSUMPTIONS:

• Standard business hours availability with extended support during exchange periods
• Margaret coordinates with estate agents and other parties with legal guidance and support
• Basic structural issue disclosure sufficient for legal compliance and commercial viability
• Transactions proceed through standard conveyancing processes with professional coordination

EXCLUSIONS:

• 24/7 availability and home visit services
• Extended post-completion monitoring and support
• Comprehensive chain management and crisis intervention
• Personal emotional support beyond professional legal guidance

COMMUNICATION STRUCTURE:

• Business hours: Direct lawyer contact for transaction matters and urgent decisions
• Bi-weekly: Progress calls covering both transactions with clear status updates
• Written: Weekly progress reports and next steps communication

BRONZE - ESSENTIAL DUAL TRANSACTION GUIDANCE SERVICE (£)

• Basic Transaction Support: Standard conveyancing for both property sale and retirement flat purchase
• Structural Disclosure Advice: Essential guidance on legal disclosure requirements
• Document Management: Standard legal documentation and contract review for both properties
• Progress Coordination: Basic liaison between transactions, ensuring legal compliance
• Legal Compliance: Fundamental conveyancing services meeting all legal requirements

ASSUMPTIONS:

• Standard office hours availability only with a 48-hour response commitment

• Margaret manages estate agents, surveyors, and timing coordination directly
• Basic legal services sufficient for straightforward property transactions
• Standard conveyancing timescales acceptable despite time-critical elements

EXCLUSIONS:

• Accelerated processing and priority handling
• Comprehensive structural issue management
• Personal support and flexible communication arrangements
• Chain management and transaction coordination services

COMMUNICATION STRUCTURE:

• Email and telephone during business hours only
• Standard progress updates as transactions develop
• Single consultation for complex matters or concerns

ASSUMPTIVE CLOSING QUESTIONS:

• "Given the significance of leaving your family home and the time pressure to secure your perfect retirement flat, shall we implement the complete Gold service to ensure everything goes smoothly?"
• "When should I begin coordinating both transactions to ensure you don't lose your ideal retirement property?"
• "Shall I start managing the structural issue disclosures immediately to protect you legally whilst maintaining your sale prospects?"
• "Should we arrange a home visit this week to review all your property documents and begin the transition process?"

VALUE-BASED QUESTIONS TO ASK:

• "What would losing your perfect retirement flat cost emotionally after searching for the right home?"
• "How much would legal problems from undisclosed structural issues cost you in future claims?"
• "What's the financial impact if your property sale falls through due to poor chain management?"
• "If the transactions don't coordinate properly, what would temporary accommodation and storage cost?"

- "How much is peace of mind worth during this major life?"

VALUE CREATED:

- Emotional Security: Provides compassionate support during a major life transition following bereavement
- Financial Protection: Safeguards Margaret from legal claims whilst maximizing property sale value
- Time Efficiency: Ensures Margaret secures her perfect retirement flat through coordinated, accelerated processing
- Stress Reduction: Manages the entire transaction process, allowing Margaret to focus on her new life chapter
- Legal Compliance: Properly handles structural issue disclosure, protecting Margaret from future legal problems
- Chain Security: Professional management prevents transaction collapse, ensuring both property deals complete
- Peace of Mind: Comprehensive service provides confidence during a vulnerable life period
- Smooth Transition: Coordinates timing, ensuring a seamless move from family home to retirement property
- Professional Excellence: Delivers exceptional service

Penguin logic... Margaret isn't buying conveyancing hours - she's purchasing emotional security, financial protection, and peace of mind during one of life's most challenging transitions.

SCENARIO 8: NEIGHBOUR DISPUTE

David Patel (52), architect. His neighbor has erected a 3-metre fence that blocks light to David's award-winning garden and home office, which is located in a conservation area. The fence breaches conservation area guidelines. Despite attempts at mediation, the neighbor refuses to compromise. David's work is suffering due to the reduced natural light.

GOLD - COMPLETE DISPUTE RESOLUTION SERVICE (£££)

- Right to Light Plan: Comprehensive legal strategy seeking to restore natural light to David's home office and award-winning garden

• Professional Environment Protection: Plan to secure optimal working conditions for the architectural practice
• Property Value Preservation: Expert intervention preventing permanent devaluation of David's property investment
• Neighbor Relationship Management: Professional mediation and negotiation, maintaining community harmony whilst achieving legal objectives
• Planning Law Enforcement: Full investigation and enforcement of planning permission requirements and building regulations
• Multi Legal Strategy: Coordinated approach using right to light claims, nuisance law, and planning enforcement simultaneously
• Expert Witness Coordination: Light assessment specialists and property valuation experts supporting comprehensive case
• Future Protection Framework: Legal safeguards preventing similar encroachments and protecting David's property rights permanently

ASSUMPTIONS:

• Full access to property deeds, planning records, and historical light enjoyment evidence
• Authority to instruct surveyors, light specialists, and expert witnesses as required
• David is available for site meetings, negotiations, and court proceedings if necessary
• Neighbor responds to professional legal communication and enforcement proceedings
• Local planning authority cooperates with investigation and enforcement action

EXCLUSIONS:

• Independent surveyor fees and expert witness costs (coordinated but separately charged)
• Court fees and disbursements if litigation becomes necessary
• Property repair or enhancement works beyond legal resolution requirements
• Ongoing property management disputes unrelated to the current fence issue

TECHNICAL DELIVERABLES:

• Comprehensive right to light assessment and legal claim preparation
• Planning law investigation and enforcement action coordination
• Professional mediation and neighbor negotiation management
• Expert witness instruction and case presentation coordination
• Property valuation protection and damage quantification
• Permanent legal framework preventing future encroachment issues
• Court representation if alternative resolution attempts fail

COMMUNICATION STRUCTURE:

• Immediate: Partner direct access for urgent negotiations and court deadlines (24/7 during active proceedings)
• Daily: Progress updates during active negotiation and enforcement periods
• Weekly: Strategic review meetings and case progression discussions
• Site visits: Senior lawyer attendance at property inspections and expert assessments

FOLLOW-UP SERVICES:

• 24-month monitoring ensuring compliance with any settlement or court orders
• Annual property rights review and boundary issue prevention advice
• Priority access for future property and neighbor dispute matters
• Preferred rates for ongoing boundary and planning law guidance

---

SILVER - ENHANCED DISPUTE RESOLUTION & PROPERTY RIGHTS SERVICE (££)

• Right to Light Strategy: Comprehensive assessment and legal action plan for light restoration
• Planning Law Investigation: Investigation of fence planning permission and building regulation compliance
• Professional Mediation: Structured negotiation with neighbor seeking practical resolution

• Property Rights Protection: Legal action to enforce David's established light rights
• Expert Assessment Coordination: Light specialist instruction and property impact evaluation
• Enforcement Action: Planning authority liaison and formal complaint coordination

ASSUMPTIONS:

• Standard business hours availability with extended support during critical negotiation phases
• David manages some direct communication with planning authorities with legal guidance
• Standard mediation and negotiation processes are sufficient for dispute resolution
• Neighbor responds reasonably to professional legal intervention

EXCLUSIONS:

• 24/7 availability for urgent developments
• Comprehensive court representation for extended litigation
• Multiple expert witness coordination
• Extended post-resolution monitoring

COMMUNICATION STRUCTURE:

• Business hours: Direct senior lawyer contact for dispute matters
• Bi-weekly: Progress calls and negotiation strategy updates
• Monthly: Written case progress reports and next steps planning

BRONZE - ESSENTIAL NEIGHBOUR DISPUTE GUIDANCE SERVICE (£)

• Legal Rights Assessment: Analysis of David's right to light and property law options
• Planning Law Guidance: Advice on fence planning permission requirements and enforcement options
• Negotiation Framework: Structured approach for neighbor discussions and resolution attempts
• Enforcement Options: Clear guidance on available legal remedies and next steps

• Action Plan: Detailed roadmap for dispute resolution and professional coordination

ASSUMPTIONS:

• Single comprehensive consultation covering essential dispute resolution options
• Standard office hours availability only
• David manages neighbor negotiations and planning authority contact with legal guidance
• Template approaches are sufficient for basic dispute resolution requirements

EXCLUSIONS:

• Direct neighbor mediation and negotiation services
• Planning authority liaison and enforcement coordination
• Expert witness instruction and case management
• Court representation and ongoing dispute management

COMMUNICATION STRUCTURE:

• Email and telephone during business hours only
• 48-hour response commitment for dispute queries
• Single follow-up consultation included for strategy clarification

ASSUMPTIVE CLOSING QUESTIONS:

• "Given the impact on your architectural practice and property value, shall we implement the complete Gold service to restore your professional environment fully?"
• "When should I begin coordinating with light specialists and planning authorities to expedite your light restoration?"
• "Shall I commence immediate negotiations with your neighbor to resolve this before it goes further?"
• "Should we start enforcement proceedings this week to protect your property rights and professional requirements?"

VALUE-BASED QUESTIONS TO ASK:

• "How much is the issue with your neighbor costing your architectural practice in lost productivity and work quality?"
• "What's your property worth, and has the neighbor's fence impacted its value?"
• "How much would relocating your home office cost if this isn't resolved quickly?"

• "What would losing your award-winning garden mean to your personal enjoyment and property appeal?"
• "How much stress and time is this dispute costing you that should be spent on your architectural work?"

VALUE CREATED:

• Professional Environment Restoration: Returns optimal natural light to the home office, enabling high-quality architectural work
• Property Value Protection: Preserves property investment, preventing permanent devaluation from light obstruction
• Work-Life Balance Recovery: Eliminates daily stress and frustration, enabling focus on professional and personal priorities
• Legal Rights Enforcement: Establishes and protects established property rights, preventing future similar issues
• Award-Winning Garden Preservation: Restores garden conditions, maintaining landscape achievement and personal satisfaction
• Neighbor Relationship Management: Achieves resolution whilst minimizing community conflict and ongoing tension
• Planning Law Compliance: Ensures neighborhood development follows proper legal processes and building regulations
• Expert Professional Support: Provides specialized knowledge in navigating complex property law and right to light issues
• Time Efficiency: Resolves dispute professionally, allowing David to focus on his architectural career rather than legal battles

SCENARIO 9: LANDLORD/TENANT

Jasmine Harper (34), private landlord. A first-time landlord facing issues with tenants who haven't paid rent for three months and have caused significant damage to her property. She's struggling with mortgage payments and needs a swift resolution.

GOLD - COMPLETE LANDLORD RESCUE & WEALTH PROTECTION SERVICE (£££)

- Emergency Property Recovery: Immediate possession proceedings using the fastest legal routes available for urgent financial relief
- Total Debt Recovery Program: Comprehensive rent arrears and damage recovery, including post-possession enforcement
- Mortgage Protection Strategy: Lender liaison preventing foreclosure and protecting Jasmine's property investment
- Property Damage Assessment: Professional coordination of damage evaluation and maximum recovery claims
- Future Landlord Shield: Complete tenancy agreement overhaul and robust tenant vetting procedures
- Emergency Financial Relief: Accelerated court proceedings and interim rent order applications where applicable
- Tenant Investigation Service: Full background checks and asset tracing for optimal debt recovery prospects
- Landlord Education Program: Comprehensive training preventing future tenancy problems and maximizing rental income

ASSUMPTIONS:

- Full access to tenancy agreements, rent records, property condition evidence, and mortgage documentation
- Authority to commence immediate possession proceedings and debt recovery action
- Property accessible for damage assessment and evidence gathering
- Jasmine is available for urgent court applications and settlement negotiations
- Mortgage lender cooperation

EXCLUSIONS:

- Property repairs and refurbishment costs (legal recovery framework provided)
- Independent property damage assessments and expert valuations (coordinated but separately charged)
- Bailiff services and enforcement costs (arranged but separately charged)

• Individual mortgage financial advice beyond legal protection strategies

TECHNICAL DELIVERABLES:

• Immediate possession proceedings using appropriate jurisdictional notices as appropriate
• Comprehensive rent arrears and damage claims with full enforcement procedures
• Emergency mortgage protection, including lender negotiation and payment arrangement strategies
• Professional property damage assessment coordination and maximum recovery claims
• Advanced tenancy agreement templates and robust tenant vetting procedures
• Complete landlord legal compliance framework preventing future disputes

COMMUNICATION STRUCTURE:

• Immediate: Partner direct access for urgent court deadlines and mortgage protection (24/7)
• Daily: Progress updates during court proceedings and enforcement phases
• Weekly: Strategic case management meetings with comprehensive progress review
• Court appearances: Senior representation with full preparation and advocacy

FOLLOW-UP SERVICES:

• 24-month post-recovery monitoring ensuring debt collection and tenancy compliance
• Annual landlord legal health checks and tenancy agreement reviews
• Priority access for future property disputes and tenant issues
• Preferred rates for portfolio expansion and additional property legal services

SILVER - ENHANCED PROPERTY RECOVERY & DEBT COLLECTION SERVICE (££)

• Property Possession Strategy: Comprehensive possession proceedings using appropriate legal routes

- Rent Recovery Program: Professional debt collection, including court judgment and enforcement
- Mortgage Protection Advice: Lender communication and payment arrangement guidance
- Damage Recovery Claims: Property damage assessment and compensation recovery
- Tenancy Agreement Review: Improved tenancy terms and basic tenant vetting procedures
- Legal Compliance Framework: Essential landlord obligations and dispute prevention advice

ASSUMPTIONS:

- Standard business hours availability with priority support during court proceedings
- Jasmine manages property access and basic tenant communications with legal guidance
- Standard possession and debt recovery procedures are sufficient for case resolution
- Mortgage protection achieved through advised communication strategies

EXCLUSIONS:

- 24/7 emergency availability for urgent decisions
- Comprehensive tenant investigation and asset tracing
- Advanced mortgage lender negotiations
- Extended post-recovery monitoring

COMMUNICATION STRUCTURE:

- Business hours: Direct senior lawyer contact for possession and debt matters
- Bi-weekly: Progress calls and case management updates
- Monthly: Written progress reports and strategy reviews

BRONZE - ESSENTIAL LANDLORD GUIDANCE SERVICE (£)

- Possession Process Guidance: Clear advice on eviction procedures and court application requirements
- Debt Recovery Framework: Basic rent arrears and damage recovery strategy, and court claim guidance

- Mortgage Communication: Essential advice on lender notification and payment arrangement discussions
- Tenancy Law Compliance: Fundamental landlord obligations and legal requirement guidance
- Template Documentation: Standard possession notices and court application forms

ASSUMPTIONS:

- Single comprehensive consultation covering essential possession and debt recovery requirements
- Standard office hours availability only
- Jasmine handles court applications and tenant communications directly with legal guidance
- Template procedures sufficient for straightforward possession and debt recovery

EXCLUSIONS:

- Court representation and advocacy services
- Complex debt enforcement and asset tracing
- Mortgage protection negotiations
- Ongoing case management support

COMMUNICATION STRUCTURE:

- Email and telephone during business hours only
- 48-hour response commitment for urgent possession queries
- Single follow-up consultation included for clarification

ASSUMPTIVE CLOSING QUESTIONS:

- "Given your mortgage situation and three months of lost rent, shall we implement the complete Gold service to protect your property investment immediately?"
- "When should I commence emergency possession proceedings?"
- "Shall I communicate with your mortgage lender immediately to prevent any foreclosure risk?"
- "Should we start comprehensive debt recovery proceedings this week to maximize your financial recovery?"

VALUE-BASED QUESTIONS TO ASK:

- "What would losing your property to mortgage foreclosure cost you financially and emotionally?"

- "How much additional rent will you lose for every month this situation continues?"
- "What's the total value of property damage that could worsen without immediate action?"
- "If this affects your credit rating, what would future mortgage applications cost?"
- "How much would replacing lost rental income cost if you can't recover the arrears?"
- "What would the stress and uncertainty cost your health and wellbeing if this drags on?"

VALUE CREATED:

- Property Investment Protection: Safeguards Jasmine's property asset through immediate legal action and mortgage protection
- Financial Recovery: Maximizes rent arrears and damage recovery through comprehensive debt collection procedures
- Speed of Resolution: Achieves the fastest possible tenant removal and financial relief through expert legal strategy
- Mortgage Security: Prevents foreclosure risk through professional lender communication and payment arrangements
- Damage Limitation: Stops ongoing property deterioration and maximizes compensation recovery
- Future Protection: Establishes robust tenancy procedures preventing repeat problems and protecting future rental income
- Stress Relief: Provides professional case management, removing the burden from the first-time landlord during the crisis
- Educational Value: Transforms Jasmine into an informed, protected landlord capable of successful property investment
- Credit Protection: Preserves financial standing through swift resolution, preventing long-term financial damage

Penguin logic… With Value-Based Pricing, Jasmine knows exactly what she's getting and what it costs. She can choose the service level that matches her budget and urgency. Most importantly, she's buying outcomes – property recovery, debt collection, mortgage protection – not lawyer timesheets.

SCENARIO 10: PLANNING PERMISSION

Robert Green (55), semi-retired consultant. Planning to build an annex for his elderly mother, but the local council rejected his application. Neighbors have objected despite similar developments nearby. He needs to appeal before his mother's health deteriorates further.

GOLD - COMPLETE PLANNING VICTORY & FAMILY CARE SOLUTION SERVICE (£££)

• Planning Strategy: Comprehensive appeal process management with expert planning law advocacy
• Urgent Care Solution: Fast-track planning appeal addressing deteriorating health timeline with priority case management
• Neighbor Relations Management: Professional community liaison resolving objections and building local support for development
• Precedent Research: Detailed analysis of similar developments nearby, building a bulletproof case for planning consistency
• Family Care Planning: Complete solution ensuring mother's care needs are met through successful annex development
• Council Relationship Reconstruction: Strategic engagement rebuilding positive relationships with planning authorities
• Construction Readiness: Complete planning framework enabling immediate building commencement upon approval

ASSUMPTIONS:

• Full access to all planning documents, rejection reasons, and neighbor correspondence
• Authority to engage directly with council planning officers and committee members
• Family cooperation in providing health evidence and care needs documentation
• Planning appeal lodged within statutory time limits with full supporting evidence
• Site access available for planning consultants and technical assessments

EXCLUSIONS:

• Architectural design services and technical drawings (coordinated but separately instructed)
• Building regulations approval process (legal framework provided)
• Construction project management and building supervision
• Individual neighbor legal disputes beyond planning objection resolution

TECHNICAL DELIVERABLES:

• Comprehensive planning appeal with expert legal advocacy and case presentation
• Detailed precedent analysis demonstrating planning policy consistency and fairness
• Professional neighbor consultation program resolving objections and building community support
• Strategic council engagement, rebuilding relationships and demonstrating development merits
• Complete care needs assessment integrating the mother's health requirements with planning justification
• Construction-ready planning framework enabling immediate project commencement
• Ongoing planning compliance monitoring and legal protection throughout development

COMMUNICATION STRUCTURE:

• Immediate: Partner direct access for urgent planning and family care decisions (24/7)
• Daily: Progress updates during critical appeal periods and council negotiations
• Weekly: Strategic planning meetings with comprehensive case development and family consultation
• Planning meetings: Senior representation with full preparation and advocacy at all council interactions

FOLLOW-UP SERVICES:

• 24-month post-approval monitoring, ensuring planning compliance and condition satisfaction
• Annual planning law updates and property development advice
• Priority access for future Green family planning and property matters

• Preferred rates for ongoing planning compliance and family care legal requirements

SILVER - ENHANCED PLANNING APPEAL & PRECEDENT ANALYSIS SERVICE (££)

• Planning Appeal Management: Comprehensive appeal process with legal advocacy and case presentation
• Precedent Research: Detailed analysis of similar developments, building strong consistency arguments
• Council Engagement: Strategic liaison with planning officers and committee members
• Neighbor Consultation: Professional approach to resolving objections and building community support
• Care Needs Integration: Health evidence coordination supporting annex necessity and planning merit
• Appeal Strategy: Expert planning law guidance maximizing approval chances

ASSUMPTIONS:

• Standard business hours availability with priority support during appeal hearings
• Robert coordinates family health evidence and care documentation with legal guidance
• Basic neighbor consultation is sufficient for objection resolution
• Planning appeal achieved through standard legal advocacy and case presentation

EXCLUSIONS:

• 24/7 availability for urgent planning crises
• Comprehensive council relationship management
• Extended community consultation programs
• Ongoing post-approval compliance monitoring

COMMUNICATION STRUCTURE:

• Business hours: Direct senior lawyer contact for planning and appeal matters
• Bi-weekly: Progress calls and appeal strategy updates
• Monthly: Written appeal progress reports and planning law guidance

BRONZE - ESSENTIAL PLANNING APPEAL GUIDANCE SERVICE (£)

• Appeal Assessment: Analysis of rejection reasons and appeal prospects with strategic recommendations
• Precedent Review: Basic research into similar developments and planning policy consistency
• Appeal Framework: Clear guidance on the appeal process and required documentation
• Council Guidance: Essential advice on engaging with planning authorities and officers
• Implementation Plan: Step-by-step appeal strategy with professional coordination requirements

ASSUMPTIONS:

• Single comprehensive consultation covering essential planning appeal requirements
• Standard office hours availability only
• Robert manages council interactions and neighbor discussions with legal guidance
• Template appeal structures sufficient for basic planning law requirements

EXCLUSIONS:

• Direct council advocacy and representation
• Comprehensive precedent research and legal analysis
• Neighbor objection resolution services
• Ongoing appeal process management and coordination

COMMUNICATION STRUCTURE:

• Email and telephone during business hours only
• 48-hour response commitment for planning queries
• Single follow-up consultation included for appeal clarification

ASSUMPTIVE CLOSING QUESTIONS:

• "Given your mother's deteriorating health and the urgent need for care accommodation, shall we implement the complete Gold service option?"
• "When should I begin coordinating with the council to fast-track your appeal?"

• "Shall I commence neighbor consultation immediately to resolve objections and build community support?"
• "Should we start building the precedent case this week using similar developments that gained approval nearby?"

VALUE-BASED QUESTIONS TO ASK:

• "What would delaying your mother's care accommodation cost in terms of her health and wellbeing?"
• "How much would alternative care arrangements cost if the annex appeal fails?"
• "What's the emotional cost to your family if your mother can't live independently near you?"
• "If the appeal fails, what would purchasing suitable alternative accommodation cost?"
• "How much would your mother's care home fees cost annually compared to home-based care?"
• "What's the property value increase if the annex is successfully built and approved?"

VALUE CREATED:

• Family Care Security: Enables proper care accommodation for the elderly mother, maintaining family proximity and independence
• Health Protection: Provides an urgent solution, addressing deteriorating health timeline with priority legal advocacy
• Emotional Wellbeing: Reduces family stress and anxiety through professional planning expertise and guaranteed outcomes
• Financial Efficiency: Avoids costly care home fees and alternative accommodation expenses through successful annex development
• Property Value Enhancement: Increases property value through successful planning permission and additional accommodation
• Community Harmony: Resolves neighbor disputes professionally, maintaining local relationships and community standing
• Planning Law Compliance: Ensures full legal compliance throughout development, preventing future planning enforcement issues

• Construction Readiness: Provides immediate development capability once planning approval is secured
• Future Planning Security: Establishes positive council relationships enabling future family planning applications

SCENARIO 11: LEASEHOLD EXTENSION

Jenny Roe (42), marketing executive. With 75 years remaining on her lease, Jenny wants to extend it after learning it's affecting her flat's value. She's worried about the costs and dealing with an unresponsive freeholder.

GOLD - COMPLETE LEASEHOLD LIBERATION & VALUE MAXIMISATION SERVICE (£££)

• Property Protection: Complete leasehold extension securing maximum property value and mortgage marketability
• Freeholder Strategy: Aggressive pursuit of unresponsive freeholder with legal enforcement and statutory compliance
• Cost Certainty Framework: Fixed-price extension process with premium cost protection and financial planning certainty
• Market Value Optimization: Strategic extension terms maximizing property value and future sale potential
• Mortgage Security: Complete lender liaison ensuring continued mortgage availability and competitive rates
• Legal Enforcement: Full statutory rights enforcement, compelling freeholder cooperation and compliance
• Future-Proofing Excellence: Extended lease terms protecting Jenny's investment for decades ahead
• Stress-Free Management: Complete process handling from initial notice through completion with zero client stress

ASSUMPTIONS:

• Full access to lease documents, property details, and freeholder information
• Authority to serve statutory notices and pursue legal enforcement against the freeholder
• Jenny's cooperation in providing property information and financial documentation
• Property valuation remains stable during the extension negotiation period

• Freeholder traced and legally compelled to respond within statutory timeframes

EXCLUSIONS:

• Independent property valuations and surveyor reports (coordinated but separately instructed)
• Leasehold tribunal representation if freeholder disputes premium (separate specialist advocacy)
• Property management and service charge disputes beyond extension requirements
• Mortgage arrangement fees and lender legal costs (legal framework provided)

TECHNICAL DELIVERABLES:

• Complete statutory leasehold extension with maximum property value protection and market enhancement
• Aggressive freeholder pursuit strategy with legal enforcement and compliance compulsion
• Fixed-cost extension framework with premium protection and financial certainty
• Strategic lease term negotiation maximizing property value and future marketability
• Comprehensive lender liaison ensuring mortgage security and competitive rate availability
• Full legal rights enforcement compelling freeholder cooperation and statutory compliance
• Extended lease documentation protecting investment and providing decades of security

COMMUNICATION STRUCTURE:

• Immediate: Partner direct access for urgent freeholder issues and extension crises (24/7)
• Weekly: Strategic progress meetings with extension development and freeholder negotiation updates
• Fortnightly: Comprehensive progress reviews with property value, legal, and financial updates
• Freeholder meetings: Senior representation with full preparation and advocacy support

FOLLOW-UP SERVICES:

- 36-month post-extension monitoring ensuring lease compliance and value protection
- Annual property value reviews and leasehold law updates
- Priority access for future Jenny Roe property and leasehold matters
- Preferred rates for ongoing lease management and property legal requirements

SILVER - ENHANCED LEASEHOLD EXTENSION & FREEHOLDER MANAGEMENT SERVICE (££)

- Leasehold Extension Management: Comprehensive extension process with legal advocacy and statutory compliance
- Freeholder Pursuit: Professional engagement strategy compelling freeholder response and cooperation
- Cost Control Framework: Extension cost management with premium negotiation and financial guidance
- Property Value Protection: Strategic extension terms protecting and enhancing flat value
- Mortgage Liaison: Lender communication ensuring continued mortgage availability
- Legal Rights Enforcement: Statutory notice service and compliance enforcement

ASSUMPTIONS:

- Standard business hours availability with priority support during critical extension phases
- Jenny coordinates property valuations and lender discussions with legal guidance
- Basic freeholder engagement is sufficient for extension completion
- Extension achieved through standard legal processes and statutory procedures

EXCLUSIONS:

- 24/7 availability for urgent freeholder crises
- Comprehensive mortgage market analysis
- Extended property value optimization strategies
- Ongoing post-extension monitoring and compliance

COMMUNICATION STRUCTURE:

• Business hours: Direct senior lawyer contact for extension and freeholder matters
• Bi-weekly: Progress calls and extension strategy updates
• Monthly: Written extension progress reports and legal compliance reviews

BRONZE - ESSENTIAL LEASEHOLD EXTENSION GUIDANCE SERVICE (£)

• Extension Assessment: Analysis of lease terms and extension options with cost estimates
• Freeholder Strategy: Basic guidance on compelling freeholder response and engagement
• Statutory Process: Clear framework for extension notices and legal requirements
• Cost Planning: Essential advice on extension premiums and negotiation strategies
• Implementation Plan: Step-by-step extension process with professional coordination guidance

ASSUMPTIONS:

• Single comprehensive consultation covering essential leasehold extension requirements
• Standard office hours availability only
• Jenny manages freeholder negotiations and property valuations with legal guidance
• Template extension procedures sufficient for basic leasehold law compliance

EXCLUSIONS:

• Direct freeholder negotiation and advocacy
• Comprehensive statutory enforcement and legal compulsion
• Property value optimization and mortgage liaison services
• Ongoing extension process management and coordination

COMMUNICATION STRUCTURE:

• Email and telephone during business hours only
• 48-hour response commitment for extension queries
• Single follow-up consultation included for process clarification

ASSUMPTIVE CLOSING QUESTIONS:

• "Given your property value concerns and the unresponsive freeholder, shall we implement the complete Gold service to start the extension success and protect the value of your property?"

• "When should I begin serving statutory notices to compel your freeholder's cooperation before further delays affect your property value?"

• "Shall I commence aggressive freeholder pursuit immediately to secure your extension and protect your investment?"

• "Should we start the fixed-cost extension process this week to provide financial certainty and value protection?"

VALUE-BASED QUESTIONS TO ASK:

• "How much property value are you losing each year with only 75 years remaining on your lease?"

• "What would it cost if mortgage lenders refuse to lend on your property due to the short lease?"

• "How much would you lose if you had to sell now at a reduced price due to lease length?"

• "What's the cost of stress and uncertainty dealing with an unresponsive freeholder yourself?"

• "If the lease continues shortening, how much more expensive will extension become in future years?"

VALUE CREATED:

• Property Value Protection: Secures and enhances flat value through strategic leasehold extension, preventing value erosion

• Financial Security: Provides cost certainty and premium protection, avoiding escalating extension costs

• Mortgage Marketability: Ensures continued lender availability and competitive rates through extended lease terms

• Stress Elimination: Removes the burden of dealing with an unresponsive freeholder through professional legal management

• Investment Protection: Safeguards Jenny's property investment, providing decades of security and value growth

• Legal Enforcement: Compels freeholder cooperation through statutory rights enforcement and legal compulsion

• Market Confidence: Creates marketable property with an extended lease attractive to future buyers and lenders

• Time Efficiency: Accelerates extension process despite freeholder non-cooperation through legal expertise
• Future-Proofing: Provides long-term property security, avoiding future extension complications and costs

Penguin logic… the traditional hourly model is completely blind to what's really happening here. We're not just drafting extension notices – we're protecting potentially tens of thousands in property value, ensuring mortgage availability, and transforming Jenny's biggest financial asset from a depreciating liability into a secure investment.

SCENARIO 12: UNFAIR DISMISSAL

Kris Harrison (45), sales director. After 15 years of service and consistently meeting targets, Kris was suddenly dismissed following a new CEO's appointment. He suspects age discrimination but has been offered a settlement agreement.

GOLD - COMPLETE EMPLOYMENT CAREER PROTECTION SERVICE (£££)

• Compensation Strategy: Comprehensive unfair dismissal and age discrimination claim maximizing financial recovery and justice
• Career Reputation: Professional reputation protection, ensuring dismissal doesn't damage future employment prospects
• Age Discrimination: Expert discrimination law advocacy proving age bias and securing substantial compensation
• Settlement Negotiation: Aggressive settlement negotiation, achieving far superior terms than the initial employer offer
• Future Employment Security: Complete career transition support, including reference management and employment law protection
• Corporate Accountability: Full investigation ensuring employer accountability and preventing similar treatment of other employees
• Financial Recovery: Maximum compensation recovery covering lost earnings, pension rights, and discrimination damages
• Executive Career Transition: Professional career coaching and employment law support for senior-level job market re-entry

ASSUMPTIONS:

• Full access to all employment records, performance reviews, communications, and dismissal documentation
• Authority to investigate discrimination claims and engage with employment tribunals
• Kris provides complete cooperation in evidence gathering and case preparation
• Employer settlement negotiations conducted through professional legal representation
• All statutory time limits met for tribunal claims and discrimination proceedings

EXCLUSIONS:

• Executive career coaching beyond employment law requirements (coordinated but separately instructed)
• New employment contract negotiation for future roles (separate service offering)
• Personal financial planning and pension advice (legal framework provided)
• Individual workplace stress counselling or medical treatment

TECHNICAL DELIVERABLES:

• Comprehensive unfair dismissal claim with expert tribunal advocacy and case presentation
• Detailed age discrimination investigation with evidence gathering and legal analysis
• Aggressive settlement negotiation, achieving maximum compensation and career protection
• Complete employment law compliance review, ensuring all claims and rights are maximized
• Professional reputation management, preventing career damage and future employment barriers
• Comprehensive discrimination case building with expert witness coordination and legal strategy
• Executive-level employment law protection for future career moves and contract negotiations

COMMUNICATION STRUCTURE:

• Immediate: Partner direct access for urgent employment and discrimination decisions (24/7)

• Daily: Progress updates during critical negotiation and tribunal periods
• Weekly: Strategic case meetings with comprehensive legal strategy and career protection planning
• Tribunal hearings: Senior representation with full preparation and advocacy at all employment proceedings

FOLLOW-UP SERVICES:

• 24-month post-settlement monitoring ensuring compliance and career protection maintenance
• Annual employment law updates and executive contract advice
• Priority access for future employment law and career protection matters
• Preferred rates for ongoing employment law compliance and executive career legal support

SILVER - ENHANCED EMPLOYMENT ADVOCACY & DISCRIMINATION CLAIM SERVICE (££)

• Employment Tribunal Representation: Comprehensive unfair dismissal claim with legal advocacy and case presentation
• Age Discrimination Analysis: Detailed discrimination investigation with evidence gathering and legal strategy
• Settlement Negotiation: Professional negotiation, improving employer settlement terms and compensation
• Career Protection: Basic reputation management and employment law guidance for future job searches
• Tribunal Strategy: Expert employment law guidance maximizing claim success and compensation recovery
• Legal Compliance: Full employment law analysis, ensuring all claims and rights are properly pursued

ASSUMPTIONS:

• Standard business hours availability with priority support during tribunal proceedings
• Kris coordinates evidence gathering and witness statements with legal guidance
• Basic settlement negotiation is sufficient for improved compensation terms
• Employment claims achieved through standard tribunal advocacy and legal representation

- 24/7 availability for urgent employment crises
- Comprehensive career reputation management
- Extended discrimination investigation and expert witness coordination
- Ongoing post-settlement compliance monitoring

COMMUNICATION STRUCTURE:

- Business hours: Direct senior lawyer contact for employment and tribunal matters
- Bi-weekly: Progress calls and case strategy updates
- Monthly: Written case progress reports and employment law guidance

BRONZE - ESSENTIAL UNFAIR DISMISSAL GUIDANCE SERVICE (£)

- Dismissal Assessment: Analysis of unfair dismissal prospects and age discrimination evidence with strategic recommendations
- Settlement Review: Professional evaluation of employer settlement offer with negotiation guidance
- Tribunal Framework: Clear guidance on the employment tribunal process and required documentation
- Legal Rights Analysis: Essential advice on employment law rights and claim procedures
- Implementation Plan: Step-by-step strategy for pursuing unfair dismissal and discrimination claims

ASSUMPTIONS:

- Single comprehensive consultation covering essential employment law requirements
- Standard office hours availability only
- Kris manages employer negotiations and tribunal interactions with legal guidance
- Template employment law strategies sufficient for basic unfair dismissal claims

EXCLUSIONS:

- Direct tribunal representation and advocacy
- Comprehensive age discrimination investigation and evidence gathering

- Settlement negotiation services and employer liaison
- Ongoing case management and tribunal coordination

COMMUNICATION STRUCTURE:

- Email and telephone during business hours only
- 48-hour response commitment for employment law queries
- Single follow-up consultation included for claim clarification

ASSUMPTIVE CLOSING QUESTIONS:

- "Given 15 years of loyal service and the suspected age discrimination, shall we implement the complete Gold service to secure justice and compensation?"
- "When should I begin the discrimination investigation to build the strongest possible case?"
- "Shall I commence settlement negotiations immediately to seek to achieve far better terms than their initial offer?"
- "Should we start protecting your career reputation this week to prevent any damage to future employment prospects?"

VALUE-BASED QUESTIONS TO ASK:

- "What would accepting an inadequate settlement cost you in lost career earnings over the next 20 years?"
- "How much would age discrimination damage your future employment prospects and earning potential?"
- "What's the emotional and financial cost of not achieving proper justice after 15 years of service?"
- "If your reputation is damaged, what would that cost in terms of executive-level job opportunities?"
- "How much would finding new employment at your level take in terms of time and cost in lost earnings during the job search?"

VALUE CREATED:

- Financial Recovery: Secures higher compensation through expert unfair dismissal and age discrimination advocacy
- Career Protection: Preserves professional reputation and future employment prospects through strategic legal representation
- Justice Achievement: Ensures proper accountability for unfair treatment after 15 years of dedicated service
- Age Discrimination Victory: Proves discriminatory treatment, securing substantial compensation and corporate accountability

• Employment Security: Provides comprehensive employment law protection for future career moves and contract negotiations
• Executive Transition: Enables confident job market re-entry with legal protection and reputation preservation
• Financial Stability: Maximizes compensation covering lost earnings, pension rights, and discrimination damages
• Corporate Responsibility: Ensures employer accountability, preventing similar unfair treatment of other employees
• Legal Precedent: Establishes a strong age discrimination precedent protecting other mature professionals
• Peace of Mind: Provides comprehensive legal expertise, removing stress and uncertainty from employment dispute

SCENARIO 13: WORKPLACE DISCRIMINATION

Amira Hassan (29), software developer. Repeatedly overlooked for promotion despite excellent performance reviews, Amira has evidence suggesting religious discrimination. She wants to stay in her job but needs the discrimination to stop.

GOLD - COMPLETE WORKPLACE EQUALITY & CAREER ADVANCEMENT SERVICE (£££)

• Discrimination Elimination: Comprehensive strategy ending religious discrimination whilst preserving employment and career prospects
• Career Advancement Protection: Strategic negotiation securing overdue promotion and fair future progression opportunities
• Evidence Preservation: Professional documentation and witness coordination building a bulletproof discrimination case
• Culture Transformation: Systematic approach changing discriminatory practices, protecting Amira and future colleagues
• Compensation: Full financial recovery for lost promotions, salary increases, and discrimination damages
• Employment Security: Complete protection against retaliation, ensuring job security throughout and after resolution
• Professional Development Restoration: Training opportunities, mentoring access, and career advancement previously denied
• Long-term Monitoring Framework: Ongoing workplace surveillance ensuring discrimination never recurs

ASSUMPTIONS:

• Full access to performance reviews, promotion criteria, and comparative employee advancement data
• Authority to engage directly with HR, senior management, and external employment tribunals
• Amira's cooperation in evidence gathering and strategic decision-making throughout the process
• Employer engagement in good faith negotiations before formal tribunal proceedings
• Workplace policies and procedures are subject to professional review and discrimination analysis

EXCLUSIONS:

• Personal counselling and therapeutic support (coordinated but separately arranged)
• Career coaching beyond legal discrimination resolution requirements
• Separate legal representation for colleague witnesses if conflicts arise
• Employment tribunal representation if concurrent personal injury claims emerge

TECHNICAL DELIVERABLES:

• Comprehensive discrimination case with expert legal advocacy and evidence presentation
• Strategic workplace negotiation securing promotion, compensation, and policy changes
• Professional evidence coordination, including witness statements and comparative analysis
• Employment security framework preventing retaliation and protecting future career progression
• Workplace culture assessment and discrimination prevention program implementation
• Financial compensation claim including back pay, promotion arrears, and discrimination damages
• Long-term monitoring system ensuring sustained workplace equality and career advancement

COMMUNICATION STRUCTURE:

• Immediate: Partner direct access for urgent discrimination incidents and workplace retaliation (24/7)

• Daily: Progress updates during critical negotiation periods and tribunal preparation phases
• Weekly: Strategic case meetings with comprehensive discrimination analysis and career advancement planning
• Workplace meetings: Senior representation with full preparation and advocacy at all employer negotiations

FOLLOW-UP SERVICES:

• 36-month post-resolution monitoring ensuring sustained workplace equality and career progression
• Annual discrimination law updates and workplace rights guidance
• Priority access for future Hassan family employment and discrimination matters
• Preferred rates for ongoing workplace monitoring and career advancement legal support

---

SILVER - ENHANCED DISCRIMINATION RESOLUTION & CAREER PROTECTION SERVICE (££)

• Discrimination Case Management: Comprehensive legal strategy addressing religious discrimination and securing fair treatment
• Promotion Negotiation: Strategic advocacy securing overdue career advancement and fair progression opportunities
• Evidence Development: Professional case building with witness coordination and comparative analysis
• Employer Engagement: Direct negotiation with management and HR resolving discrimination and advancement issues
• Compensation Recovery: Financial claim for lost promotions, salary increases, and discrimination damages
• Retaliation Protection: Employment security measures preventing workplace retaliation throughout resolution

ASSUMPTIONS:

• Standard business hours availability with priority support during critical negotiations
• Amira coordinates evidence gathering and witness cooperation with legal guidance

• Basic employer engagement is sufficient for discrimination resolution and promotion achievement
• Workplace discrimination resolved through professional negotiation and legal advocacy

EXCLUSIONS:

• 24/7 availability for urgent workplace crises
• Comprehensive workplace culture transformation programs
• Extended monitoring and long-term discrimination prevention services
• Complex tribunal advocacy if the case requires specialist employment court representation

COMMUNICATION STRUCTURE:

• Business hours: Direct senior lawyer contact for discrimination and employment matters
• Bi-weekly: Progress calls and case strategy updates
• Monthly: Written case progress reports and employment law guidance

BRONZE - ESSENTIAL DISCRIMINATION GUIDANCE SERVICE (£)

• Discrimination Assessment: Analysis of religious discrimination evidence and legal options with strategic recommendations
• Rights Education: Comprehensive guidance on employment rights and discrimination law protections
• Evidence Framework: Clear strategy for documenting discrimination and building a legal case
• Employer Approach: Essential advice on engaging with management and HR regarding discrimination concerns
• Resolution Strategy: Step-by-step approach to addressing discrimination whilst protecting employment security

ASSUMPTIONS:

• Single comprehensive consultation covering essential discrimination law requirements
• Standard office hours availability only
• Amira manages employer discussions and evidence gathering with legal guidance

• Template discrimination approaches are sufficient for basic employment law protection

EXCLUSIONS:

• Direct employer advocacy and representation
• Comprehensive evidence development and witness coordination
• Employment tribunal representation and formal legal proceedings
• Ongoing case management and discrimination resolution support

COMMUNICATION STRUCTURE:

• Email and telephone during business hours only
• 48-hour response commitment for employment queries
• Single follow-up consultation included for discrimination case clarification

ASSUMPTIVE CLOSING QUESTIONS:

• "Shall we implement the complete Gold service to guarantee workplace equality and secure your overdue promotion?"
• "When should I begin engaging with your employer to address this discrimination before it further damages your career prospects?"
• "Shall I commence evidence preservation immediately to build the strongest possible case for your promotion and compensation?"
• "Should we start the strategic negotiation process this week to attempt to resolve the discrimination?"

VALUE-BASED QUESTIONS TO ASK:

• "What has the lost promotion already cost you in salary increases and career advancement over the past year?"
• "How much will continued discrimination cost your long-term earning potential if left unaddressed?"
• "What's the emotional and professional cost of working in a discriminatory environment daily?"
• "If you're forced to leave this job due to discrimination, what would finding equivalent employment cost?"

• "How much would the stress and anxiety of ongoing discrimination cost your health and wellbeing?"
• "What's the financial value of securing fair promotion opportunities and workplace equality going forward?"

VALUE CREATED:

• Career Justice: Eliminates religious discrimination, ensuring fair treatment and equal opportunities in workplace advancement
• Financial Recovery: Secures compensation for lost promotions, salary increases, and discrimination damages, restoring career trajectory
• Employment Security: Protects job stability whilst addressing discrimination, ensuring continued income and career development
• Professional Dignity: Restores workplace respect and equal treatment, ending discriminatory practices and behavior
• Future Opportunity Protection: Establishes fair promotion processes, preventing future discrimination and ensuring career advancement
• Workplace Culture Improvement: Creates positive change benefiting Amira and protecting future colleagues from discrimination
• Stress Elimination: Removes daily discrimination anxiety, enabling a focus on professional performance and career development
• Legal Precedent: Establishes workplace equality standards preventing future religious discrimination in the organization
• Personal Empowerment: Provides confidence and legal protection, ensuring Amira's rights are respected and enforced

SCENARIO 14: SETTLEMENT AGREEMENT

Lucy Waters (41), finance manager. Offered redundancy during maternity leave, Lucy suspects discrimination but wants to handle things diplomatically. She needs the agreement reviewed and negotiated while maintaining her professional reputation.

GOLD - COMPLETE DISCRIMINATION PROTECTION & REPUTATION PRESERVATION SERVICE (£££)

- Discrimination Shield: Expert analysis of potential discrimination claims with strategic protection ensuring maximum compensation
- Diplomatic Negotiation: Sophisticated settlement negotiation preserving professional relationships whilst securing optimal financial outcomes
- Reputation Protection: Complete professional reputation management, ensuring future career prospects remain pristine
- Maternity Rights Maximization: Full exploitation of maternity and equality legislation, securing enhanced settlement terms
- Career Transition: Strategic career planning and professional network preservation during the transition period
- Financial Security: Optimal settlement negotiation ensuring maximum compensation and financial protection for the family
- Future Employment Shield: Complete reference management and professional reputation protection for subsequent roles
- Stress-Free Resolution: Complete case management allowing Lucy to focus on the new baby whilst experts handle employer negotiations

ASSUMPTIONS:

- Full access to employment records, HR communications, and maternity leave documentation
- Authority to negotiate directly with employer legal representatives and HR management
- Lucy provides complete discrimination evidence and timeline with professional support
- Settlement negotiations conclude within the maternity leave period, protecting employment rights
- Employer engagement in good faith settlement discussions with professional mediation

EXCLUSIONS:

- Employment tribunal representation if settlement negotiations fail (separate engagement available)
- Career coaching and professional development beyond reputation protection requirements

• Tax advice on settlement payments (coordinated with tax specialists but separately charged)

TECHNICAL DELIVERABLES:

• Comprehensive discrimination analysis with expert legal assessment and strategic claim evaluation
• Sophisticated settlement negotiation securing maximum compensation and professional reputation protection
• Complete maternity rights exploitation, ensuring enhanced settlement terms and employment law compliance
• Strategic career transition planning with professional network preservation and reference management
• Financial security optimization through expert settlement negotiation and compensation maximization
• Reputation protection program ensuring pristine professional standing for future employment
• Stress-free case management enabling family focus during the precious maternity period

COMMUNICATION STRUCTURE:

• Immediate: Partner direct access for urgent discrimination and negotiation decisions (sensitive timing respected)
• Daily: Progress updates during critical negotiation periods with employer representatives
• Weekly: Strategic planning meetings with comprehensive case development and family-friendly scheduling
• Employer meetings: Senior representation with full preparation and diplomatic advocacy throughout negotiations

FOLLOW-UP SERVICES:

• 24-month post-settlement monitoring ensuring agreement compliance and reputation protection
• Annual employment law updates and discrimination protection advice
• Priority access for future Lucy Waters family employment and legal matters
• Preferred rates for ongoing employment law requirements and career transition support

SILVER - ENHANCED SETTLEMENT NEGOTIATION & REPUTATION MANAGEMENT SERVICE (££)

- Settlement Agreement Optimization: Comprehensive review and negotiation securing fair compensation and terms
- Discrimination Assessment: Professional analysis of potential claims and strategic settlement positioning
- Reputation Management: Professional approach to employer negotiations, preserving career prospects
- Maternity Rights Protection: Employment law expertise ensuring maternity rights are respected throughout the process
- Diplomatic Negotiation: Expert settlement discussions, maintaining professional relationships where possible
- Reference Security: Professional management ensuring positive employment references for future roles

ASSUMPTIONS:

- Standard business hours availability with flexible scheduling for maternity leave requirements
- Lucy coordinates employer communications with professional legal guidance and support
- Basic reputation management is sufficient for settlement objectives and career protection
- Settlement achieved through standard negotiation processes without complex discrimination claims

EXCLUSIONS:

- 24/7 availability for urgent discrimination crises
- Comprehensive career transition planning and network preservation
- Extended employer relationship management beyond settlement requirements
- Ongoing post-settlement reputation monitoring and employment law updates

COMMUNICATION STRUCTURE:

- Business hours: Direct senior lawyer contact for settlement and discrimination matters (maternity-friendly timing)
- Bi-weekly: Progress calls and settlement negotiation updates

• Monthly: Written settlement progress reports and employment law guidance

BRONZE - ESSENTIAL SETTLEMENT AGREEMENT REVIEW SERVICE (£)

• Agreement Assessment: Professional review of settlement terms with strategic recommendations for improvement
• Discrimination Evaluation: Basic analysis of potential discrimination claims and settlement positioning
• Negotiation Guidance: Clear advice on settlement discussion strategy and professional approach
• Maternity Rights Advice: Essential guidance on employment law protection during maternity leave
• Implementation Framework: Step-by-step settlement process with professional coordination requirements

ASSUMPTIONS:

• Single comprehensive consultation covering essential settlement agreement requirements
• Standard office hours availability only (with reasonable maternity leave flexibility)
• Lucy manages employer negotiations directly with legal guidance and strategic advice
• Template settlement review sufficient for basic employment law protection requirements

EXCLUSIONS:

• Direct employer negotiation and settlement advocacy
• Comprehensive discrimination claim analysis and strategic positioning
• Professional reputation management and reference coordination
• Ongoing settlement implementation support and employer relationship management

COMMUNICATION STRUCTURE:

• Email and telephone during business hours only (maternity-friendly scheduling where possible)
• 48-hour response commitment for settlement queries

• Single follow-up consultation included for agreement clarification

ASSUMPTIVE CLOSING QUESTIONS:

• "Given the potential discrimination during maternity leave and your professional reputation at stake, shall we implement the complete Gold service to secure maximum protection?"
• "When should I begin diplomatic negotiations with your employer to ensure optimal settlement whilst preserving your career prospects?"
• "Shall I commence comprehensive discrimination analysis immediately to strengthen your negotiating position?"
• "Should we start protecting your professional reputation now to ensure seamless future career progression?"

VALUE-BASED QUESTIONS TO ASK:

• "What would inadequate settlement compensation cost your family's financial security during this crucial time?"
• "How much would professional reputation damage cost in terms of future career earnings?"
• "What's the emotional cost of handling employer negotiations yourself whilst caring for a new baby?"
• "If discrimination claims aren't properly pursued, how much potential compensation could you lose?"
• "What would poor employment references cost in terms of future job opportunities?"
• "How much would a career setback cost over the next decade of professional progression?"

VALUE CREATED:

• Financial Security: Maximizes settlement compensation, ensuring family financial stability during the maternity period
• Discrimination Protection: Expert legal analysis and claim pursuit securing enhanced compensation for potential discrimination
• Professional Reputation: Preserves pristine career standing, enabling seamless future employment and career progression
• Maternity Peace: Enables complete focus on the new baby whilst experts handle complex employer negotiations

• Career Preservation: Protects future earning potential through strategic reputation management and reference security
• Diplomatic Resolution: Maintains professional relationships where possible, preserving industry networks and opportunities
• Legal Compliance: Ensures full employment law protection during the vulnerable maternity leave period
• Stress Elimination: Removes negotiation burden

SCENARIO 15: REDUNDANCY

Sarah Ball (52), HR director. After being made redundant following a company merger, Sarah believes her role has been given to a younger, less qualified male colleague. She needs to negotiate her package while maintaining industry connections.

GOLD - COMPLETE CAREER PROTECTION & MAXIMUM COMPENSATION SERVICE (£££)

• Discrimination Strategy: Comprehensive age and sex discrimination case building maximum compensation through legal expertise and evidence analysis
• Career Reputation: Professional reputation management ensuring industry relationships are preserved whilst securing maximum financial settlement
• Package Optimization: Expert negotiation maximizing redundancy package, pension benefits, and post-employment compensation
• Confidential Settlement: Discreet legal advocacy securing substantial settlement without damaging professional standing
• Industry Network Preservation: A strategic approach, maintaining HR director relationships and future career opportunities
• Legal Protection Architecture: Complete employment law protection, including tribunal representation and appellate advocacy if required
• Financial Security: Comprehensive compensation strategy covering lost earnings, pension rights, and discrimination damages
• Executive Reference: Professional reference protection and industry reputation management throughout the process

ASSUMPTIONS:
• Full access to employment records, merger documentation, and colleague comparison evidence
• Authority to negotiate directly with company legal teams and senior management
• Sarah provides complete discrimination evidence and timeline documentation
• Confidential settlement preferred, maintaining professional industry relationships
• Company merger documentation and decision-making processes available for legal analysis

EXCLUSIONS:
• Executive career coaching and job placement services (professional connections provided)
• Personal financial planning and pension advice (legal framework secured)
• Tax advice on settlement payments (coordination with specialist advisers)
• Ongoing employment disputes unrelated to current redundancy and discrimination issues

TECHNICAL DELIVERABLES:
• Comprehensive discrimination case with expert legal analysis and maximum compensation strategy
• Executive redundancy package negotiation securing enhanced financial settlement and benefits protection
• Professional reputation management, ensuring industry relationships are preserved throughout the legal process
• Strategic settlement negotiation balancing maximum compensation with career preservation objectives
• Complete employment law protection, including tribunal representation and appellate advocacy capacity
• Confidentiality framework protecting both financial settlement and professional standing
• Industry reference protection and professional recommendation management

COMMUNICATION STRUCTURE:
• Immediate: Partner direct access for urgent discrimination and negotiation decisions (24/7)

• Daily: Progress updates during critical settlement negotiations and company discussions
• Weekly: Strategic case meetings with comprehensive discrimination analysis and settlement strategy
• Company meetings: Senior representation with full preparation and expert advocacy at all negotiations

FOLLOW-UP SERVICES:

• 24-month post-settlement monitoring ensuring compliance and ongoing legal protection
• Annual employment law updates and executive protection advice
• Priority access for future Sarah Ball employment and discrimination matters
• Preferred rates for ongoing career legal protection and industry relationship management

SILVER - ENHANCED REDUNDANCY NEGOTIATION & DISCRIMINATION PROTECTION SERVICE (££)

• Redundancy Package Enhancement: Professional negotiation securing improved financial settlement and benefits protection
• Discrimination Assessment: Legal analysis of age and sex discrimination evidence with strategic case development
• Settlement Strategy: Expert negotiation balancing compensation maximization with professional reputation protection
• Industry Relationship Management: Guidance on maintaining HR director networks whilst pursuing legal rights
• Employment Law Protection: Comprehensive legal advocacy and tribunal preparation if settlement negotiations fail
• Reference Security: Professional approach ensuring positive references and industry reputation preservation

ASSUMPTIONS:

• Standard business hours availability with priority support during settlement negotiations
• Sarah coordinates evidence gathering and company interactions with legal guidance

- Settlement achieved through professional negotiation without extended tribunal proceedings
- Basic reputation management is sufficient for industry relationship preservation

EXCLUSIONS:

- 24/7 availability for urgent settlement crises
- Comprehensive discrimination tribunal representation
- Extended industry reputation management
- Ongoing post-settlement legal monitoring

COMMUNICATION STRUCTURE:

- Business hours: Direct senior lawyer contact for redundancy and discrimination matters
- Bi-weekly: Progress calls and settlement strategy updates
- Monthly: Written case progress reports and employment law guidance

BRONZE - ESSENTIAL REDUNDANCY GUIDANCE & SETTLEMENT ADVICE SERVICE (£)

- Redundancy Assessment: Analysis of redundancy process and potential discrimination claims with strategic recommendations
- Settlement Framework: Essential guidance on negotiating an enhanced redundancy package and protecting employment rights
- Discrimination Review: Basic legal analysis of age and sex discrimination evidence and tribunal prospects
- Industry Guidance: Advice on maintaining professional relationships whilst pursuing legal rights
- Implementation Plan: Clear redundancy negotiation strategy with professional coordination requirements

ASSUMPTIONS:

- Single comprehensive consultation covering essential redundancy and discrimination requirements
- Standard office hours availability only
- Sarah manages company negotiations and evidence gathering with legal guidance
- Template settlement approaches are sufficient for basic employment law protection

EXCLUSIONS:

• Direct company negotiation and legal representation
• Comprehensive discrimination case building and tribunal advocacy
• Professional reputation management services
• Ongoing settlement negotiation support and legal advocacy

COMMUNICATION STRUCTURE:

• Email and telephone during business hours only
• 48-hour response commitment for redundancy queries
• Single follow-up consultation included for settlement clarification

ASSUMPTIVE CLOSING QUESTIONS:

• "Given the clear evidence and your senior HR director position, shall we implement the complete Gold service to maximize your compensation whilst protecting your reputation?"
• "When should I begin building the discrimination case to ensure maximum leverage in settlement negotiations?"
• "Shall I commence confidential negotiations immediately to try to resolve this professionally and quickly?"

VALUE-BASED QUESTIONS TO ASK:

• "What would losing your senior HR director career trajectory cost in lifetime earnings?"
• "What's the financial impact if your industry reputation is damaged?"
• "If settlement negotiations fail, what would extended tribunal proceedings cost in time and stress?"
• "How much would enhanced redundancy package terms be worth compared to statutory minimums?"
• "What would losing positive industry references cost in future executive opportunities?"

VALUE CREATED:

• Financial Justice: Maximizes compensation for clear discrimination, ensuring appropriate financial recognition of legal wrongs
• Career Protection: Preserves senior HR director reputation, enabling continued executive career progression

- Industry Relationship Security: Maintains professional networks and industry standing whilst pursuing legitimate legal rights
- Executive Settlement Excellence: Negotiates enhanced redundancy terms exceeding statutory minimums through expert advocacy
- Legal Rights Vindication: Ensures age and sex discrimination are properly addressed through professional legal expertise
- Confidentiality Management: Protects both settlement terms and professional reputation through strategic confidential resolution
- Reference Security: Preserves positive professional references essential for continued HR director career opportunities
- Financial Security: Provides a substantial compensation package protecting immediate and long-term financial wellbeing
- Professional Dignity: Ensures executive-level treatment throughout the legal process, maintaining personal and professional respect

SCENARIO 16: NON-COMPETE CLAUSE

Vincent Anderson (35), recruitment consultant. Offered his dream job but is currently restricted by a 12-month non-compete clause. The new employer wants him to start in 3 months. Needs to negotiate his exit from his current role without breaching his contract.

GOLD - COMPLETE CAREER FREEDOM & STRATEGIC TRANSITION SERVICE (£££)

- Career Liberation: Complete non-compete clause analysis and strategic negotiation, ensuring dream job opportunity secured
- Dual Employer Management: Professional relationship management with both current and future employers, preserving all professional relationships
- Legal Risk Elimination: Comprehensive contract analysis with a bulletproof exit strategy preventing litigation and financial exposure
- Strategic Negotiation: Expert commercial negotiation securing optimal exit terms and non-compete modification or waiver

• Career Protection: Complete legal framework protecting future career moves and professional advancement opportunities
• Timeline Management: Fast-track negotiation process meeting a 3-month deadline whilst maximizing negotiation outcomes
• Industry Reputation Preservation: Discreet professional handling, maintaining Vincent's market reputation and industry relationships
• Transition Optimization: Complete career transition strategy maximizing new role success and minimizing exit complications

ASSUMPTIONS:

• Full access to employment contracts, non-compete clauses, and new job offer documentation
• Authority to negotiate directly with the current employer's legal counsel and senior management
• Current employer willing to engage in commercial discussions regarding contract modification
• New employer supportive of negotiation process and flexible on start date within reasonable parameters
• Vincent provides complete disclosure of client relationships and competitive considerations

EXCLUSIONS:

• Employment tribunal representation if current employer initiates legal proceedings (separate matter)
• Career coaching and professional development services beyond legal transition requirements
• Ongoing employment law advice for new role beyond initial transition period
• Individual client relationship management and business transfer coordination

TECHNICAL DELIVERABLES:

• Comprehensive non-compete clause analysis with enforceability assessment and negotiation strategy
• Strategic dual-employer negotiation securing optimal exit terms and career freedom
• Complete legal risk assessment with detailed transition plan, preventing litigation exposure
• Professional relationship management, preserving industry reputation and future opportunities

- Commercial negotiation achieving non-compete modification, waiver, or acceptable restriction terms
- Timeline-critical project management, ensuring Vincent's dream job opportunity is secured within the deadline
- Career protection framework enabling future professional moves without legal constraints

COMMUNICATION STRUCTURE:

- Immediate: Partner direct access for urgent negotiation decisions and employer communications (24/7)
- Daily: Progress updates during critical negotiation periods and employer discussions
- Weekly: Strategic planning meetings with comprehensive negotiation updates and tactical adjustments
- Employer meetings: Senior representation with full preparation and commercial negotiation expertise

FOLLOW-UP SERVICES:

- 18-month post-transition monitoring ensuring non-compete compliance and career protection
- Annual employment law updates and career advancement legal advice
- Priority access for future career and employment matters
- Preferred rates for ongoing employment law requirements and professional development

SILVER - ENHANCED NON-COMPETE NEGOTIATION & TRANSITION SERVICE (££)

- Non-Compete Resolution: Comprehensive clause analysis with strategic negotiation for modification or release
- Employer Liaison: Professional negotiation with current employer, securing reasonable exit terms
- Legal Risk Management: Contract analysis with transition strategy minimizing litigation exposure
- Timeline Coordination: Project management ensuring negotiation completion within a 3-month deadline
- Career Transition Support: Strategic advice enabling a smooth move to the new role with legal protection
- Industry Relationship Preservation: Professional handling, maintaining market reputation and connections

ASSUMPTIONS:

• Standard business hours availability with priority support during employer negotiations
• Vincent coordinates with his new employer and manages timeline expectations with legal guidance
• Basic negotiation strategy sufficient for non-compete modification and career transition
• Current employer willing to engage in reasonable commercial discussions

EXCLUSIONS:

• 24/7 availability for urgent career crises
• Comprehensive dual-employer relationship management
• Extended industry reputation protection services
• Ongoing post-transition legal monitoring

COMMUNICATION STRUCTURE:

• Business hours: Direct senior lawyer contact for negotiation and employment matters
• Bi-weekly: Progress calls and negotiation strategy updates
• Monthly: Written transition progress reports and legal risk assessments

BRONZE - ESSENTIAL NON-COMPETE GUIDANCE SERVICE (£)

• Contract Assessment: Analysis of non-compete enforceability and negotiation prospects
• Exit Strategy Framework: Basic guidance on approaching current employer and managing transition
• Legal Risk Review: Essential advice on contract breach implications and mitigation strategies
• Negotiation Guidance: Clear recommendations for non-compete discussions and compromise options
• Implementation Plan: Step-by-step transition strategy with professional coordination requirements

ASSUMPTIONS:

• Single comprehensive consultation covering essential non-compete requirements
• Standard office hours availability only

- Vincent manages employer negotiations and his career transition with legal guidance
- Template negotiation approaches are sufficient for basic non-compete resolution

EXCLUSIONS:
- Direct employer negotiation and representation
- Comprehensive contract analysis and legal risk assessment
- Timeline management and project coordination services
- Ongoing transition support and legal monitoring

COMMUNICATION STRUCTURE:
- Email and telephone during business hours only
- 48-hour response commitment for employment queries
- Single follow-up consultation included for negotiation clarification

ASSUMPTIVE CLOSING QUESTIONS:
- "Given this job opportunity and the 3-month deadline, shall we implement the complete Gold service to seek to secure your career freedom?"
- "When should I begin negotiations with your current employer to secure the non-compete release before your new opportunity disappears?"
- "Shall I commence dual-employer liaison immediately to preserve all professional relationships?"
- "Should we start the legal risk analysis this week to ensure a transition without litigation exposure?"

VALUE-BASED QUESTIONS TO ASK:
- "What would losing this dream job opportunity cost your career progression and lifetime earnings?"
- "How much would a 12-month career delay cost in terms of salary, bonuses, and professional advancement?"
- "What's the financial impact if your current employer sues for contract breach and wins?"
- "If this opportunity passes, when might another similar role become available in your market?"
- "What would the reputational damage cost if this transition goes wrong and becomes industry gossip?"

• "How much additional earning potential does this new role offer over your current position?"

VALUE CREATED:

• Career Liberation: Secures dream job opportunity through successful non-compete negotiation and strategic legal planning
• Future Earnings Protection: Preserves significant salary increase and career advancement potential worth potentially hundreds of thousands
• Professional Reputation: Maintains industry standing and market relationships through discreet, professional transition management
• Legal Risk Elimination: Prevents costly litigation, financial penalties, and career-damaging contract breach allegations
• Timeline Security: Meets critical 3-month deadline, ensuring new employer commitment and opportunity realization
• Relationship Preservation: Maintains positive connections with current employer, enabling future industry collaboration
• Career Freedom: Establishes a legal framework preventing future non-compete restrictions limiting professional advancement
• Commercial Negotiation: Achieves optimal exit terms, potentially including financial settlement or reduced restriction periods
• Industry Expertise: Provides specialist employment law knowledge, ensuring maximum negotiation leverage and outcome optimization
• Peace of Mind: Delivers complete confidence in career transition without ongoing legal anxiety or professional uncertainty

Penguin logic… Vincent isn't purchasing legal time – he's buying his professional freedom, career advancement, and financial future!

SCENARIO 17: TRAFFIC OFFENCE

Daniel Kelly (37), pharmaceutical sales representative. Facing potential disqualification under "totting up" after being caught doing 88mph in a 50mph zone. Already has 6 points on his license from previous minor speeding offences. His employer has made it clear that his role cannot be adapted to accommodate a driving ban. Desperately seeking legal help to avoid disqualification through exceptional hardship arguments, as public transport isn't viable in his territory.

GOLD - COMPLETE CAREER PROTECTION & LICENCE RETENTION SERVICE (£££)

- License Retention Strategy: Expert exceptional hardship advocacy seeking driving license preservation and career continuity
- Employment Protection: Comprehensive career safeguarding, preventing job loss through professional legal representation
- Expert Advocacy: Senior motoring law specialist with proven exceptional hardship success record and magistrate relationships
- Total Case Management: Complete preparation including witness statements, employment evidence, and territory analysis
- Employer Liaison Service: Professional coordination with the pharmaceutical company, ensuring maximum corporate support and understanding
- Alternative Defense Analysis: Comprehensive review of technical defenses, procedural challenges, and mitigation opportunities
- Reputation Management: Discreet handling, preserving professional standing within the pharmaceutical industry and client relationships
- Future Compliance Program: Ongoing advice preventing further driving infractions and career-threatening situations

ASSUMPTIONS:

- Full access to employment contract, territory requirements, and employer correspondence regarding driving restrictions
- Authority to coordinate with the pharmaceutical company's HR and management for supporting evidence
- Daniel provides a complete driving history, speed awareness courses, and mitigating circumstances
- Court hearing attended with full preparation and professional advocacy representation
- Access to employer witnesses and territory analysis supporting exceptional hardship arguments

EXCLUSIONS:

• Employment law advice beyond motoring law intersection and career protection requirements
• Appeal to the Crown Court if the magistrates' court application is unsuccessful (quoted separately)

TECHNICAL DELIVERABLES:

• Expert exceptional hardship application with comprehensive supporting evidence and legal precedent analysis
• Professional employment impact assessment demonstrating career and financial consequences of disqualification
• Territory analysis proving public transport inadequacy and employment impossibility without a driving license
• Comprehensive mitigation presentation including character references and professional standing evidence
• Technical defense review exploring all possible challenges to speeding prosecution and points validity
• Employer coordination, ensuring maximum corporate support and witness availability for the court hearing
• Future driving compliance program preventing career-threatening traffic violations

COMMUNICATION STRUCTURE:

• Immediate: Partner direct access for urgent court and employment matters (24/7 before hearing)
• Daily: Progress updates during case preparation and employer coordination phases
• Weekly: Strategic meetings with comprehensive case development and exceptional hardship preparation
• Court representation: Senior partner advocacy with full preparation and pharmaceutical industry expertise

FOLLOW-UP SERVICES:

• Priority access for future Kelly family motoring law and employment protection matters
• Preferred rates for ongoing driving compliance and professional development support

SILVER - ENHANCED EXCEPTIONAL HARDSHIP DEFENCE & EMPLOYMENT PROTECTION SERVICE (££)

• Exceptional Hardship Advocacy: Comprehensive court representation with detailed hardship arguments and employment evidence
• Employment Impact Analysis: Professional assessment of career consequences and territory requirements
• Court Preparation: Expert case preparation with witness coordination and supporting documentation
• Employer Coordination: Strategic liaison ensuring corporate support and evidence provision
• Mitigation Strategy: Character references and professional standing presentation
• Technical Review: Basic analysis of possible defenses and procedural challenges

ASSUMPTIONS:

• Standard business hours availability with priority support during court preparation
• Daniel coordinates employer witnesses and territory evidence with legal guidance
• Basic exceptional hardship arguments are sufficient for license retention objectives
• Court representation achieved through standard motoring law advocacy and case presentation

EXCLUSIONS:

• 24/7 availability for urgent court preparation crises
• Comprehensive technical defense analysis and procedural challenge review
• Extended employer liaison and pharmaceutical industry relationship management
• Ongoing post-hearing driving compliance monitoring

COMMUNICATION STRUCTURE:

• Business hours: Direct senior lawyer contact for court preparation and exceptional hardship matters
• Bi-weekly: Progress calls and case preparation updates

• Monthly: Written case progress reports and motoring law guidance

BRONZE - ESSENTIAL EXCEPTIONAL HARDSHIP GUIDANCE SERVICE (£)

• Hardship Assessment: Analysis of exceptional hardship prospects with employment evidence requirements
• Court Guidance: Basic advice on magistrates' court procedure and exceptional hardship applications
• Employment Evidence: Essential guidance on gathering territory analysis and employer support documentation
• Mitigation Framework: Template approach to character references and professional standing presentation
• Implementation Plan: Step-by-step exceptional hardship strategy with court preparation requirements

ASSUMPTIONS:

• Single comprehensive consultation covering essential exceptional hardship application requirements
• Standard office hours availability only
• Daniel manages employer coordination and witness preparation with legal guidance
• Template exceptional hardship applications sufficient for basic career protection objectives

EXCLUSIONS:

• Direct court advocacy and representation
• Comprehensive case preparation and evidence coordination
• Employer liaison services and professional relationship management
• Ongoing court preparation support and case management

COMMUNICATION STRUCTURE:

• Email and telephone during business hours only
• 48-hour response commitment for exceptional hardship queries
• Single follow-up consultation included for court preparation clarification

ASSUMPTIVE CLOSING QUESTIONS:

• "Given your career depends entirely on keeping your license, shall we implement the complete Gold service?"
• "When should I begin coordinating with your company to build the strongest possible exceptional hardship case?"
• "Shall I commence comprehensive case preparation immediately to explore every possible defense and hardship argument?"
• "Should we start gathering territory analysis and employer evidence this week to demonstrate the impossibility of your role without driving?"

VALUE-BASED QUESTIONS TO ASK:

• "What would losing your pharmaceutical sales job cost in annual salary and career progression?"
• "How much would retraining for a non-driving career cost in time and lost earnings?"
• "What's the financial impact of unemployment while seeking alternative employment in your field?"
• "If you lost your license, what would alternative transportation cost for your current territory?"
• "How much would your family's financial security be affected by sudden job loss?"
• "What would the long-term career damage cost if you couldn't work in pharmaceutical sales?"

VALUE CREATED:

• Career Preservation: Protects Daniel's pharmaceutical sales career and prevents immediate unemployment through license retention
• Financial Security: Maintains family income and prevents devastating financial consequences of job loss
• Employment Continuity: Enables continued territory management and client relationship maintenance in the pharmaceutical industry
• Professional Reputation: Preserves standing within the pharmaceutical sector and prevents a career-limiting record
• Family Stability: Protects household financial security and prevents disruption to family life and commitments

• Future Earning Potential: Maintains career trajectory and promotional opportunities within pharmaceutical sales
• Transportation Freedom: Preserves driving independence essential for territory-based employment and family responsibilities
• Legal Compliance: Ensures proper court representation, preventing worse outcomes through inadequate self-representation

SCENARIO 18: DEFAMATION

Dr. Rachel Mason (45), veterinarian. False social media posts accusing her of animal cruelty are destroying her practice's reputation. Immediate action is needed to remove posts and restore reputation before the business fails.

GOLD - COMPLETE REPUTATION RESCUE & PRACTICE PRESERVATION SERVICE (£££)

• Immediate Crisis Response: Emergency 24/7 legal action securing rapid removal of defamatory posts and preventing further damage
• Reputation Restoration Campaign: Comprehensive digital reputation management rebuilding professional standing and client trust
• Practice Protection: Complete business preservation strategy, maintaining veterinary practice viability and client relationships
• Legal Action Guarantee: Full defamation litigation action seeking damages, injunctions, and public vindication of professional integrity
• Digital Fortress Creation: Advanced online reputation monitoring and protection, preventing future defamatory attacks
• Professional Standing Recovery: Industry relationship restoration and veterinary community confidence rebuilding
• Client Retention Program: Strategic communication, maintaining existing client relationships and rebuilding lost custom
• Media Management: Professional PR coordination ensuring positive coverage and narrative control

ASSUMPTIONS:

• Full access to all social media evidence, defamatory posts, and platform communications
• Authority to engage directly with social media platforms, internet service providers, and defamatory posters
• Veterinary practice records available demonstrating professional competence and animal welfare standards
• Immediate action authorized for emergency injunction applications and platform takedown requests
• Cooperation with reputation management specialists and PR professionals as required

EXCLUSIONS:

• Professional indemnity insurance claim management (legal framework provided)
• Veterinary regulatory body representation (coordinated but separately instructed if required)
• Business coaching and practice management consultancy beyond reputation recovery
• Individual client relationship counselling and veterinary service improvements

TECHNICAL DELIVERABLES:

• Emergency injunction applications securing immediate removal of defamatory content and preventing republication
• Comprehensive defamation action with damages claims and full legal vindication
• Advanced digital reputation management program rebuilding online presence and professional standing
• Social media platform engagement, securing content removal and account restrictions
• Professional reputation restoration campaign demonstrating veterinary competence and animal welfare commitment
• Client communication strategy, maintaining practice relationships and rebuilding customer confidence
• Ongoing reputation monitoring and legal protection against future defamatory attacks

COMMUNICATION STRUCTURE:

• Immediate: Partner direct access for urgent reputation crises and emergency legal action (24/7)

• Daily: Crisis management updates during critical defamation response and content removal periods
• Weekly: Strategic reputation meetings with comprehensive progress reviews and client relationship management
• Media coordination: Senior representation managing all press interactions and public communications

FOLLOW-UP SERVICES:

• 12-month reputation monitoring and legal protection against future defamatory attacks
• Annual digital presence reviews and reputation management optimization
• Priority access for future Dr. Mason professional and business legal matters
• Preferred rates for ongoing reputation protection and veterinary practice legal requirements

SILVER - ENHANCED DEFAMATION ACTION & REPUTATION MANAGEMENT SERVICE (££)

• Defamation Legal Action: Comprehensive legal proceedings securing content removal, damages, and professional vindication
• Reputation Recovery: Strategic digital management rebuilding professional standing and online presence
• Practice Protection: Business continuity support, maintaining client relationships and veterinary service delivery
• Content Removal: Platform engagement securing takedown of defamatory posts and preventing republication
• Professional Restoration: Industry relationship rebuilding and veterinary community confidence recovery
• Client Communication: Strategic messaging, maintaining practice relationships and customer trust

ASSUMPTIONS:

• Standard business hours availability with priority support during reputation crises
• Dr. Mason coordinates practice management and client communications with legal guidance
• Basic reputation management is sufficient for professional standing recovery

• Defamation action achieved through standard legal proceedings and platform negotiations

EXCLUSIONS:

• 24/7 emergency crisis response and immediate legal action
• Comprehensive PR management and media coordination
• Extended digital reputation monitoring and protection
• Ongoing post-resolution reputation management services

COMMUNICATION STRUCTURE:

• Business hours: Direct senior lawyer contact for defamation and reputation matters
• Bi-weekly: Progress calls and reputation recovery updates
• Monthly: Written defamation progress reports and practice protection guidance

---

BRONZE - ESSENTIAL DEFAMATION GUIDANCE & CONTENT REMOVAL SERVICE (£)

• Defamation Assessment: Analysis of defamatory content and legal remedies with strategic action recommendations
• Content Removal Guidance: Platform takedown procedures and legal notice requirements
• Legal Action Framework: Clear guidance on defamation proceedings and damages recovery options
• Reputation Advice: Essential strategies for professional standing recovery and practice protection
• Implementation Plan: Step-by-step defamation response with professional coordination requirements

ASSUMPTIONS:

• Single comprehensive consultation covering essential defamation law requirements
• Standard office hours availability only
• Dr. Mason manages platform communications and practice relationships with legal guidance
• Template defamation responses are sufficient for basic content removal and legal protection

EXCLUSIONS:

• Direct platform advocacy and takedown management
• Comprehensive reputation restoration and digital management

- Emergency legal action and injunction applications
- Ongoing defamation proceedings management and coordination

COMMUNICATION STRUCTURE:

- Email and telephone during business hours only
- 48-hour response commitment for defamation queries
- Single follow-up consultation included for action clarification

ASSUMPTIVE CLOSING QUESTIONS:

- "Given that your veterinary practice could fail without immediate action, shall we implement the complete Gold service to guarantee reputation recovery?"
- "When should I commence emergency legal action to remove these defamatory posts before more clients see them?"
- "Shall I begin coordinating with social media platforms immediately to secure content takedown and prevent republication?"
- "Should we start the reputation restoration campaign this week to rebuild client confidence and professional standing?"

VALUE-BASED QUESTIONS TO ASK:

- "What's your annual practice revenue that's at risk from these false animal cruelty accusations?"
- "How many clients have you already lost due to these defamatory social media posts?"
- "What would closing your veterinary practice permanently cost in terms of career and livelihood?"
- "How much would rebuilding your professional reputation cost if these posts remain online indefinitely?"
- "What's the emotional cost to you and your family of these false accusations about animal welfare?"
- "If you can't practice veterinary medicine, what alternative career income could you realistically achieve?"

VALUE CREATED:

- Career Preservation: Protects veterinary career and professional standing from malicious defamatory attacks
- Business Continuity: Maintains practice viability and client relationships, preventing business failure and revenue loss

- **Professional Vindication:** Achieves full legal clearance demonstrating veterinary competence and animal welfare commitment
- **Financial Recovery:** Secures damages compensation for business losses and reputation damage whilst preventing future income destruction
- **Emotional Wellbeing:** Reduces personal stress and family anxiety through professional legal advocacy and reputation restoration
- **Industry Standing:** Rebuilds veterinary community relationships and professional network confidence
- **Digital Protection:** Creates ongoing reputation monitoring and legal protection, preventing future defamatory attacks
- **Client Confidence:** Restores customer trust and practice relationships, enabling business growth and professional development
- **Legal Precedent:** Establishes a strong defamation deterrent protecting against future malicious online attacks on professional reputation

Penguin logic… Dr. Mason isn't purchasing legal time – she's buying back her entire career, professional reputation, and life's work from malicious online destruction!

SCENARIO 19: INHERITANCE DISPUTE

Victoria Davies (48), accountant. Excluded from father's will after a recent family argument, despite his verbal promises about inheriting the family home. Suspects undue influence from her stepmother.

GOLD - COMPLETE INHERITANCE JUSTICE & LEGACY RESTORATION SERVICE (£££)

- **Inheritance Recovery Strategy:** A comprehensive will challenge with expert probate litigation seeking rightful inheritance restoration
- **Undue Influence Investigation:** Professional forensic analysis uncovering evidence of stepmother manipulation and coercion
- **Family Legacy Protection:** Complete estate reconstruction preserving Victoria's father's true intentions and family heritage

• Advocacy Support: Relentless advocacy seeking fair inheritance settlement and family honor restoration
• Emotional Support Framework: Compassionate legal guidance managing family trauma whilst pursuing rightful claims
• Evidence Program: Comprehensive witness coordination and documentation, building a detailed inheritance case
• Settlement Negotiations: Strategic mediation achieving optimal inheritance recovery without prolonged court trauma
• Family Relationship Management: Professional guidance preserving salvageable family connections whilst pursuing justice

ASSUMPTIONS:

• Full access to all estate documents, will versions, and family correspondence
• Authority to investigate stepmother's actions and father's mental capacity at will-making
• Family members and friends willing to provide witness evidence regarding the father's true intentions
• Victoria's emotional resilience is supported through professional legal advocacy and family counselling coordination
• Proceedings commenced within any statutory time limits with full supporting evidence

EXCLUSIONS:

• Independent forensic accounting of estate assets (coordinated but separately instructed)
• Private investigation services for evidence gathering (arranged but separately charged)
• Family therapy and counselling services (recommended and coordinated)
• Stepmother's separate legal costs if settlement negotiations are successful

TECHNICAL DELIVERABLES:

• Comprehensive will challenge with expert probate litigation and undue influence evidence
• Professional investigation uncovering coercion evidence and mental capacity concerns
• Strategic settlement negotiation, achieving optimal inheritance recovery and family justice

• Complete estate analysis, ensuring all assets are properly considered and fairly distributed
• Witness coordination program building compelling case for Victoria's father's true intentions
• Family mediation framework preserving relationships whilst achieving settlement
• Ongoing probate management ensuring efficient estate resolution and inheritance recovery

COMMUNICATION STRUCTURE:

• Immediate: Partner direct access for urgent inheritance and family crisis support (24/7)
• Daily: Progress updates during critical evidence gathering and court proceedings
• Weekly: Strategic case meetings with comprehensive inheritance strategy and emotional support
• Court appearances: Senior representation with full preparation and advocacy at all hearings

FOLLOW-UP SERVICES:

• 24-month post-settlement monitoring, ensuring inheritance received and family relationships managed
• Annual estate planning advice preventing future inheritance disputes
• Priority access for future Davies family legal and inheritance matters
• Preferred rates for ongoing family legal requirements and estate planning

---

SILVER - ENHANCED INHERITANCE DISPUTE & EVIDENCE BUILDING SERVICE (££)

• Inheritance Challenge Management: A comprehensive will dispute with legal advocacy and case presentation
• Undue Influence Analysis: Professional investigation into the stepmother's actions and the father's mental capacity
• Evidence Coordination: Strategic witness gathering and documentation, building a strong inheritance case
• Settlement Strategy: Expert negotiation achieving fair inheritance recovery through mediation

- Family Guidance: Professional support managing family relationships during the inheritance dispute
- Probate Navigation: Complete estate proceedings management, ensuring efficient resolution

ASSUMPTIONS:

- Standard business hours availability with priority support during court hearings
- Victoria coordinates family witness evidence with professional legal guidance
- Basic investigation sufficient for undue influence evidence gathering
- Inheritance dispute resolved through standard legal advocacy and case presentation

EXCLUSIONS:

- 24/7 availability for urgent family crises
- Comprehensive forensic investigation services
- Extended family mediation programs
- Ongoing post-settlement family relationship management

COMMUNICATION STRUCTURE:

- Business hours: Direct senior lawyer contact for inheritance and probate matters
- Bi-weekly: Progress calls and case strategy updates
- Monthly: Written inheritance dispute reports and legal guidance

BRONZE - ESSENTIAL INHERITANCE DISPUTE GUIDANCE SERVICE (£)

- Inheritance Assessment: Analysis of will challenge prospects and undue influence evidence
- Legal Strategy Framework: Clear guidance on probate dispute process and required evidence
- Evidence Guidelines: Essential advice on gathering witness statements and supporting documentation
- Settlement Options: Basic negotiation strategy and family mediation recommendations
- Implementation Plan: Step-by-step inheritance dispute strategy with court procedure guidance

ASSUMPTIONS:

• Single comprehensive consultation covering essential inheritance dispute requirements
• Standard office hours availability only
• Victoria manages family relationships and evidence gathering with legal guidance
• Template dispute structures sufficient for basic probate challenge requirements

EXCLUSIONS:

• Direct court representation and advocacy
• Comprehensive undue influence investigation
• Family mediation and relationship management services
• Ongoing probate proceedings management and coordination

COMMUNICATION STRUCTURE:

• Email and telephone during business hours only
• 48-hour response commitment for inheritance queries
• Single follow-up consultation included for strategy clarification

ASSUMPTIVE CLOSING QUESTIONS:

• "Given the suspected undue influence, shall we implement the complete Gold service to preserve your inheritance?"
• "When should I begin investigating your stepmother's actions to uncover evidence of coercion and manipulation?"
• "Shall I commence gathering witness evidence immediately to build your case before memories fade?"
• "Should we start settlement negotiations this week whilst preserving what family relationships remain?"

VALUE-BASED QUESTIONS TO ASK:

• "What's the financial value of the family home and inheritance you've been denied?"
• "How much would losing your father's legacy and family heritage cost emotionally?"
• "What would accepting this injustice cost in terms of family honor and your father's memory?"
• "How much would alternative housing cost if you lose the family home inheritance?"

- "What's the long-term financial impact of losing your rightful inheritance on your retirement planning?"

VALUE CREATED:

- Inheritance Justice: Restores rightful inheritance, ensuring Victoria's father's true intentions are honored and the family legacy is preserved
- Financial Recovery: Recovers significant inheritance value, including family home and estate assets denied through manipulation
- Family Honor: Upholds family integrity and the father's memory against suspected undue influence and coercion
- Emotional Healing: Provides professional advocacy enabling focus on grieving whilst pursuing justice through expert legal representation
- Evidence Excellence: Uncovers truth about undue influence through professional investigation and witness coordination
- Settlement Efficiency: Achieves optimal inheritance recovery through strategic negotiation, avoiding prolonged court trauma
- Relationship Preservation: Manages family dynamics professionally, maintaining salvageable connections whilst pursuing rightful claims
- Future Security: Establishes proper inheritance, providing financial security and family legacy continuation for Victoria's future
- Legal Protection: Prevents the stepmother benefiting from suspected manipulation whilst ensuring the estate is distributed according to the father's true wishes

SCENARIO 20: PROFESSIONAL NEGLIGENCE - LAWYER MISCONDUCT

Amy Richardson (42), marketing director. Victim of catastrophic legal negligence where a solicitor missed a crucial personal injury deadline, then covered up the mistake by forging a witness signature. Original £100,000 claim now statute-barred due to the lawyer's misconduct and deception.

GOLD - COMPLETE PROFESSIONAL JUSTICE & MISCONDUCT RECOVERY SERVICE (£££)

• Professional Negligence Mastery: Comprehensive claim against the negligent solicitor with expert advocacy seeking full compensation recovery

• Misconduct Investigation Program: Forensic analysis exposing forgery evidence and cover-up deception with regulatory reporting

• Financial Recovery Strategy: Complete compensation pursuit, including original claim value plus additional misconduct damages

• Regulatory Action Coordination: Strategic SRA complaint ensuring professional accountability and preventing future victim creation

• Trauma Support Framework: Compassionate legal guidance managing betrayal trauma whilst pursuing maximum financial recovery

• Evidence Reconstruction: Comprehensive document analysis and witness coordination, rebuilding original personal injury case strength

• Settlement Maximization: Strategic negotiation achieving optimal compensation recovery, including aggravated damages for misconduct

• Future Protection Guidance: Professional advice preventing similar legal negligence and ensuring proper representation standards

ASSUMPTIONS:

• Full access to original case files, correspondence, and forged documentation evidence

• Authority to pursue both financial compensation and regulatory sanctions against the negligent solicitor

• Original personal injury case documentation available for reconstruction and damage assessment

• Amy's emotional resilience is supported through professional legal advocacy and trauma counselling coordination

• Professional indemnity insurance available from the negligent solicitor's firm for compensation recovery

EXCLUSIONS:

- Independent forensic document analysis for forgery evidence (coordinated but separately instructed)
- Private investigation services for additional misconduct evidence (arranged but separately charged)
- Trauma therapy and psychological support services (recommended and coordinated)
- Negligent solicitor's defense costs if settlement negotiations are successful

TECHNICAL DELIVERABLES:

- Comprehensive professional negligence claim with expert legal advocacy and misconduct evidence presentation
- Forensic investigation exposing forgery and cover-up with detailed regulatory complaint submission
- Strategic settlement negotiation achieving maximum compensation recovery, including aggravated damages
- Complete original case reconstruction demonstrating full financial loss and missed opportunities
- Witness coordination program building compelling negligence case and misconduct evidence
- Regulatory proceedings management, ensuring professional accountability and sanctions
- Ongoing claim management ensuring efficient compensation recovery and justice delivery

COMMUNICATION STRUCTURE:

- Immediate: Partner direct access for urgent negligence and misconduct crisis support (24/7)
- Daily: Progress updates during critical evidence gathering and regulatory proceedings
- Weekly: Strategic case meetings with a comprehensive recovery strategy and emotional support
- Court appearances: Senior representation with full preparation and advocacy at all hearings

FOLLOW-UP SERVICES:

- 24-month post-settlement monitoring, ensuring compensation received and regulatory action completed
- Annual legal service audit preventing future professional negligence exposure

• Priority access for future Amy Richardson legal matters and professional guidance
• Preferred rates for ongoing legal requirements and professional representation needs

SILVER - ENHANCED PROFESSIONAL NEGLIGENCE & EVIDENCE BUILDING SERVICE (££)

• Negligence Claim Management: Comprehensive professional negligence action with legal advocacy and case presentation
• Misconduct Evidence Analysis: Professional investigation into forgery and cover-up with regulatory complaint preparation
• Financial Recovery Coordination: Strategic compensation pursuit, building a strong negligence case
• Settlement Strategy: Expert negotiation achieving fair compensation recovery through mediation
• Regulatory Guidance: Professional support managing the SRA complaint during negligence proceedings
• Case Reconstruction: Complete original claim analysis, ensuring efficient compensation assessment

ASSUMPTIONS:

• Standard business hours availability with priority support during court hearings
• Amy coordinates evidence gathering with professional legal guidance and support
• Basic investigation sufficient for negligence and misconduct evidence presentation
• Compensation dispute resolved through standard legal advocacy and case presentation

EXCLUSIONS:

• 24/7 availability for urgent misconduct crisis support
• Comprehensive forensic document analysis services
• Extended trauma support programs
• Ongoing post-settlement regulatory monitoring and guidance

COMMUNICATION STRUCTURE:

• Business hours: Direct senior lawyer contact for negligence and compensation matters

- Bi-weekly: Progress calls and case strategy updates
- Monthly: Written negligence claim reports and legal guidance

BRONZE - ESSENTIAL PROFESSIONAL NEGLIGENCE GUIDANCE SERVICE (£)

- Negligence Assessment: Analysis of professional negligence prospects and misconduct evidence strength
- Legal Strategy Framework: Clear guidance on the negligence claim process and required evidence gathering
- Evidence Guidelines: Essential advice on gathering documentation and supporting misconduct evidence
- Settlement Options: Basic negotiation strategy and regulatory complaint recommendations
- Implementation Plan: Step-by-step negligence claim strategy with court procedure guidance

ASSUMPTIONS:

- Single comprehensive consultation covering essential negligence claim requirements
- Standard office hours availability only
- Amy manages evidence coordination and regulatory matters with legal guidance
- Template claim structures sufficient for basic professional negligence requirements

EXCLUSIONS:

- Direct court representation and advocacy services
- Comprehensive misconduct investigation and forgery analysis
- Regulatory proceedings management and SRA complaint coordination
- Ongoing negligence claim management and strategic guidance

COMMUNICATION STRUCTURE:

- Email and telephone during business hours only
- 48-hour response commitment for negligence queries
- Single follow-up consultation included for strategy clarification

ASSUMPTIVE CLOSING QUESTIONS:

- "Given the clear forgery evidence, shall we implement the complete Gold service to expose this misconduct fully?"

- "When should I begin the forensic investigation to uncover all evidence of this cover-up and deception?"
- "Shall I commence the SRA complaint immediately whilst pursuing maximum financial compensation?"
- "Should we start settlement negotiations this week to secure your £100,000 plus aggravated damages?"

VALUE-BASED QUESTIONS TO ASK:

- "What's the total financial impact of losing your £100,000 personal injury compensation?"
- "How much has this betrayal and misconduct cost you emotionally and professionally?"
- "What would accepting this injustice cost in terms of allowing other victims to suffer similarly?"
- "How much additional financial hardship has the delayed justice caused your family?"
- "What's the long-term impact of this professional betrayal on your trust in legal services?"

VALUE CREATED:

- Compensation Restoration: Recovers the full £100,000 personal injury compensation wrongfully lost through negligence
- Interest Recovery: Claims statutory interest on delayed payments from the missed deadline onwards
- Cost Protection: Amy pays nothing for justice delivery
- Truth Vindication: Exposes the lies and cover-up, validating Amy's suspicions and concerns
- Control Restoration: Returns power and agency after feeling helpless against professional deception
- Closure Achievement: Provides definitive resolution to the trauma and betrayal experienced
- Future Planning: Enables Amy to move forward with her life rather than dwelling on unresolved injustice

Penguin logic... Peace of Mind knowing that justice has been served, the truth has been exposed, and Amy can finally move forward with her life. That's what real value looks like – it's not just about the money, it's about restoring Amy's entire world!

COMMERCIAL CLIENT EXAMPLES

SCENARIO 21: BREACH OF CONTRACT

Iceberg Ltd contracted to supply Titanic Bergs 4 U Ltd with 1,000 marine safety beacons at £500 each (total: £500,000). After accepting and paying for the first delivery of 250 units, Titanic Bergs 4 U Ltd breached the contract by refusing further deliveries and switched to a cheaper supplier. Iceberg Ltd is left with 750 unwanted beacons and seeks to recover its losses.

GOLD – COMPLETE LITIGATION RECOVERY SERVICE (£££)

STRATEGIC PLANNING, SCOPING & ANALYSIS

- Comprehensive contract analysis and breach assessment
- Multi-scenario damages modelling
- Evidence preservation strategy
- Witness identification and preparation
- Alternative dispute resolution pathway analysis
- Litigation risk assessment matrix
- Cost-benefit analysis at each stage
- Settlement negotiation strategy development
- Enforcement route planning
- Asset investigation of defendant
- International recovery options assessment
- Interim relief strategy (if applicable)

DEDICATED SENIOR LEADERSHIP

- Senior Commercial Litigation Partner as lead lawyer
- Dedicated Counsel on standby
- Commercial Contracts Specialist
- Damages Assessment Expert
- Enforcement & Recovery Specialist
- Dedicated Case Manager
- Personal mobile access to Partner
- Weekend/evening availability
- Emergency response capability

ASSUMPTIONS

- Contract is governed by English law

- All parties are solvent and trading
- Original contract documentation is available
- Key witnesses are accessible
- Beacons remain in sellable condition
- No cross-claims exist
- Insurance policies do not restrict litigation
- Time limits for claims have not expired

EXCLUSIONS

- Product liability claims
- Employment law issues
- Regulatory compliance matters
- Tax advice on settlements
- Insolvency proceedings
- International arbitration
- Criminal law implications
- Intellectual property disputes
- Environmental compliance issues

TECHNICAL EXCELLENCE

- Expert contract interpretation and analysis
- Sophisticated damages quantification
- Loss of profit calculations with expert economists
- Mitigation of loss strategy implementation
- Comprehensive evidence bundle preparation
- Expert witness instruction and management
- Advanced legal research and precedent analysis
- Complex procedural applications
- Interim applications for urgent relief
- Asset tracing and recovery mechanisms
- International enforcement if required
- Settlement agreement drafting and negotiation

CLIENT COMMUNICATION & SUPPORT

- Weekly strategy calls with senior team
- 24/7 secure client portal access
- Daily email updates during active phases
- Comprehensive monthly reports
- Direct Partner mobile access
- Video conference facilities
- Stakeholder presentation services

- Board-level briefings
- Crisis communication management
- Media liaison if required
- Regular cost updates and budgeting

POST-CASE SUPPORT

- Judgment enforcement services
- Asset recovery assistance
- Settlement implementation monitoring
- Future contract drafting improvements
- Legal process review and learning
- Ongoing relationship management
- Annual contract review service
- Dispute prevention advisory
- Training for commercial teams

TECHNOLOGY & INNOVATION

- AI-powered document review
- Secure digital case management
- Virtual court hearing facilities
- Electronic bundle preparation
- Advanced costs tracking software
- Settlement negotiation platforms
- Secure communication channels
- Satisfaction guarantee
- Transparent costs reporting

SILVER - THE ENHANCED COMMERCIAL DISPUTE SERVICE (££)

DEDICATED SENIOR LEADERSHIP

- Senior Associate lead lawyer
- Commercial litigation specialist backup
- Dedicated paralegal support
- Standard business hours availability

STRATEGIC PLANNING, SCOPING & ANALYSIS

- Contract review and breach analysis
- Basic damages assessment
- Standard evidence gathering
- Settlement negotiation support

- Monthly strategy reviews

TECHNICAL EXCELLENCE

- Contract analysis and advice
- Standard damages calculations
- Court documentation preparation
- Basic expert witness coordination
- Settlement agreement drafting

CLIENT COMMUNICATION & SUPPORT

- Bi-weekly updates
- Standard email communication
- Monthly progress reports
- Business hours telephone access

POST-CASE SUPPORT

- Basic enforcement assistance
- Settlement monitoring
- Annual review meeting

BRONZE - THE ESSENTIAL DISPUTE SERVICE (£)
DEDICATED SENIOR LEADERSHIP

- Associate lawyer
- Paralegal assistance
- Standard business hours only

STRATEGIC PLANNING, SCOPING & ANALYSIS

- Basic contract review
- Simple damages assessment
- Standard court procedures

TECHNICAL EXCELLENCE

- Standard litigation procedures
- Basic documentation
- Settlement negotiation support

CLIENT COMMUNICATION & SUPPORT

- Monthly updates
- Email communication
- Standard reporting

ASSUMPTIVE CLOSING QUESTIONS

- "When would you like us to commence the Gold comprehensive recovery service?"
- "Should I begin the immediate evidence preservation process today?"
- "Shall we schedule the first strategy session for this week or next?"
- "Are you ready for me to instruct our damages expert to begin the assessment?"
- "Would you prefer morning or afternoon for our kick-off meeting?"
- "Should I prepare the engagement letter for the Gold service now?"
- "When can we arrange the initial case conference with the senior team?"

VALUE-BASED QUESTIONS TO ASK

- "What would successful recovery of your losses mean for your business?"
- "How important is speed of resolution versus maximizing recovery?"
- "Would you prefer to focus on settlement or pursue full litigation?"
- "What level of involvement do you want in the day-to-day case management?"
- "How critical is maintaining business relationships during this dispute?"
- "What concerns you most about the litigation process?"
- "Would having senior Partner/Lawyer involvement give you greater confidence?"

VALUE CREATED

- Recovery of £375,000 contract losses plus interest
- Mitigation of storage and disposal costs for 750 beacons
- Protection of business reputation and commercial relationships
- Precedent setting for future contract enforcement
- Deterrent effect on other potential contract breaches
- Peace of mind through expert legal guidance
- Risk mitigation through professional case management
- Cost certainty through fixed-fee arrangements

- Time savings through dedicated expert handling
- Strategic business advice beyond just legal recovery
- Future contract improvement recommendations
- Enhanced commercial negotiation position

SCENARIO 22: SHAREHOLDER DISPUTE

Mike Getz, CEO of DigiTechFlow Ltd. Mike founded the successful app development company 5 years ago with a university friend. The company is now valued at £8M with 45 employees. The co-founder, with a 30% shareholding, is going through a divorce and is threatening to sell their shares to their biggest competitor. This would block a crucial £2M investment opportunity that would double the company's size. The relationship between Mike and the co-founder has completely broken down. The existing shareholders' agreement is poorly drafted, and Mike needs urgent advice on share valuation, preventing the sale, and forcing through investment. Time is critical as potential investors want a decision within 30 days.

GOLD - COMPLETE SHAREHOLDER CRISIS RESOLUTION SERVICE (£££)

DEDICATED SENIOR LEADERSHIP

- Senior Corporate Partner as lead strategist
- Specialist Shareholder Disputes KC on standby
- Company Law Expert
- Corporate Finance Specialist
- Commercial Litigation Partner
- Valuation Expert Coordinator
- Crisis Management Director
- 24/7 emergency response team
- Direct Partner mobile access
- Weekend/evening availability
- Boardroom crisis meetings capability

STRATEGIC PLANNING, SCOPING & ANALYSIS

- Immediate restraint strategy development
- Comprehensive shareholder agreement analysis
- Emergency injunction assessment and preparation
- Investment opportunity protection planning

- Share valuation methodology review
- Competitor threat analysis and countermeasures
- Divorce proceedings impact assessment
- Alternative resolution pathway mapping
- Timeline management and critical path analysis
- Stakeholder communication strategy
- Board resolution planning and execution
- Emergency general meeting preparation
- Investment agreement restructuring options
- Exit strategy alternatives assessment

ASSUMPTIONS

- Company is incorporated in England & Wales
- Shareholders' agreement is enforceable despite drafting issues
- Co-founder's divorce proceedings are in English courts
- Investment opportunity remains available within the timeframe
- Company records and financial information are accessible
- No other hidden agreements or side letters exist
- Board has the authority to act decisively
- Potential investors are genuine and solvent
- No regulatory approvals required for investment

EXCLUSIONS

- Family law divorce proceedings
- Employment law matters
- Tax advice on restructuring
- Financial services regulation
- Competition law clearances
- International law aspects
- Intellectual property disputes
- Data protection compliance
- Criminal law implications
- Insolvency proceedings
- Property transactions

TECHNICAL EXCELLENCE

- Emergency court applications for injunctive relief
- Sophisticated share valuation analysis with expert valuers
- Pre-emption rights enforcement strategy
- Drag-along and tag-along rights analysis
- Investment agreement restructuring

- New shareholders' agreement drafting
- Corporate governance restructuring
- Board resolution strategy and implementation
- Emergency general meeting coordination
- Minority shareholder protection mechanisms
- Deadlock-breaking provisions implementation
- Corporate restructuring for investment readiness
- Due diligence coordination for investors
- Settlement negotiation and mediation
- Expert witness instruction and management

CLIENT COMMUNICATION & SUPPORT

- Daily progress calls during crisis phase
- Hourly updates during critical negotiations
- 24/7 secure messaging platform
- Emergency boardroom presentations
- Investor liaison and communication
- Stakeholder management coordination
- Employee communication strategy
- Media management if required
- Crisis communication protocols
- Regular strategy review sessions
- Cost tracking and budget management
- Decision tree analysis presentations

POST-CASE SUPPORT

- New corporate governance implementation
- Investment completion oversight
- Ongoing shareholder relationship management
- Corporate structure optimization
- Annual governance health checks
- Future dispute prevention mechanisms
- Board effectiveness reviews
- Succession planning advisory
- Exit strategy development
- Ongoing legal risk assessment

TECHNOLOGY & INNOVATION

- Secure digital war room platform
- Real-time document collaboration
- AI-powered contract analysis

- Virtual board meeting facilities
- Encrypted communication channels
- Digital signature platforms
- Share registry management systems
- Investor portal development
- Crisis management dashboards
- Automated compliance monitoring

SILVER - THE ENHANCED SHAREHOLDER DISPUTE SERVICE (££)

DEDICATED SENIOR LEADERSHIP

- Senior Associate lead lawyer
- Corporate law specialist support
- Litigation backup available
- Business hours priority access

STRATEGIC PLANNING, SCOPING & ANALYSIS

- Shareholders' agreement review and analysis
- Share valuation options assessment
- Investment protection strategy
- Basic restraint mechanisms
- Standard resolution pathways

TECHNICAL EXCELLENCE

- Shareholders' agreement interpretation
- Share valuation coordination
- Standard court applications
- Investment documentation review
- Settlement negotiation support

CLIENT COMMUNICATION & SUPPORT

- Daily updates during critical phases
- Standard business hours access
- Weekly strategy reviews
- Email and telephone communication
- Regular progress reporting

POST-CASE SUPPORT

- Settlement implementation monitoring
- Basic governance improvements
- Quarterly review meetings

BRONZE - THE ESSENTIAL SHAREHOLDER SUPPORT SERVICE (£)

DEDICATED SENIOR LEADERSHIP

- Associate lawyer
- Paralegal support
- Standard business hours only

STRATEGIC PLANNING, SCOPING & ANALYSIS

- Basic shareholders' agreement review
- Standard dispute resolution options
- Simple strategic planning

TECHNICAL EXCELLENCE

- Standard legal documentation
- Basic court procedures
- Settlement facilitation

CLIENT COMMUNICATION & SUPPORT

- Weekly updates
- Email communication
- Standard reporting procedures

ASSUMPTIVE CLOSING QUESTIONS

- "When shall we activate the Gold crisis resolution service to protect your investment opportunity?"
- "Should I begin preparing the emergency injunction application today?"
- "Are you ready for me to convene the senior team for an immediate strategy session?"
- "Shall we schedule the emergency board meeting for tomorrow morning?"
- "Would you like me to instruct our valuation experts to begin work immediately?"
- "Should I prepare the engagement terms for our comprehensive service now?"
- "When can we arrange the crisis team briefing - this afternoon or first thing tomorrow?"

VALUE-BASED QUESTIONS TO ASK

• "What would losing this £2M investment opportunity cost your business in growth and competitive advantage?"
• "How important is maintaining control and preventing competitor acquisition of shares?"
• "What's the impact on your 45 employees if this crisis isn't resolved quickly?"
• "How critical is it to resolve this within the 30-day investor deadline?"
• "What would happen to company morale and stability if this dispute becomes public?"
• "How important is preserving any possibility of future relationship repair?"
• "What's your biggest fear about how this situation could unfold?"

VALUE CREATED

• Protection of £2M investment opportunity and future company growth
• Prevention of competitor acquisition of strategic shareholding
• Preservation of £8M company valuation and growth trajectory
• Protection of 45 jobs and company stability
• Resolution of crisis within the critical 30-day timeframe
• Enhanced corporate governance for future protection
• Elimination of ongoing shareholder disputes and deadlock
• Maintenance of CEO control and strategic direction
• Professional reputation and credibility protection
• Investor confidence preservation and enhancement
• Long-term business relationship strategy development
• Risk mitigation through proper legal structures
• Peace of mind through expert crisis management
• Cost certainty in a high-stakes situation
• Strategic advantage through professional guidance

SCENARIO 23: EMPLOYEE THEFT

Sarah Williams, MD of Williams, Williams & Williams Retail, runs a successful chain of 12 high-end fashion boutiques. A trusted store manager of eight years has been discovered systematically stealing through an elaborate false refund scheme totaling £50,000. Sarah has evidence from CCTV and an internal investigation. The police are involved, but Sarah is worried about publicity damaging the brand. Three other employees might be implicated. Sarah needs guidance on the dismissal process, criminal proceedings, recovering money, and protecting her brand's reputation. Also needs to review all financial procedures.

GOLD - COMPLETE CRISIS PROTECTION & RECOVERY SERVICE (£££)

DEDICATED SENIOR LEADERSHIP

- Senior Employment Partner as crisis lead
- Criminal Defense/Prosecution Specialist
- Brand Protection & Media Law Expert
- Corporate Investigation Specialist
- Asset Recovery & Civil Litigation Partner
- Crisis Communications Director
- HR Policy Specialist
- Dedicated Crisis Manager
- 24/7 emergency response capability
- Direct Partner mobile access
- Weekend crisis support available
- Boardroom crisis meetings on-demand

STRATEGIC PLANNING, SCOPING & ANALYSIS

- Immediate damage limitation strategy
- Comprehensive evidence preservation and analysis
- Criminal proceedings coordination and strategy
- Employment law compliance roadmap
- Brand protection and reputation management plan
- Internal investigation expansion and methodology
- Asset recovery and civil claim assessment
- Insurance claim strategy and coordination
- Stakeholder communication planning
- Media response strategy development
- Employee morale and retention planning
- Financial control system overhaul design
- Whistleblower protection implementation
- Future prevention mechanism development

ASSUMPTIONS

- All employees are UK-based with standard contracts
- CCTV evidence is legally obtained and admissible
- The company has appropriate insurance coverage
- Police investigation is ongoing and cooperative
- No other significant frauds are discovered
- Company records are complete and accessible
- Management has the authority to implement changes
- No regulatory investigations are triggered
- Union involvement is not anticipated

EXCLUSIONS

- Tax advice on stolen amounts
- Regulatory compliance beyond employment law
- Property law matters
- Intellectual property issues
- Competition law implications
- International law aspects
- Family law matters affecting employees
- Immigration law issues
- Health and safety prosecutions
- Environmental compliance

TECHNICAL EXCELLENCE

- Emergency dismissal procedure implementation
- Criminal proceedings liaison and victim impact coordination
- Civil recovery claim preparation and pursuit
- Comprehensive internal investigation management
- Evidence gathering and forensic analysis coordination
- Employment tribunal defense preparation
- Disciplinary hearing management for all implicated staff
- Settlement negotiation and recovery agreements
- Insurance claim preparation and pursuit
- Restraining order applications if required
- Asset tracing and freezing mechanisms
- Expert witness instruction for financial analysis
- ACAS early conciliation management
- Grievance procedure navigation
- Whistleblower policy implementation

CLIENT COMMUNICATION & SUPPORT

- Daily crisis briefings during active phase
- 24/7 crisis hotline access
- Secure encrypted communication platform
- Regular stakeholder briefings
- Employee communication strategy and scripts
- Customer communication planning
- Media statement preparation and management
- Insurance company liaison
- Police liaison and coordination
- Regular legal risk assessments
- Cost tracking and budget management
- Strategic decision-making support

POST-CASE SUPPORT

- Financial controls system implementation
- Staff training program development
- Ongoing HR policy review and updates
- Annual fraud risk assessments
- Insurance policy optimization
- Reputation monitoring and management
- Employee relations ongoing support
- Future investigation protocol establishment
- Whistleblower system maintenance
- Legal compliance monitoring
- Crisis response plan updates

TECHNOLOGY & INNOVATION

- Secure digital evidence management
- Encrypted crisis communication platform
- AI-powered document review for investigations
- Digital forensics coordination
- Secure client portal with real-time updates
- Employee communication management systems
- Media monitoring and alert systems
- Financial analysis and recovery tracking
- Compliance monitoring dashboards
- Training delivery platforms

SILVER - THE ENHANCED EMPLOYEE CRISIS SERVICE (££)

DEDICATED SENIOR LEADERSHIP

- Senior Associate lead lawyer
- Employment law specialist
- Criminal law advisory support
- Business hours priority support

STRATEGIC PLANNING, SCOPING & ANALYSIS

- Employment dismissal strategy
- Criminal proceedings support
- Basic reputation management
- Standard investigation oversight
- Recovery claim assessment

TECHNICAL EXCELLENCE

- Dismissal procedure implementation
- Employment tribunal preparation
- Basic civil recovery claims
- Standard disciplinary procedures
- Settlement negotiation support

CLIENT COMMUNICATION & SUPPORT

- Daily updates during critical phases
- Business hours telephone access
- Weekly progress reports
- Email communication priority
- Basic stakeholder liaison

POST-CASE SUPPORT

- Basic policy review recommendations
- Settlement monitoring
- Quarterly check-in meetings

BRONZE - THE ESSENTIAL EMPLOYEE SUPPORT SERVICE (£)

DEDICATED SENIOR LEADERSHIP

- Associate lawyer
- Employment paralegal support
- Standard business hours only

STRATEGIC PLANNING, SCOPING & ANALYSIS
- Basic dismissal guidance
- Standard employment procedures
- Simple recovery options

TECHNICAL EXCELLENCE
- Standard dismissal documentation
- Basic employment law compliance
- Simple settlement facilitation

CLIENT COMMUNICATION & SUPPORT
- Weekly updates
- Email communication
- Standard progress reporting

ASSUMPTIVE CLOSING QUESTIONS
- "When shall we activate the Gold crisis protection service to safeguard your brand?"
- "Should I begin coordinating with the police immediately to protect your interests?"
- "Are you ready for me to implement the emergency dismissal procedures today?"
- "Shall we schedule the crisis team briefing for this afternoon?"
- "Would you like me to prepare the media protection strategy before any publicity emerges?"
- "Should I start the asset recovery process while the evidence is fresh?"
- "When can we convene the senior team to begin damage limitation - today or tomorrow morning?"

VALUE-BASED QUESTIONS TO ASK
- "What would negative publicity about employee theft do to your high-end brand reputation?"
- "How important is recovering the £50,000 versus preventing further losses?"
- "What's the potential impact on customer confidence if this becomes public?"
- "How critical is maintaining employee morale and trust across your 12 stores?"

- "What would happen to your business if more employees are found to be involved?"
- "How important is setting a deterrent example versus resolving this quietly?"
- "What's your biggest concern about how this crisis could unfold?"

VALUE CREATED

- Protection of premium brand reputation and customer confidence
- Recovery of £50,000 stolen funds plus interest and costs
- Prevention of future theft through robust system implementation
- Legal compliance and protection from employment tribunal claims
- Employee confidence restoration across all 12 stores
- Insurance claim maximization and coverage protection
- Criminal proceedings coordination for deterrent effect
- Crisis management, preventing business disruption
- Media protection preserving marketing investment
- Customer retention through reputation management
- Competitive advantage protection in a high-end market
- Peace of mind through expert crisis handling
- Long-term fraud prevention system implementation
- Staff loyalty and morale preservation
- Professional evidence gathering for maximum recovery
- Cost certainty during uncertain times
- Strategic guidance through a complex legal maze

SCENARIO 24: LEASE RENEWAL

James McEvoy, owner of 'Hillary Patterson's Kitchen', has had an award-winning restaurant in a prime high street location for 15 years. The landlord is refusing to renew his lease, wanting to redevelop. The business is valued at £2M, employs 30 staff, and has invested £300,000 in a recent kitchen renovation. Bookings taken for the next 6 months include weddings. The landlord has suggested a 300% rent increase to stay. James needs to understand his rights under the Landlord & Tenant Act and negotiate new terms or compensation for leaving.

GOLD - COMPLETE BUSINESS PRESERVATION & LEASE STRATEGY SERVICE (£££)

DEDICATED SENIOR LEADERSHIP

- Senior Commercial Property Partner as lead lawyer
- Landlord & Tenant Act 1954 Specialist KC
- Business Valuation Expert Coordinator
- Commercial Litigation Partner
- Employment Law Advisory Support
- Licensing Law Specialist
- Compensation Claim Expert
- Crisis Management Director
- 24/7 emergency response capability
- Direct Partner mobile access
- Weekend negotiation availability
- Site visit capability for negotiations

STRATEGIC PLANNING, SCOPING & ANALYSIS

- Comprehensive Landlord & Tenant Act 1954 rights analysis
- Security of tenure assessment and protection strategy
- Lease renewal negotiation strategy and tactics
- Compensation claim evaluation and maximization
- Alternative premises search and evaluation strategy
- Business continuity and preservation planning
- Employee retention and protection strategy
- Customer booking management and mitigation
- Redevelopment challenge assessment
- Market rent analysis and benchmarking
- Investment recovery and improvement compensation
- Future business protection and lease structuring
- Timeline management and critical deadline tracking
- Stakeholder communication and crisis management

ASSUMPTIONS

- Current lease is protected under the Landlord & Tenant Act 1954
- Business is legitimately conducted from premises
- Landlord's redevelopment intentions are genuine
- Planning permission requirements apply to redevelopment
- Recent kitchen investment is properly documented
- Employment contracts are standard UK agreements

- No breach of lease terms by tenant
- Licensing is up to date and transferable
- Financial records are complete and accessible
- No other legal disputes exist with the landlord

EXCLUSIONS

- Planning law advice on redevelopment proposals
- Tax advice on compensation payments
- Corporate restructuring advice
- Immigration law for staff
- Food safety and environmental health matters
- Intellectual property in recipes/brand
- Competition law issues
- Insolvency advice
- Family law matters
- Criminal law implications

TECHNICAL EXCELLENCE

- Landlord & Tenant Act 1954 analysis
- Court application preparation for lease renewal
- Compensation calculation
- Improvement compensation claim calculation
- Interim rent application strategy
- Counter-notice preparation and service
- Expert valuation instruction and coordination
- Market rent analysis and comparable evidence gathering
- Lease negotiation and heads of terms drafting
- Business rates and service charge analysis
- Alternative dispute resolution and mediation
- High Court proceedings management if required
- Settlement negotiation and documentation
- New lease documentation and clause negotiation
- Assignment and subletting rights protection

CLIENT COMMUNICATION & SUPPORT

- Daily updates during critical negotiation phases
- 24/7 crisis communication availability
- Secure client portal with real-time case updates
- Regular strategy meetings and decision consultations
- Employee communication strategy development
- Customer communication template provision

- Supplier and creditor liaison support
- Media management if required
- Insurance claim coordination support
- Financial impact analysis and reporting
- Alternative venue search coordination
- Booking management strategy advice

POST-CASE SUPPORT

- New lease implementation and compliance monitoring
- Ongoing landlord relationship management
- Rent review preparation and strategy for the future
- Business expansion legal support
- Annual lease health checks and advice
- Succession planning and lease assignment advice
- Insurance optimization review
- Future renewal preparation (if applicable)
- Alternative premises evaluation for expansion
- Ongoing commercial property portfolio advice

TECHNOLOGY & INNOVATION

- Secure digital case management platform
- Property search and analysis tools
- Financial modelling and compensation calculators
- Market rent analysis databases
- Document automation for lease documentation
- Client communication portal with real-time updates
- Expert valuation coordination platform
- Court filing and case management systems
- Settlement negotiation tracking tools
- Compliance monitoring dashboards

SILVER - THE ENHANCED LEASE RENEWAL SERVICE (££)

DEDICATED SENIOR LEADERSHIP

- Senior Associate lead lawyer
- Commercial property specialist
- L&T Act expertise available
- Business hours priority support

STRATEGIC PLANNING, SCOPING & ANALYSIS

- L&T Act rights assessment
- Basic renewal negotiation strategy
- Compensation evaluation
- Market rent analysis
- Standard business continuity planning

TECHNICAL EXCELLENCE

- Statutory notice response
- Court application preparation
- Basic compensation claims
- Standard lease negotiation
- Settlement documentation

CLIENT COMMUNICATION & SUPPORT

- Daily updates during negotiations
- Business hours telephone access
- Weekly progress meetings
- Email priority communication
- Basic stakeholder liaison support

POST-CASE SUPPORT

- Lease implementation monitoring
- Quarterly review meetings
- Basic ongoing advice

BRONZE - THE ESSENTIAL LEASE SUPPORT SERVICE (£)

DEDICATED SENIOR LEADERSHIP

- Associate lawyer
- Property paralegal support
- Standard business hours only

STRATEGIC PLANNING, SCOPING & ANALYSIS

- Basic L&T Act rights review
- Standard renewal procedures
- Simple compensation assessment

TECHNICAL EXCELLENCE

- Basic statutory compliance
- Standard negotiation support

• Simple documentation review

CLIENT COMMUNICATION & SUPPORT

• Weekly updates
• Email communication
• Standard progress reporting

ASSUMPTIVE CLOSING QUESTIONS

• "When shall we activate the Gold service to protect your £2M business and 30 employees?"
• "Should I begin the comprehensive L&T Act analysis today to secure your position?"
• "Are you ready for me to instruct the valuation experts to maximize your compensation?"
• "Shall we schedule the emergency strategy meeting for this afternoon?"
• "Would you like me to prepare the counter-offensive to your landlord's demands immediately?"
• "Should I start coordinating the court application to protect your lease rights?"
• "When can we convene the senior team to develop your negotiation strategy - today or tomorrow?"

VALUE-BASED QUESTIONS TO ASK

• "What would losing this prime location after 15 years do to your £2M business value?"
• "How critical is protecting the jobs of your 30 loyal employees?"
• "What's the reputational impact of cancelling 6 months of bookings, including weddings?"
• "How important is recovering your £300,000 recent kitchen investment?"
• "What would a 300% rent increase do to your business profitability and viability?"
• "How difficult would it be to recreate your award-winning reputation in a new location?"
• "What's your biggest fear about how this landlord situation could unfold?"
• "How important is maintaining your competitive advantage in this prime location?"

VALUE CREATED

- Protection of £2M business value and going concern
- Preservation of 30 jobs and employee livelihoods
- Recovery of £300,000 kitchen renovation investment
- Protection of 6 months forward bookings and customer relationships
- Legal rights maximization under the Landlord & Tenant Act 1954
- Compensation maximization for business loss and improvements
- Award-winning reputation and location preservation
- Competitive advantage maintenance in a prime high street location
- Customer confidence and booking security protection
- Professional negotiation leverage against landlord pressure
- Alternative exit strategy with maximum compensation if required
- Peace of mind through expert legal representation
- Cost certainty during business-critical negotiations
- Strategic guidance through complex commercial property law
- Long-term business security and lease protection
- Professional valuation and evidence gathering for maximum recovery

SCENARIO 25: INTELLECTUAL PROPERTY THEFT

Dr. Emma Jones, Founder of BioGenRayner Solutions, has developed a revolutionary cancer screening process over 5 years with £3M investment. Her former Head of Research left six months ago, and has now launched a competing business using suspiciously similar processes. Emma has evidence of downloaded files before departure. The new competitor is already approaching their clients. Patents pending but not yet granted. Emma needs urgent action to protect her IP and stop the competitor from trading.

GOLD - COMPLETE IP FORTRESS & RECOVERY SERVICE (£££)

DEDICATED SENIOR LEADERSHIP

- Senior IP Partner as strategic lead
- Patent Attorney (Chartered/European)
- Trade Secrets & Confidentiality Specialist
- Employment Law Partner for breach of duty claims
- Commercial Litigation KC for urgent injunctions
- Forensic IT Investigation Specialist
- Crisis Management Director
- International IP Coordinator
- 24/7 emergency injunction capability
- Direct Partner mobile access
- Weekend urgent court applications
- Boardroom war room facilities

STRATEGIC PLANNING, SCOPING & ANALYSIS

- Immediate injunction strategy and emergency court applications
- Comprehensive IP audit and protection mapping
- Trade secret identification and classification
- Employment contract breach analysis
- Forensic IT investigation and evidence preservation
- Patent acceleration and strengthening strategy
- Client retention and protection program
- Competitor intelligence and market analysis
- International IP protection strategy
- Licensing and commercialization optimization
- IP valuation for damages and investment protection
- Media and stakeholder communication strategy
- Insurance claim coordination (if applicable)
- Investment protection and recovery planning

ASSUMPTIONS

- Company is UK-based with English law employment contracts
- Digital evidence is recoverable and admissible
- Patents are properly filed and prosecutable
- Former employee had access to confidential information
- Competition is within the UK jurisdiction initially
- The company has proper confidentiality agreements

- No international treaty complications
- Research data is properly documented
- Investment agreements don't restrict IP actions

EXCLUSIONS

- Regulatory approvals for medical devices
- Clinical trials and medical compliance
- Tax implications of IP exploitation
- Corporate finance and investment advice
- Competition/antitrust law clearances
- Data protection compliance beyond IP
- International trade regulations
- Product liability issues
- Medical malpractice considerations
- Environmental compliance

TECHNICAL EXCELLENCE

- Emergency injunction applications
- Patent prosecution acceleration and strategic filing
- Trade secret protection and confidentiality enforcement
- Employment law breach claims and restrictive covenant enforcement
- Forensic IT investigation and digital evidence recovery
- Copyright and database rights protection
- Passing off and unfair competition claims
- Client anti-solicitation enforcement
- Springboard injunction applications
- Damages quantification and expert valuation
- Cross-border enforcement coordination
- Settlement negotiation from a position of strength
- Licensing strategy and commercialization planning
- IP portfolio optimization and strategic development

CLIENT COMMUNICATION & SUPPORT

- Hourly updates during emergency applications
- 24/7 crisis communication platform
- Daily war room briefings during active litigation
- Investor and stakeholder briefing coordination
- Client communication and retention strategy
- Media management and reputation protection
- Regular IP strategy reviews and updates

- Cost tracking with litigation funding options
- Decision tree analysis and risk assessment
- Commercial impact monitoring and reporting

POST-CASE SUPPORT

- Comprehensive IP protection system implementation
- Employee training on confidentiality and IP protection
- Enhanced employment contracts and restrictive covenants
- IP monitoring and enforcement protocols
- Patent portfolio management and prosecution
- Licensing and commercialization strategy
- Annual IP audits and protection reviews
- Competitor monitoring and intelligence systems
- Crisis response protocol development
- Investment protection ongoing advisory

TECHNOLOGY & INNOVATION

- Advanced forensic IT investigation tools
- Secure digital evidence preservation platforms
- AI-powered patent landscape analysis
- Encrypted crisis communication systems
- IP monitoring and alert systems
- Digital watermarking and protection technologies
- Secure client portal with real-time case updates
- Patent prosecution management platforms
- Competitor intelligence gathering systems
- IP valuation and damages calculation tools

SILVER - THE ENHANCED IP PROTECTION SERVICE (££)

DEDICATED SENIOR LEADERSHIP

- Senior Associate IP specialist
- Patent attorney support
- Employment law backup
- Business hours priority access

STRATEGIC PLANNING, SCOPING & ANALYSIS

- Standard injunction assessment
- IP protection strategy
- Employment breach analysis

- Basic forensic investigation
- Patent filing coordination

TECHNICAL EXCELLENCE

- Standard injunction applications
- Patent prosecution support
- Employment law claims
- Basic IP enforcement
- Settlement negotiation facilitation

CLIENT COMMUNICATION & SUPPORT

- Daily updates during active phases
- Business hours telephone access
- Weekly strategy meetings
- Email priority communication
- Regular progress reporting

POST-CASE SUPPORT

- Basic IP protection recommendations
- Standard employment contract review
- Quarterly IP health checks

BRONZE - THE ESSENTIAL IP SUPPORT SERVICE (£)

DEDICATED SENIOR LEADERSHIP

- Associate lawyer
- Patent attorney (junior)
- Standard business hours only

STRATEGIC PLANNING, SCOPING & ANALYSIS

- Basic IP assessment
- Standard protection options
- Simple enforcement strategy

TECHNICAL EXCELLENCE

- Standard legal documentation
- Basic patent filing support
- Simple dispute resolution

CLIENT COMMUNICATION & SUPPORT

- Weekly updates
- Email communication

• Standard reporting procedures

ASSUMPTIVE CLOSING QUESTIONS

• "When shall we activate the Gold IP fortress service to protect your £3M investment?"
• "Should I begin preparing the emergency injunction application today?"
• "Are you ready for me to coordinate the forensic IT investigation immediately?"
• "Shall we schedule the urgent court application for tomorrow morning?"
• "Would you like me to instruct our patent attorney to accelerate your patent applications?"
• "Should I start the asset freezing procedures before they hide more evidence?"
• "When can we convene the IP war room - this afternoon or first thing tomorrow?"

VALUE-BASED QUESTIONS TO ASK

• "What would losing your competitive advantage in cancer screening mean to your business future?"
• "How critical is protecting your £3M investment and 5 years of development work?"
• "What's the potential market value of your revolutionary screening process?"
• "How important is stopping them from approaching more of your clients?"
• "What would happen if competitors gain access to your proprietary processes?"
• "How vital is maintaining your first-mover advantage in this breakthrough technology?"
• "What's your biggest fear about how this IP theft could impact your business?"

VALUE CREATED

• Protection of £3M investment and 5 years of development work
• Prevention of competitor advantage using stolen IP
• Recovery of confidential information and trade secrets
• Client base protection and retention

- Patent portfolio acceleration and strengthening
- Competitive market position preservation
- Investment value protection and enhancement
- Licensing and commercialization opportunity optimization
- Deterrent effect preventing future IP theft
- Employee loyalty and confidentiality reinforcement
- Professional reputation and credibility protection
- Peace of mind through expert IP warfare management
- Long-term IP strategy development and implementation
- International protection coordination
- Damages recovery for losses and future profits
- Crisis management, preventing business disruption
- Evidence preservation for maximum legal leverage
- Strategic advantage through sophisticated IP enforcement

SCENARIO 26: COMMERCIAL CONTRACT BREACH

Raj Patel, CEO of CloudServe4U IT. A major client (25% of revenue) suddenly terminated a £500K annual contract, claiming service failures. No formal complaints had been previously raised. Raj suspects they've been approached by a cheaper competitor. CloudServe4U has a perfect service record and all KPIs are met, with 20 staff dedicated to this contract. Raj needs to recover losses while maintaining the company's reputation in a small industry where everyone knows each other.

GOLD - THE COMPREHENSIVE CONTRACT RECOVERY & REPUTATION FORTRESS SERVICE (£££)

DEDICATED SENIOR LEADERSHIP

- Senior Commercial Litigation Partner as strategic lead.
- Contract Law KC for complex breach analysis
- IT & Technology Law Specialist
- Employment Law Partner for workforce restructuring
- Reputation Management & Crisis Communications Director
- Commercial Mediation Specialist
- Industry Relations Advisor
- Forensic IT Evidence Specialist

- 24/7 urgent response capability
- Direct Partner mobile access
- Weekend crisis strategy sessions
- Executive boardroom war room facilities

STRATEGIC PLANNING, SCOPING & ANALYSIS

- Immediate contract breach analysis and legal position assessment
- Comprehensive damages quantification and loss calculation
- Reputation protection strategy for small industry dynamics
- Workforce restructuring and employment law compliance
- Evidence gathering and KPI documentation compilation
- Competitor intelligence and market analysis
- Client relationship forensics and communication audit
- Settlement strategy with relationship preservation options
- Alternative dispute resolution pathway planning
- Industry network protection and stakeholder management
- Future contract fortification and protection mechanisms
- Crisis communication and media management strategy
- Insurance claim coordination (if applicable)
- Business continuity and recovery planning

ASSUMPTIONS

- Contract contains proper termination and dispute clauses
- KPI measurements are documented and verifiable
- All parties are UK-based under English law
- Service records are comprehensive and accessible
- Employment contracts allow flexible redeployment
- No regulatory compliance issues affecting services
- Client's termination notice follows contractual procedures
- Industry relationships are commercially important
- No conflicts of interest with other clients

EXCLUSIONS

- Data protection compliance beyond contract breach
- Cybersecurity incident investigation
- Regulatory compliance in specific IT sectors
- Tax implications of contract termination
- Corporate restructuring and insolvency advice
- Intellectual property disputes
- International jurisdiction complications

- Employment tribunal costs for redundancies
- Professional indemnity insurance claims
- Competition law implications

TECHNICAL EXCELLENCE

- Urgent injunction applications to prevent unlawful termination
- Comprehensive contract breach claim preparation and pursuit
- Damages quantification, including lost profits and consequential losses
- Evidence preservation and digital forensics coordination
- Employment law compliance for workforce restructuring
- Alternative dispute resolution and commercial mediation
- Settlement negotiation with a reputation preservation focus
- Industry arbitration procedures (if applicable)
- Restraint of trade and anti-competitive behavior claims
- Professional negligence defense (if counter-claimed)
- Urgent interim relief and asset protection measures
- Expert witness instruction for technical and financial analysis
- Cross-examination preparation for service quality defense
- Commercial relationship restoration where viable

CLIENT COMMUNICATION & SUPPORT

- Hourly updates during critical negotiation phases
- 24/7 crisis communication platform
- Daily strategy briefings during active litigation
- Workforce communication and change management support
- Industry stakeholder liaison and reputation management
- Client communication strategy and relationship preservation
- Regular legal and commercial risk assessments
- Cost tracking with litigation funding options available
- Decision tree analysis for strategic choices
- Commercial impact monitoring and business continuity support

POST-CASE SUPPORT

- Enhanced contract templates and protection mechanisms
- Client relationship management system implementation
- Early warning systems for contract disputes
- Industry reputation monitoring and management
- Employment policy review for flexible workforce management
- Alternative revenue stream development advisory

- Annual contract health checks and risk assessments
- Crisis response protocol development
- Industry networking and relationship building support
- Future dispute prevention training and systems

TECHNOLOGY & INNOVATION

- Advanced KPI tracking and evidence compilation systems
- Secure digital evidence preservation platforms
- AI-powered contract analysis and risk identification
- Encrypted crisis communication systems
- Reputation monitoring and industry intelligence platforms
- Workforce management and redeployment optimization tools
- Settlement calculation and scenario modelling systems
- Industry network mapping and relationship tracking
- Secure client portal with real-time case updates
- Commercial litigation management platforms

SILVER - THE ENHANCED CONTRACT RECOVERY SERVICE (££)

DEDICATED SENIOR LEADERSHIP

- Senior Associate commercial litigation specialist
- Contract law expert support
- Employment law backup
- Business hours priority access

STRATEGIC PLANNING, SCOPING & ANALYSIS

- Contract breach assessment
- Standard damages calculation
- Basic reputation management
- Workforce restructuring guidance
- Settlement strategy development

TECHNICAL EXCELLENCE

- Standard breach of contract claims
- Employment law compliance support
- Basic settlement negotiations
- Evidence gathering coordination
- Alternative dispute resolution facilitation

CLIENT COMMUNICATION & SUPPORT

- Daily updates during active phases

- Business hours telephone access
- Weekly strategy meetings
- Email priority communication
- Regular progress reporting

POST-CASE SUPPORT

- Basic contract template improvements
- Standard employment policy review
- Quarterly business relationship check-ins

BRONZE - THE ESSENTIAL CONTRACT SUPPORT SERVICE (£)

DEDICATED SENIOR LEADERSHIP

- Associate lawyer
- Contract paralegal support
- Standard business hours only

STRATEGIC PLANNING, SCOPING & ANALYSIS

- Basic contract review
- Simple breach assessment
- Standard recovery options

TECHNICAL EXCELLENCE

- Standard legal documentation
- Basic settlement facilitation
- Simple dispute guidance

CLIENT COMMUNICATION & SUPPORT

- Weekly updates
- Email communication
- Standard reporting procedures

ASSUMPTIVE CLOSING QUESTIONS

- "When shall we activate the Gold contract recovery service to protect your £500K and reputation?"
- "Should I begin the urgent contract breach analysis today to preserve your legal position?"
- "Are you ready for me to start the evidence preservation process immediately?"

• "Shall we schedule the crisis strategy session for this afternoon?"
• "Would you like me to coordinate the workforce restructuring while we pursue the claim?"
• "Should I start the reputation protection measures before word spreads further?"
• "When can we convene the recovery war room - today or first thing tomorrow?"

VALUE-BASED QUESTIONS TO ASK

• "What would losing £500K annually do to your business cash flow and growth plans?"
• "How critical is maintaining your reputation in this small, interconnected industry?"
• "What's the potential impact on your other clients if they hear negative rumors?"
• "How important is keeping your 20 staff engaged and productive?"
• "What would happen if competitors gain an unfair advantage through wrongful termination?"
• "How vital is preventing this client from bad-mouthing you to industry contacts?"
• "What's your biggest concern about how this contract breach could spiral?"

VALUE CREATED

• Recovery of £500K+ annual contract value plus damages and costs
• Protection of professional reputation in a small industry network
• Workforce stability and morale preservation for 20 dedicated staff
• Prevention of unfair competitive advantage to rival providers
• Industry credibility and relationship network protection
• Client relationship restoration where commercially viable
• Professional standards enforcement and precedent-setting
• Business continuity during crisis and recovery period
• Enhanced contract protection for future client relationships
• Crisis management, preventing business disruption

- Evidence-based defense of service quality and KPI performance
- Strategic positioning for industry leadership
- Employment law compliance during workforce restructuring
- Peace of mind through expert commercial warfare management
- Long-term contract fortification and risk mitigation
- Alternative revenue stream identification and development
- Industry intelligence and competitive positioning

SCENARIO 27: BUSINESS SALE

David Foster, Owner of DR.Foster Engineering Ltd, a third-generation family manufacturing business established in 1945. Approaching retirement, the company received a £5M offer from an American competitor. DR.Foster Engineering employs 85 staff, many of whom are long-serving. David is concerned about staff retention, protecting the company's pension scheme, and maintaining the family name. His son works in business but doesn't want to take over. David needs guidance on due diligence, warranties, and staff protection. Tax implications are significant.

GOLD - THE FAMILY LEGACY GUARDIAN SERVICE
Complete Third-Generation Business Transition Protection
(£££)

DEDICATED SENIOR LEADERSHIP

- Partner with 20+ years M&A experience leading entire process
- Dedicated Senior Corporate Associate as daily transaction manager
- Employment Law Partner for comprehensive staff protection strategy
- Tax Planning Partner for complex structuring and optimization
- Company Secretary expertise for corporate governance matters
- Direct mobile access to all senior team members 24/7
- Weekend and evening availability for urgent family consultations
- On-site meetings at DR.Foster Engineering premises
- Personal relationship manager assigned to the Foster family
- Quarterly strategy sessions with the entire leadership team

STRATEGIC PLANNING, SCOPING & ANALYSIS

- Comprehensive pre-sale business diagnostic and preparation audit
- Strategic transaction structuring analysis across multiple scenarios
- Complete due diligence defense preparation program
- Multi-layered risk assessment covering legal, commercial, and reputational risks
- Advanced tax optimization strategy development and implementation
- Detailed staff retention and protection planning with HR consultation
- Family legacy preservation strategy creation and documentation
- Son's future interests protection and planning framework
- Pension scheme protection mechanism design and implementation
- Regular strategic review meetings with monthly progress assessments
- Competitive bid management if additional offers emerge
- Post-completion integration planning with the American buyer

ASSUMPTIONS

- Business books and records are substantially complete and accessible
- The management team will be available for an extended due diligence process
- No material adverse changes occur during the 12-16 week transaction period
- Existing professional advisers (accountants, actuaries) will cooperate fully
- All regulatory licenses, permits, and consents are current and transferable
- No ongoing material litigation or regulatory investigations
- Foster family will participate in the handover and transition process
- American buyer will proceed with standard corporate acquisition structure
- Current employment contracts and pension arrangements are documented

EXCLUSIONS

• Specialist environmental compliance surveys beyond desktop analysis
• US tax and corporate law advice regarding the buyer's jurisdiction
• Individual pension transfer advice for employees
• Post-completion business integration consulting services
• Property valuations and building surveys
• Actuarial advice on pension scheme calculations
• Competition law merger clearance if the transaction exceeds thresholds
• Individual employment contract renegotiations post-completion
• Overseas regulatory filing requirements in the buyer's jurisdiction

TECHNICAL EXCELLENCE

• Comprehensive Share Purchase Agreement drafting and aggressive negotiation
• Advanced warranty and indemnity package with sophisticated limitation strategies
• Detailed disclosure letter preparation with defensive positioning
• Complete due diligence response coordination across all business areas
• Complex corporate tax structuring implementation and documentation
• Employment law compliance audit and protection mechanism design
• Pension scheme legal protection framework and documentation
• Advanced completion accounts mechanism with dispute resolution procedures
• Sophisticated escrow and retention arrangements negotiation
• Comprehensive corporate governance restructuring pre-completion
• Advanced data protection and IP transfer protocols
• Regulatory compliance verification and transfer procedures

CLIENT COMMUNICATION & SUPPORT

- Weekly family strategy video conferences with all stakeholders
- Dedicated secure family portal with real-time transaction visibility
- Daily progress updates during critical negotiation phases
- WhatsApp group for immediate family communication
- Face-to-face meetings at DR.Foster premises or family convenience
- Staff communication strategy development and implementation support
- Regular tri-party calls with accountants, tax advisers, and pension consultants
- Buyer relationship management and communication coordination
- Crisis communication planning and media liaison if required
- Family member individual consultation sessions as needed

POST-CASE SUPPORT

- Comprehensive 18-month post-completion support and monitoring package
- Warranty claim management and defense service with dedicated resource
- Staff transition monitoring with quarterly welfare assessments
- Earn-out monitoring, calculation verification, and collection services
- Annual business performance review meetings with the American buyer
- Tax efficiency monitoring and ongoing optimization advice
- Son's career planning and future business opportunity consultation
- Family wealth management coordination with private banking introductions
- Legacy preservation monitoring with annual family strategy reviews
- Pension scheme ongoing compliance monitoring and member liaison

TECHNOLOGY & INNOVATION

- AI-powered due diligence response management system
- Secure family business portal with multi-user access controls

- Advanced document automation and version control systems
- Digital signature integration with secure authentication protocols
- Virtual data room management with granular access permissions
- Real-time transaction milestone tracking with automated alerts
- Completion timeline visualization with critical path analysis
- Secure communication platform with encryption and audit trails
- Mobile app access for real-time updates and document review

---

SILVER - THE PROFESSIONAL TRANSITION SERVICE Enhanced Corporate Sale Support with Family Focus (££)

DEDICATED SENIOR LEADERSHIP

- Senior Associate-led team with regular Partner oversight and involvement
- Employment law specialist consultation for staff matters
- Tax planning coordination with external advisers
- Direct line access during extended business hours
- Monthly family progress meetings with the senior team

STRATEGIC PLANNING, SCOPING & ANALYSIS

- Standard pre-sale preparation and business review
- Due diligence preparation with template-based approach
- Basic tax planning coordination and advice
- Staff communication planning and template development
- Standard commercial risk assessment and mitigation planning

TECHNICAL EXCELLENCE

- Share Purchase Agreement drafting with standard terms
- Comprehensive warranty and disclosure process management
- Due diligence coordination across key business areas
- Employment law compliance review and basic protection measures
- Standard completion mechanics and documentation

CLIENT COMMUNICATION & SUPPORT

- Bi-weekly family progress calls with written summaries
- Email communication for queries and updates

- Standard client portal access for document review
- Coordination with accountants and other professional advisers

---

BRONZE - THE ESSENTIAL TRANSACTION SERVICE Core Legal Sale Support (£)

DEDICATED SENIOR LEADERSHIP

- Qualified Associate with Partner supervision
- Standard business hours availability
- Email and telephone communication

TECHNICAL EXCELLENCE

- Basic Share Purchase Agreement preparation
- Essential due diligence support and coordination
- Standard document review and completion services
- Core legal compliance verification

CLIENT COMMUNICATION & SUPPORT

- Regular email communication and progress updates
- Scheduled telephone consultations
- Standard completion meeting and handover

GOLD SERVICE UNIQUE FEATURES:

- Three-Generation Family Legacy Protection Program
- 85-Employee Retention Strategy Development
- Personal Family Wealth Transition Planning
- Crisis Management Hotline for Sensitive Matters
- Bespoke Family Meeting Facilitation Service
- American Buyer Relationship Management
- Post-Sale Success Monitoring and Support
- Son's Future Business Planning Framework

ASSUMPTIVE CLOSING QUESTIONS

- "Given the American buyer's timeline, shall we start the comprehensive Gold service this week?"
- "With 85 staff members depending on this transaction, are you ready to proceed with the full Legacy Guardian protection?"
- "Would you like me to schedule the first strategy session to map out your family's transition plan?"
- "Should I begin coordinating with your accountants today using our Gold service integration approach?"

- "Are you comfortable moving forward with the complete staff protection program included in Gold?"
- "Shall I prepare the comprehensive engagement letter that covers all aspects of your business sale?"

VALUE-BASED QUESTIONS

- "If this transaction fails, what would that cost you in terms of retirement planning?"
- "How much would you invest to guarantee your employees' job security through this transition?"
- "What's the value of ensuring your son's interests are properly protected even though he's not taking over?"
- "How important is maintaining DR.Foster Engineering's reputation with the local community?"
- "What would it be worth to have complete peace of mind throughout this process?"
- "How valuable would it be to have experts managing every aspect so you can focus on your family?"

VALUE CREATED ANALYSIS

FINANCIAL VALUE:

- Tax optimization potentially saving £200K-£500K
- Warranty protection securing millions in potential claims
- Structured deal terms maximizing sale proceeds
- Pension scheme protection preserving staff benefits

OPERATIONAL VALUE:

- Business continuity during sensitive transition period
- Staff retention, reducing operational disruption
- Professional management maintaining productivity
- Regulatory compliance, ensuring smooth completion

EMOTIONAL VALUE:

- Family legacy preservation protecting its 75-year heritage
- Peace of mind during once-in-a-lifetime transaction
- Staff loyalty maintained, protecting long-term relationships
- Reputation protection in the local community

STRATEGIC VALUE:

- Son's future interests protected despite non-participation
- American buyer relationship optimally structured
- Post-completion position maximized for all stakeholders

• Risk mitigation, protecting against unforeseen issues

Penguin logic… There we go! A complete, comprehensive service structure that shows David exactly why the Gold service isn't just legal work – it's legacy protection with value creation! The beauty of this approach? David can see exactly what he's getting at each level, and more importantly, what he's NOT getting if he chooses Bronze over Gold. That's the power of proper option structuring!

SCENARIO 28: GDPR BREACH — YOUR STYLEBOX ONLINE

Linda Kang, CEO of Your StyleBox Online (a subscription-based fashion retailer), has discovered a hack of their customer database, potentially exposing the credit card details of 10,000 clients. The IT team is still assessing the damage. Complaints are already surfacing on social media, and Linda urgently needs advice on notification requirements, regulatory compliance, and crisis management. The business is valued at £4M with an IPO planned next year.

GOLD - COMPLETE IPO-SAFE BREACH RESPONSE SERVICE (£££)

• Crisis Command Centre: 24/7 senior partner availability for 72 hours
• IPO Protection Strategy: Bespoke investor communication plan to safeguard listing
• Regulatory Shield: Direct ICO liaison and representation throughout investigation
• Media Crisis Management: Professional PR firm coordination and messaging control
• Legal Immunity Assessment: Full liability evaluation and mitigation strategy
• Customer Retention Program: Template communications to preserve customer loyalty
• Board Governance Support: Emergency board meeting facilitation and legal briefings

ASSUMPTIONS:

- Single breach incident affecting up to 10,000 records
- No previous regulatory breaches
- Cooperation from the IT team and management
- Access to all relevant systems and documentation

EXCLUSIONS:

- Criminal defense representation
- Ongoing litigation beyond regulatory matters
- IT system remediation costs
- Third-party PR agency fees (coordinated but separately charged)

COMMUNICATION STRUCTURE:

- Immediate: Senior partner direct mobile access
- Daily: Morning briefings (07:30) and evening updates (18:00)
- Weekly: Board-level strategy reviews

FOLLOW-UP SERVICES:

- 6-month regulatory monitoring
- Annual GDPR compliance health check
- IPO readiness documentation review

SILVER - ENHANCED COMPLIANCE & REPUTATION SERVICE (££)

- Rapid Response Team: Senior associate lead with partner oversight
- Regulatory Compliance: ICO notification and correspondence handling
- Stakeholder Communications: Template letters for customers, suppliers, investors
- Legal Risk Assessment: Comprehensive liability evaluation
- Crisis Management: Basic media response guidance and holding statements
- Documentation Package: All required legal notices and regulatory submissions

ASSUMPTIONS:

- Standard working hours response (extended hours charged separately)
- Breach affects up to 10,000 records

- Basic cooperation from internal teams

EXCLUSIONS:

- 24/7 availability
- Direct ICO representation at hearings
- PR agency coordination
- Ongoing litigation support

COMMUNICATION STRUCTURE:

- Business hours: Direct associate contact
- Daily: End-of-day email updates
- Weekly: Partner review calls

BRONZE - ESSENTIAL GDPR COMPLIANCE SERVICE (£)

- Regulatory Notification: ICO breach reporting and initial correspondence
- Legal Guidance: Essential compliance advice and next steps
- Template Documents: Standard customer notification letters
- Basic Risk Assessment: Initial legal exposure evaluation
- Compliance Checklist: Step-by-step internal action plan

ASSUMPTIONS:

- Standard office hours only
- Single consultation and document review
- Client handles internal communications

EXCLUSIONS:

- Ongoing support beyond initial notification
- Media guidance
- ICO representation
- Crisis management support

COMMUNICATION STRUCTURE:

- Email and phone during business hours
- 48-hour response time for queries

ASSUMPTIVE CLOSING QUESTIONS:

- "Given your IPO timeline, I assume protecting investor confidence is your top priority - shall we implement the Gold service immediately?"

- "When would you like us to start the ICO notification process?"
- "Who should I coordinate with from your board for the emergency briefing?"
- "Shall I arrange the crisis PR team introduction for this afternoon?"

VALUE-BASED QUESTIONS TO ASK:

- "What would a successful outcome look like for you in 6 months' time?"
- "How would a regulatory fine or delayed IPO impact your business valuation?"
- "What's the cost to Your StyleBox if customer confidence is permanently damaged?"
- "How important is it that your investors see this handled professionally?"
- "What would missing your IPO window cost the business?"

VALUE CREATED:

- IPO Protection: Safeguards £4M+ business valuation and listing timeline
- Regulatory Shield: Minimizes ICO penalties and investigation scope
- Reputation Preservation: Maintains customer trust and market confidence
- Crisis Leadership: Provides expert guidance during a high-stress period
- Legal Certainty: Clear compliance pathway and risk mitigation
- Time Savings: Handles all regulatory complexity while you run the business
- Peace of Mind: 24/7 support when you need it most

SCENARIO 29: FRANCHISE DISPUTE

Mohammed Ali, Owner of a 2UQuickServe Logistics Franchise, has invested £250,000 of his life savings in a logistics franchise. The franchisor is not providing promised territory protection, training, or marketing support. Now, they are changing the operating manual terms unilaterally, increasing costs. A five-year contract was signed, but the business is becoming unviable. Mohammed has taken out a large loan and employed 15 staff. He needs to either enforce the franchise agreement or exit without losing everything.

GOLD - COMPLETE FRANCHISE RESCUE & RECOVERY SERVICE (£££)

- Business Survival Strategy: Comprehensive franchise enforcement or strategic exit plan
- Investment Recovery Program: Maximum asset protection and compensation pursuit
- Staff Protection Plan: Employment law guidance to safeguard your team's positions
- Franchisor Negotiation: Senior partner-led direct negotiations with franchisor management
- Litigation Management: Full dispute resolution, including court representation if required
- Financial Recovery Assessment: Detailed loss calculation and recovery strategy
- Alternative Business Planning: New venture structuring if exit becomes optimal
- Creditor Protection: Liaison with lenders and suppliers during transition

ASSUMPTIONS:
- Single franchise agreement dispute
- Access to all franchise documentation and financial records
- Mohammed's full cooperation and decision-making authority
- Franchisor based in the UK jurisdiction

EXCLUSIONS:
- Insolvency proceedings (coordinated but separately charged)
- Property lease renegotiations beyond franchise context
- Individual employment tribunal claims
- Tax advice on business restructuring

TECHNICAL DELIVERABLES:
- Forensic franchise agreement analysis
- Breach of contract assessment and evidence compilation
- Financial loss calculation and supporting documentation
- Settlement negotiation strategy and execution
- Court pleadings and litigation strategy (if required)

COMMUNICATION STRUCTURE:

- Immediate: Direct partner mobile access for urgent decisions
- Weekly: Progress meetings with full status updates
- Monthly: Strategic review and next-phase planning

FOLLOW-UP SERVICES:

- 12-month post-resolution monitoring
- New business venture legal setup (if applicable)
- Ongoing relationship management with resolved parties

SILVER - FRANCHISE ENFORCEMENT & NEGOTIATION SERVICE (££)

- Contract Analysis: Detailed franchise agreement review and breach identification
- Negotiation Support: Senior lawyer-led settlement discussions
- Loss Assessment: Professional valuation of damages and recovery prospects
- Strategic Options: Clear pathway analysis for enforcement vs. exit
- Documentation Package: All legal notices and formal communications
- Basic Litigation Prep: Initial court preparation if negotiations fail

ASSUMPTIONS:

- Standard business hours availability
- Negotiation-focused resolution preferred
- Basic franchisor cooperation expected
- Mohammed handles day-to-day business operations

EXCLUSIONS:

- Extended litigation beyond initial proceedings
- Complex financial restructuring
- Detailed employment law advice
- 24/7 availability

COMMUNICATION STRUCTURE:

- Business hours: Direct senior lawyer contact
- Bi-weekly: Progress calls and strategy updates
- Monthly: Written progress reports

BRONZE - ESSENTIAL FRANCHISE ADVICE SERVICE (£)

• Legal Assessment: Initial franchise agreement review and key issues identification
• Options Analysis: Basic guidance on potential remedies and next steps
• Template Documents: Standard legal notices and correspondence templates
• Settlement Framework: Basic negotiation structure and approach
• Resource Guidance: Signposting to relevant support organizations

ASSUMPTIONS:
• Single consultation and document review
• Standard office hours only
• Mohammed manages most communications directly

EXCLUSIONS:
• Ongoing negotiation support
• Litigation representation
• Complex financial analysis
• Direct franchisor contact

COMMUNICATION STRUCTURE:
• Email and telephone during business hours
• 48-hour response commitment
• Single follow-up consultation included

ASSUMPTIVE CLOSING QUESTIONS:
• "Given that 15 jobs depend on getting this right, shall we start the comprehensive Gold service immediately?"
• "When would you like me to begin the direct negotiations with the franchisor?"
• "Should I prepare both enforcement and exit strategies so you have maximum flexibility?"
• "Shall I coordinate with your accountant to begin the financial loss assessment this week?"

VALUE-BASED QUESTIONS TO ASK:

• "What would saving your business and protecting those 15 jobs be worth to you?"
• "How much of your £250,000 investment could you afford to lose?"
• "What's the monthly cost of keeping this situation unresolved?"
• "If we could recover 80% of your losses, what would that mean for your family's future?"
• "How important is it to you that your staff keep their jobs through this?"
• "What would walking away from this business cost you financially and personally?"

VALUE CREATED:

• Investment Protection: Safeguards up to £250,000 life savings from total loss
• Employment Security: Protects 15 jobs and maintains staff loyalty during the crisis
• Business Survival: Transforms failing franchise into viable operation or strategic exit
• Financial Recovery: Maximizes compensation for franchisor breaches and failures
• Stress Relief: Expert handling allows Mohammed to focus on running the business
• Future Security: Creates a foundation for either the business's success or a new venture
• Family Protection: Prevents financial ruin and secures the family's livelihood
• Professional Vindication: Holds franchisor accountable for broken promises

SCENARIO 30: SUPPLIER DISPUTE

Gaby Smith, Director of Smith Construction Ltd. A key supplier has delivered defective steel beams for a £3M office development. The project is now eight weeks behind schedule, incurring £100K client penalties. The supplier is denying responsibility despite an independent expert report, whilst an alternative supplier is charging a premium for quick delivery. The company's professional reputation is at risk with an important client. Gaby needs to recover losses and manage project delays.

GOLD - COMPLETE PROJECT RESCUE & REPUTATION PROTECTION SERVICE (£££)

- Crisis Project Management: Immediate legal intervention to minimize further delays
- Client Relationship Preservation: Direct client communication and expectation management
- Maximum Recovery Strategy: Full cost recovery, including penalties, premiums, and consequential losses
- Reputation Shield: Professional PR guidance and industry relationship protection
- Supplier Enforcement: Aggressive pursuit of defective supplier, including immediate injunctive relief
- Alternative Supplier Protection: Legal review of premium supplier contracts and risk mitigation
- Expert Witness Coordination: Technical expert management and evidence compilation
- Future Contract Bulletproofing: Enhanced supplier agreement templates for future projects

ASSUMPTIONS:

- Single £3M project dispute with one defective supplier
- Independent expert report available and supportive
- Access to all project documentation and supplier contracts
- Gaby has the authority to make strategic decisions
- Alternative supplier available for completion

EXCLUSIONS:

- Criminal investigations or health & safety prosecutions
- Additional project disputes beyond this supplier issue
- Employment disputes arising from project delays
- Insurance claim management (coordinated but separately charged)

TECHNICAL DELIVERABLES:

- Forensic contract analysis and breach documentation
- Comprehensive loss calculation including all consequential damages

- Expert evidence coordination and presentation strategy
- Settlement negotiation framework and execution
- Court proceedings preparation and litigation management
- Client communication templates and relationship strategy

COMMUNICATION STRUCTURE:

- Immediate: Partner direct mobile for urgent project decisions
- Daily: Morning briefings during critical phases (07:30)
- Weekly: Strategic progress meetings with full team updates
- Client meetings: Joint attendance at all critical client discussions

FOLLOW-UP SERVICES:

- 6-month project completion monitoring
- Annual supplier contract reviews
- Relationship management with resolved parties
- Future project legal support at preferential rates

SILVER - ENHANCED RECOVERY & CLIENT PROTECTION SERVICE (££)

- Dispute Resolution: Comprehensive supplier dispute management and settlement pursuit
- Loss Recovery: Professional damages calculation and negotiation strategy
- Client Communication: Template communications and basic relationship guidance
- Expert Evidence: Coordination of existing expert report and additional evidence gathering
- Legal Documentation: All formal notices, letters before action, and settlement agreements
- Contract Protection: Review of alternative supplier agreements

ASSUMPTIONS:

- Standard business hours availability with some extended support
- Existing expert report sufficient for initial proceedings
- Gaby manages day-to-day client relationships with legal guidance
- Settlement-focused approach preferred over extended litigation

EXCLUSIONS:

- 24/7 availability for project crises

- Direct client meeting attendance
- Complex PR or reputation management
- Extended litigation beyond initial proceedings

COMMUNICATION STRUCTURE:

- Business hours: Direct senior lawyer contact
- Weekly: Progress calls and strategy updates
- Monthly: Written progress reports and next-phase planning

BRONZE - ESSENTIAL DISPUTE GUIDANCE SERVICE (£)

- Legal Assessment: Initial contract review and breach analysis
- Recovery Options: Basic guidance on potential damages and recovery prospects
- Template Documents: Standard legal notices and correspondence templates
- Settlement Framework: Basic negotiation approach and strategy
- Next Steps Guidance: Clear action plan for dispute resolution

ASSUMPTIONS:

- Single consultation and document review
- Standard office hours availability only
- Gaby handles most communications and negotiations directly
- Limited ongoing support required

EXCLUSIONS:

- Ongoing negotiation representation
- Court proceedings and litigation
- Client relationship management
- Complex damages calculations

COMMUNICATION STRUCTURE:

- Email and telephone during business hours
- 48-hour response commitment
- Single follow-up consultation included

ASSUMPTIVE CLOSING QUESTIONS:

- "Given your client relationship is at stake, shall we implement the full Gold service immediately to protect your reputation?"

• "When should I begin direct discussions with your client to manage their expectations professionally?"
• "Shall I coordinate with the alternative supplier today to review their premium contract terms?"
• "Should we commence formal proceedings against the defective supplier this week?"

VALUE-BASED QUESTIONS TO ASK:

• "What would losing this £3M client relationship cost your business long-term?"
• "How much is your professional reputation in the construction industry worth?"
• "What's the impact on Smith Construction if this project failure becomes industry knowledge?"
• "If we could recover all your losses and preserve the client relationship, what would that be worth?"
• "How many future projects could be at risk if your reputation is damaged?"
• "What would it cost to replace this client with an equivalent business?"

VALUE CREATED:

• Business Survival: Protects £3M project and prevents business-threatening losses
• Reputation Preservation: Maintains professional standing in the competitive construction industry
• Client Relationship: Saves a valuable long-term client worth multiple future projects
• Financial Recovery: Recovers penalties, premiums, and consequential losses from defective supplier
• Project Completion: Ensures successful delivery despite supplier failures
• Industry Standing: Demonstrates professional crisis management to the wider market
• Future Protection: Creates bulletproof supplier agreements preventing repeat issues
• Peace of Mind: Expert handling allows Gaby to focus on running her business

Penguin logic... Gaby isn't buying legal hours, she's buying her business survival, reputation protection, and client relationships! The stakes are massive here – lose this client and her reputation could be ruined in a tight-knit industry. The Gold service pricing reflects that reality, not some arbitrary time-based calculation.

SCENARIO 31: DIRECTOR DUTIES

Robert Johnson, Director of Jonno Brothers Manufacturing, a £10M family business facing a modernization crisis. One sibling is pushing for automation and redundancies, another wants to maintain traditional methods. The board is deadlocked. The father (majority shareholder) is recently deceased, and his will is in probate. Robert needs clarity on director responsibilities, shareholder rights, and managing family dynamics without destroying the business.

GOLD - COMPLETE FAMILY BUSINESS RESCUE & GOVERNANCE SERVICE (£££)

• Business Survival Strategy: Comprehensive family business restructuring and strategic direction
• Family Harmony Program: Professional family mediation and relationship preservation
• Director Protection Shield: Complete director duties guidance and legal compliance assurance
• Succession Planning: Probate coordination and ownership transition management
• Board Governance Rebuild: New articles, decision-making frameworks, and deadlock resolution mechanisms
• Strategic Business Planning: Independent commercial assessment of automation vs traditional approaches
• Employment Law Integration: Staff consultation strategies and redundancy protection planning
• Legacy Preservation: Family constitution creation, ensuring multi-generational business survival

ASSUMPTIONS:

• Single-family business with identifiable shareholding structure
• Access to all business financial records and constitutional documents

- Robert has the authority to engage legal representation for the business
- Probate proceedings are of standard complexity
- Family members willing to engage in the mediation process

EXCLUSIONS:

- Individual family member personal legal advice (potential conflict)
- Complex tax planning beyond basic succession issues
- Employment tribunal proceedings (coordinated but separately charged)
- Property/asset valuations (arranged but separately charged)

TECHNICAL DELIVERABLES:

- Comprehensive director duties audit, and compliance framework
- Shareholder agreement restructuring with deadlock resolution mechanisms
- Family business constitution and governance charter
- Strategic business options analysis with commercial viability assessment
- Board meeting protocols and decision-making procedures
- Succession planning documentation and probate coordination

COMMUNICATION STRUCTURE:

- Immediate: Direct partner access for urgent family/business crises
- Weekly: Strategic progress meetings with all key stakeholders
- Monthly: Board meeting facilitation and governance reviews
- Family sessions: Neutral venue mediation and relationship rebuilding

FOLLOW-UP SERVICES:

- 12-month governance monitoring and board support
- Annual family business health checks
- Ongoing succession planning reviews
- Priority access for future family business issues

SILVER - ENHANCED DIRECTOR GUIDANCE & FAMILY MEDIATION SERVICE (££)

• Director Duties Framework: Comprehensive guidance on legal responsibilities and compliance
• Family Business Mediation: Professional facilitation of family discussions and dispute resolution
• Shareholder Rights Analysis: Clear explanation of rights, obligations, and voting procedures
• Basic Governance Structure: Template articles and board procedures for family businesses
• Strategic Options Review: Independent assessment of business direction options
• Succession Coordination: Basic probate liaison and ownership transition guidance

ASSUMPTIONS:

• Standard business hours availability with extended support during critical phases
• Family members are generally cooperative in the mediation process
• Basic business restructuring is sufficient for resolution
• Robert manages day-to-day business operations during transition

EXCLUSIONS:

• 24/7 crisis availability
• Complex family therapy or extended relationship counselling
• Detailed commercial business planning
• Individual family member representation

COMMUNICATION STRUCTURE:

• Business hours: Direct senior lawyer contact
• Bi-weekly: Progress calls and strategy updates
• Monthly: Family mediation sessions and governance reviews

BRONZE - ESSENTIAL DIRECTOR ADVICE SERVICE (£)

• Director Duties Briefing: Basic guidance on legal responsibilities and key compliance requirements

- Shareholder Rights Summary: Clear explanation of current rights and voting procedures
- Deadlock Options: Basic guidance on potential resolution mechanisms
- Template Documentation: Standard board meeting procedures and basic governance templates
- Next Steps Framework: Clear action plan for addressing immediate issues

ASSUMPTIONS:

- Single consultation covering key legal and governance issues
- Standard office hours availability only
- Family manages mediation and relationship aspects independently
- Basic documentation sufficient for immediate needs

EXCLUSIONS:

- Ongoing family mediation or dispute resolution
- Complex governance restructuring
- Detailed succession planning
- Strategic business planning

COMMUNICATION STRUCTURE:

- Email and telephone during business hours
- 48-hour response commitment
- Single follow-up consultation included

ASSUMPTIVE CLOSING QUESTIONS:

- "Given that a £10M family legacy is at stake, shall we implement the complete Gold service to save both the business and family relationships?"
- "When should I begin the family mediation sessions to get everyone working together again?"
- "Shall I coordinate with the probate lawyers immediately to ensure the succession planning protects the business?"
- "Should we schedule the first family governance meeting for next week to start rebuilding the board structure?"

VALUE-BASED QUESTIONS TO ASK:

- "What would losing this £10M family business mean to the Johnson family legacy?"

• "How much is preserving family relationships worth while saving the business?"
• "What's the cost of continued deadlock - lost opportunities, declining performance, staff uncertainty?"
• "If we could create a governance structure that preserves both family harmony and business success, what would that be worth?"
• "How many jobs and livelihoods depend on resolving this family business crisis?"
• "What would your father want most - family unity or business success - and can we achieve both?"

VALUE CREATED:

• Business Survival: Saves £10M family enterprise from destruction through deadlock
• Family Harmony: Preserves precious family relationships while enabling business success
• Legacy Protection: Ensures the father's life's work continues and thrives for future generations
• Legal Compliance: Eliminates director liability risks and ensures proper governance
• Strategic Clarity: Provides clear business direction, ending destructive uncertainty
• Employment Security: Protects jobs and livelihoods dependent on business stability
• Succession Success: Smooth transition of ownership, preventing further family conflict
• Multi-generational Planning: Creates a framework for long-term family business success

SCENARIO 32: DEBT RECOVERY

Anna Murphy, Owner of DeclanSoft Solutions, a fast-growing software company with three major clients owing £300K in unpaid invoices. The largest debtor (£150K) is claiming software bugs, despite signing off on acceptance testing. Cash flow is critical as the company needs to pay developers for an upcoming large healthcare contract worth £2M. One debtor is showing signs of insolvency. Anna has 45 staff relying on regular payroll. She needs a strategic approach to recover debt without destroying client relationships.

GOLD - COMPLETE CASH FLOW RESCUE & BUSINESS PROTECTION SERVICE (£££)

• Business Survival Strategy: Emergency cash flow management and immediate payment acceleration
• Relationship Preservation Program: Strategic debt recovery, maintaining ongoing client partnerships
• Healthcare Contract: Legal framework to seek to protect the contract without cash flow disruption
• Staff Security Shield: Payroll protection strategies and employment law compliance during crisis
• Insolvency Defense: Early intervention with distressed debtor, including asset tracing and recovery
• Technical Dispute Resolution: Software acceptance evidence compilation and bug claim refutation
• Future Cash Flow Protection: Enhanced contract terms and payment security for ongoing business
• Growth Strategy Support: Legal framework enabling continued expansion despite the current crisis

ASSUMPTIONS:

• Three identifiable major debtors with documented payment obligations
• Access to all contracts, acceptance testing records, and correspondence
• Anna has the authority to pursue recovery action and negotiate settlements
• Healthcare contract negotiations can be coordinated with a debt recovery strategy
• Software acceptance documentation available to counter bug claims

EXCLUSIONS:

• Employee personal financial advice or redundancy costs
• Complex software technical expert evidence (arranged but separately charged)
• Insolvency practitioner fees for any formal proceedings
• Corporate finance or investment banking services

TECHNICAL DELIVERABLES:

- Forensic contract analysis and payment obligation documentation
- Strategic debt recovery roadmap preserving client relationships
- Emergency cash flow projections and payment acceleration strategy
- Software acceptance evidence compilation and legal defense framework
- Insolvency monitoring and early intervention protocols
- Enhanced contract templates with improved payment security

COMMUNICATION STRUCTURE:

- Immediate: Partner direct access for urgent cash flow decisions (24/7)
- Daily: Morning briefings during critical payment phases
- Weekly: Strategic progress meetings with full business impact assessment
- Client meetings: Joint attendance at all sensitive debtor negotiations

FOLLOW-UP SERVICES:

- 12-month cash flow monitoring and debt management support
- Annual contract reviews and payment terms optimization
- Priority access for future business growth legal needs
- Healthcare contract ongoing legal support at preferential rates

---

SILVER - ENHANCED DEBT RECOVERY & CASH FLOW SERVICE (££)

- Strategic Debt Recovery: Professional multi-debtor recovery program with relationship management
- Cash Flow Support: Payment acceleration strategies and emergency cash flow planning
- Technical Defense: Software acceptance documentation and bug claim counter-arguments
- Insolvency Monitoring: Early warning system and protective action for distressed debtor
- Contract Enhancement: Improved payment terms and security for future agreements
- Business Continuity: Legal guidance ensuring operations continue during recovery

ASSUMPTIONS:

• Standard business hours availability with extended support during critical phases
• Anna manages day-to-day client relationships with legal strategy guidance
• Basic cash flow planning is sufficient for immediate needs
• Settlement-focused approach preferred over extended litigation

EXCLUSIONS:

• 24/7 availability for cash flow crises
• Complex business restructuring or corporate finance
• Extended litigation beyond initial enforcement
• Individual employment law advice for staff concerns

COMMUNICATION STRUCTURE:

• Business hours: Direct senior lawyer contact
• Bi-weekly: Progress calls and strategy updates
• Monthly: Written progress reports and cash flow reviews

BRONZE - ESSENTIAL DEBT RECOVERY GUIDANCE SERVICE (£)

• Debt Recovery Assessment: Analysis of recovery prospects and legal options for each debtor
• Payment Demand Strategy: Template letters and formal notices for immediate use
• Software Defense Brief: Basic guidance on countering bug claims with acceptance evidence
• Insolvency Alert: Warning signs checklist and immediate protective actions
• Next Steps Framework: Clear action plan for debt recovery and cash flow improvement

ASSUMPTIONS:

• Single consultation covering all three debtors and recovery strategy
• Standard office hours availability only
• Anna handles most debtor communications and negotiations directly
• Template documents sufficient for initial recovery attempts

EXCLUSIONS:

- Ongoing negotiation representation
- Court proceedings and enforcement action
- Complex cash flow planning
- Business continuity strategies

COMMUNICATION STRUCTURE:

- Email and telephone during business hours
- 48-hour response commitment
- Single follow-up consultation included

ASSUMPTIVE CLOSING QUESTIONS:

- "Given that 45 jobs and a £2M healthcare contract depend on resolving this cash flow crisis, shall we implement the full Gold service immediately?"
- "When should I begin negotiations with your largest debtor to secure the £150K payment this month?"
- "Shall I coordinate the debt recovery strategy with your healthcare contract timeline to ensure no disruption?"
- "Should we commence immediate action against the potentially insolvent debtor to protect your position?"

VALUE-BASED QUESTIONS TO ASK:

- "What would losing the £2M healthcare contract cost DeclanSoft's future growth plans?"
- "How much is keeping your 45-person team employed worth to your business reputation?"
- "What's the real cost if cash flow problems force you to miss developer payments and breach the healthcare contract?"
- "If we could recover the £300K debt while preserving all client relationships, what would that mean for DeclanSoft?"
- "How many months can the business survive without this £300K in current cash flow?"
- "What would your competitors pay to secure your healthcare contract if DeclanSoft failed?"

VALUE CREATED:

- Business Survival: Saves a fast-growing software company from cash flow collapse

• Staff Security: Protects 45 jobs and maintains team stability during critical growth phase
• Contract Protection: Ensures £2M healthcare contract proceeds without financial disruption
• Relationship Preservation: Recovers debts while maintaining valuable ongoing client partnerships
• Growth Enablement: Provides cash flow stability, allowing continued business expansion
• Technical Defense: Protects company reputation by successfully countering unfounded bug claims
• Future Security: Creates robust payment systems, preventing future cash flow crises
• Market Position: Maintains competitive advantage and industry credibility

SCENARIO 33: COMMERCIAL PROPERTY

Tom Wilson, MD of Wilson Developments, has a £2M retail park development halted by planning issues. A local residents group is mounting a social media campaign, claiming environmental impact. The company has already spent £400K on groundworks, and holding costs are £20K monthly. Three pre-let agreements with national retailers are at risk if delayed beyond September, and bank funding is dependent on planning resolution. Twenty contractors are on hold. Tom needs a solution to save the project.

GOLD - COMPLETE PROJECT RESCUE & DEVELOPMENT PROTECTION SERVICE (£££)

• Project Salvation Strategy: Comprehensive planning resolution and development rescue program
• Stakeholder Management Program: Professional community engagement and resident relations management
• Environmental Defense Shield: Technical environmental impact assessment and expert evidence coordination
• Retail Tenant Protection: Legal strategies preserving pre-let agreements and preventing contract breaks
• Bank Relationship Management: Funding coordination and lender communication throughout resolution

- Contractor Crisis Management: Legal framework protecting contractor relationships and minimizing delay costs
- PR & Reputation Management: Social media strategy coordination and public relations guidance
- Future Development Protection: Enhanced planning processes, preventing similar issues on future projects

ASSUMPTIONS:

- Planning applications and objections are clearly documented and accessible
- Environmental impact claims can be technically assessed and countered
- Pre-let agreements contain manageable delay provisions
- Bank funding terms allow reasonable extension periods
- Tom has the authority to engage in community consultation processes

EXCLUSIONS:

- Environmental consultancy and technical surveys (coordinated but separately charged)
- PR agency services and social media management (arranged but separately charged)
- Additional groundwork or construction costs due to delays
- Bank facility renegotiation fees or additional interest charges

TECHNICAL DELIVERABLES:

- Comprehensive planning objection analysis and response strategy
- Environmental impact technical defense and expert evidence coordination
- Pre-let agreement protection strategy and tenant relationship management
- Community consultation framework and stakeholder engagement plan
- Bank communication strategy ensuring funding continuation
- Contractor relationship management and delay mitigation protocols

COMMUNICATION STRUCTURE:

- Immediate: Partner direct access for urgent planning and funding decisions (24/7)

• Daily: Morning briefings during critical planning committee phases
• Weekly: Stakeholder management meetings with full project progress review
• Community sessions: Professional facilitation of resident consultation meetings

FOLLOW-UP SERVICES:

• 12-month development monitoring and planning compliance support
• Annual planning review and risk assessment for future projects
• Priority access for subsequent development legal needs
• Preferred rates for Wilson Developments expansion projects

SILVER - ENHANCED PLANNING RESOLUTION & STAKEHOLDER SERVICE (££)

• Planning Resolution Strategy: Professional planning objection response and committee presentation
• Community Engagement: Structured resident consultation and objection management
• Environmental Response: Basic environmental impact defense and technical coordination
• Tenant Communication: Pre-let agreement management and delay notification protocols
• Project Continuity: Legal guidance ensuring development proceeds with minimal disruption
• Bank Liaison: Basic lender communication and funding protection strategies

ASSUMPTIONS:

• Standard business hours availability with extended support during planning committee meetings
• Tom manages day-to-day contractor and tenant relationships with legal guidance
• Basic community consultation is sufficient for resident engagement
• Planning resolution achievable through the standard objection response process

EXCLUSIONS:

- 24/7 availability for project crises
- Complex environmental expert evidence
- Extended community relations management
- Detailed contractor delay negotiations

COMMUNICATION STRUCTURE:

- Business hours: Direct senior lawyer contact
- Bi-weekly: Progress calls and planning strategy updates
- Monthly: Written progress reports and stakeholder reviews

BRONZE - ESSENTIAL PLANNING GUIDANCE SERVICE (£)

- Planning Assessment: Analysis of objections and available resolution options
- Response Strategy: Template objection responses and planning committee guidance
- Environmental Brief: Basic guidance on addressing environmental impact claims
- Tenant Protection: Standard delay notification templates and contract review
- Next Steps Framework: Clear action plan for planning resolution and project continuation

ASSUMPTIONS:

- Single consultation covering planning issues and resolution strategy
- Standard office hours availability only
- Tom handles community engagement and contractor management directly
- Template responses are sufficient for the initial planning objection process

EXCLUSIONS:

- Planning committee representation
- Ongoing stakeholder management
- Complex environmental defense
- Extended project management support

COMMUNICATION STRUCTURE:

- Email and telephone during business hours

- 48-hour response commitment
- Single follow-up consultation included

ASSUMPTIVE CLOSING QUESTIONS:

- "Given that £2M of development value and £400K of investment are at risk, shall we implement the complete Gold service to save your project immediately?"
- "When should I begin the community consultation process to turn residents from opponents into supporters?"
- "Shall I coordinate with your environmental consultants this week to build the technical defense against these claims?"
- "Should we commence immediate liaison with your bank to ensure funding remains secure throughout resolution?"

VALUE-BASED QUESTIONS TO ASK:

- "What would losing this £2M retail park development mean to Wilson Developments' future growth?"
- "How much are those three pre-let agreements with national retailers worth in ongoing rental income?"
- "What's the real cost of £20K monthly holding costs if this drags on for six more months?"
- "If the bank withdraws funding, what would sourcing alternative finance cost in today's market?"
- "How many future development opportunities depend on successfully completing this project?"
- "What would your competitors pay to secure those prime retail tenants if your project fails?"

VALUE CREATED:

- Project Salvation: Saves £2M retail development from planning failure and financial collapse
- Investment Protection: Preserves £400K already invested in groundwork and development costs
- Revenue Security: Protects pre-let rental income streams worth potentially millions over lease terms
- Funding Preservation: Maintains bank relationships and secures continued project financing
- Reputation Management: Transforms community opposition into development support

• Contractor Relations: Preserves valuable contractor partnerships and prevents penalty costs
• Future Opportunities: Establishes a successful development track record, enabling future projects
• Market Position: Maintains Wilson Developments' credibility with retailers and investors

SCENARIO 34: EMPLOYMENT TRIBUNAL

Grace Wong, HR Director at Penguin TechGlobal Ltd. A senior female manager is claiming £150K for sex discrimination after redundancy. She was selected from a three-person team, but was the only woman and the highest performer. Internal emails discovered have suggested "family commitments" were discussed in the selection process. A national tech magazine is now requesting comment. Two similar roles were recently advertised. Need to manage legal and PR response.

GOLD - COMPLETE DISCRIMINATION DEFENCE & REPUTATION PROTECTION SERVICE (£££)

• Total Liability Defense: Comprehensive tribunal strategy minimizing financial exposure and reputational damage
• Crisis Communication Management: Professional media response and reputation protection throughout proceedings
• Evidence Forensics Program: Email audit, witness preparation, and documentation strategy to counter discrimination claims
• Business Continuity Shield: Internal process review preventing copycat claims and regulatory investigation
• Executive Protection Strategy: Leadership team coaching and testimony preparation for tribunal appearances
• Settlement Negotiation Excellence: Strategic settlement discussions protecting both finances and reputation
• Future-Proofing Program: Complete HR policy overhaul and discrimination prevention systems
• Industry Reputation Management: Tech sector relationship preservation and talent acquisition protection

ASSUMPTIONS:

• Full access to all internal communications, HR records, and decision-making documentation
• Executive team availability for witness preparation and strategic consultations
• Authority to engage settlement discussions within reasonable parameters
• Cooperation with coordinated media strategy and communication protocols
• Access to all redundancy selection criteria and alternative role documentation

EXCLUSIONS:

• PR agency services and social media monitoring (coordinated but separately charged)
• Employment investigation consultancy for internal processes (arranged but separately charged)
• Executive coaching beyond tribunal preparation requirements
• Additional tribunal costs if the case extends beyond standard timescales

TECHNICAL DELIVERABLES:

• Comprehensive discrimination defense strategy and evidence compilation
• Media response framework and reputation protection protocols
• Internal investigation review and witness testimony coordination
• Settlement negotiation strategy with optimal financial and reputational outcomes
• HR policy reformation and discrimination prevention system implementation
• Executive team tribunal preparation and coaching program

COMMUNICATION STRUCTURE:

• Immediate: Partner direct access for urgent media and settlement decisions (24/7)
• Daily: Morning briefings during active tribunal periods and media engagement
• Weekly: Strategic progress meetings with full business impact assessment

• Tribunal hearings: Senior representation with comprehensive preparation and support

FOLLOW-UP SERVICES:

• 12-month employment compliance monitoring and policy implementation support
• Annual discrimination prevention training and HR review programs
• Priority access for future employment law needs across the Penguin TechGlobal group
• Preferred rates for ongoing employment tribunal insurance and prevention services

---

SILVER - ENHANCED TRIBUNAL DEFENCE & MEDIA MANAGEMENT SERVICE (££)

• Tribunal Defense Strategy: Professional discrimination claim defense with evidence preparation
• Media Response Management: Coordinated press statement and reputation protection guidance
• Evidence Preparation: Email review, witness coordination, and documentation analysis
• Settlement Support: Negotiation guidance and financial exposure minimization
• Policy Review: Basic HR process assessment and discrimination prevention recommendations
• Executive Briefing: Senior team preparation for tribunal testimony and media queries

ASSUMPTIONS:

• Standard business hours availability with extended support during tribunal hearings
• Grace manages internal communications and staff relations with legal guidance
• Basic media response sufficient for reputation protection
• Settlement achievable through standard negotiation processes

EXCLUSIONS:

• 24/7 availability for crisis management
• Comprehensive internal investigation review
• Extended media relations management

- Detailed HR policy reformation program

COMMUNICATION STRUCTURE:

- Business hours: Direct senior lawyer contact
- Bi-weekly: Progress calls and tribunal strategy updates
- Monthly: Written progress reports and settlement discussions

BRONZE - ESSENTIAL TRIBUNAL GUIDANCE SERVICE (£)

- Defense Assessment: Analysis of discrimination claim and available defense options
- Evidence Review: Basic guidance on email disclosure and witness requirements
- Media Guidance: Template press responses and reputation protection basics
- Settlement Framework: Initial negotiation parameters and financial exposure assessment
- Next Steps Plan: Clear action framework for tribunal defense and claim resolution

ASSUMPTIONS:

- Single comprehensive consultation covering claim defense and media response
- Standard office hours availability only
- Grace handles internal coordination and stakeholder management directly
- Template responses sufficient for initial media and tribunal requirements

EXCLUSIONS:

- Tribunal representation and hearing attendance
- Ongoing settlement negotiations
- Complex evidence preparation
- Extended reputation management

COMMUNICATION STRUCTURE:

- Email and telephone during business hours
- 48-hour response commitment
- Single follow-up consultation included

ASSUMPTIVE CLOSING QUESTIONS:

• "Given the £150K claim exposure plus potential reputation damage to Penguin TechGlobal's brand, shall we implement the complete Gold service to protect both your finances and market position?"
• "When should I begin coordinating with your PR team to manage the national media interest professionally?"
• "Shall I commence immediate review of those internal emails to build the strongest possible defense strategy?"
• "Should we start settlement discussions this week to minimize both financial exposure and ongoing reputation damage?"

VALUE-BASED QUESTIONS TO ASK:

• "What would a £150K tribunal award plus legal costs mean to Penguin TechGlobal's annual budget?"
• "How much is Penguin TechGlobal's reputation in the competitive tech talent market worth?"
• "What's the cost if this case triggers claims from other employees?"
• "If the national tech magazine runs a negative story, how would that impact recruitment and client relationships?"
• "What would losing your top-performing managers cost in terms of diversity targets and team performance?"
• "How much would a discrimination finding cost Penguin TechGlobal in future insurance premiums?"

VALUE CREATED:

• Financial Protection: Minimizes £150K claim exposure through strategic defense and settlement
• Reputation Preservation: Protects Penguin TechGlobal's brand and talent attraction capabilities in a competitive tech market
• Crisis Management: Transforms potential PR disaster into a managed resolution with minimal business impact
• Legal Compliance: Strengthens internal processes, preventing future discrimination claims and regulatory issues
• Executive Confidence: Provides leadership team with skills and strategies for handling sensitive employment matters
• Industry Standing: Maintains Penguin TechGlobal's position as a progressive employer in the diversity-conscious tech sector

• Risk Mitigation: Prevents copycat claims and similar future employment disputes
• Talent Retention: Preserves relationships with remaining staff and broader workforce confidence

SCENARIO 35: MERGER ACQUISITION

Paul O'Brien, Founder of the Spy Case SecureChat App, has received a £15M buyout offer from a Silicon Valley tech giant. Spy Case SecureChat has innovative encryption technology, but its patents are still pending. There are 30 employees with share options. Concerns about earn-out structure and protecting UK jobs. Personal tax implications are significant as the founder owns 60%. Paul needs guidance on valuation, IP protection, and structuring a deal.

GOLD - COMPLETE M&A OPTIMISATION & WEALTH PROTECTION SERVICE (£££)

• Deal Value Maximization Strategy: Comprehensive valuation analysis and negotiation tactics to optimize final acquisition price
• Tax Efficiency Architecture: Advanced tax planning maximizing Paul's net proceeds from 60% shareholding through optimal deal structuring
• IP Protection Excellence: Patent portfolio strategy ensuring maximum value extraction for encryption technology and future developments
• Employee Safeguarding Program: Share option optimization and job protection negotiation, preserving team retention and morale
• Earn-Out Structure: Strategic earn-out design protecting future value whilst minimizing performance risk exposure
• Due Diligence: Comprehensive buyer due diligence management, minimizing disruption and protecting confidential technology
• Negotiation Leadership: Senior partner-led acquisition negotiation maximizing terms, conditions, and final consideration
• Post-Completion Protection: Ongoing support ensuring earn-out achievements and warranty claim defense

ASSUMPTIONS:

• Full access to Spy Case SecureChat's financial records, IP documentation, and employee contracts
• Paul has the authority to negotiate terms and engage in structured tax planning
• Silicon Valley buyer proceeding in good faith with standard M&A timescales
• Patent applications progressing normally through UK and international filing systems
• Employee share option scheme documentation available and properly structured

EXCLUSIONS:

• Tax advisory services beyond legal structuring (coordinated with specialist tax advisors)
• Patent prosecution and IP filing costs (managed but separately charged)
• Financial due diligence and valuation consultancy (arranged but separately charged)
• US legal counsel for Silicon Valley buyer coordination (facilitated but separately charged)

TECHNICAL DELIVERABLES:

• Comprehensive acquisition agreement with optimized terms and maximum price protection
• Advanced tax-efficient deal structure minimizing Paul's personal tax liability
• IP protection framework preserving encryption technology value and future development rights
• Employee protection package ensuring job security and share option maximization
• Earn-out structure design with achievable targets and risk mitigation provisions
• Due diligence coordination protecting business confidentiality and operational continuity

COMMUNICATION STRUCTURE:

• Immediate: Partner direct access for critical deal decisions and buyer negotiations (24/7)
• Daily: Deal progress briefings during active negotiation and due diligence phases

• Weekly: Strategic meetings covering valuation, structure, and tax optimization progress
• Completion support: Comprehensive transaction management and post-deal implementation

FOLLOW-UP SERVICES:

• 24-month earn-out monitoring and achievement support, including dispute resolution
• Annual tax planning review optimizing ongoing wealth management strategies
• Priority IP counselling for future technology development and patent filings
• Preferred rates for subsequent investment opportunities and business ventures

SILVER - ENHANCED M&A GUIDANCE & DEAL PROTECTION SERVICE (££)

• Deal Structure Optimization: Professional acquisition negotiation and contract structuring guidance
• Tax Planning Support: Basic tax-efficient structuring advice coordinated with specialist advisors
• IP Value Protection: Patent strategy guidance and technology transfer agreement review
• Employee Protection: Share option review and job security negotiation support
• Earn-Out Design: Standard earn-out structure with performance target assessment
• Due Diligence Management: Buyer information request coordination and confidentiality protection

ASSUMPTIONS:

• Standard business hours availability with extended support during critical negotiation phases
• Paul manages day-to-day operational continuity with legal guidance during due diligence
• Basic tax structuring is sufficient for transaction efficiency
• Standard M&A documentation adequate for deal completion

EXCLUSIONS:

• 24/7 availability for urgent deal crises

- Complex advanced tax planning strategies
- Extended post-completion earn-out support
- Detailed IP portfolio development guidance

COMMUNICATION STRUCTURE:

- Business hours: Direct senior lawyer contact
- Bi-weekly: Progress calls and deal structure updates
- Monthly: Written progress reports and negotiation summaries

BRONZE - ESSENTIAL M&A ADVICE SERVICE (£)

- Deal Assessment: Analysis of £15M offer terms and key negotiation priorities
- Structure Guidance: Basic tax and legal structuring recommendations for acquisition
- IP Review: Essential patent and technology transfer considerations
- Employee Impact: Share option implications and job protection basics
- Next Steps Framework: Clear action plan for deal negotiation and completion

ASSUMPTIONS:

- Single comprehensive consultation covering deal structure and key considerations
- Standard office hours availability only
- Paul handles buyer negotiations and employee communications directly
- Template agreements sufficient for basic transaction requirements

EXCLUSIONS:

- Deal negotiation and buyer liaison
- Complex tax planning implementation
- Extended due diligence support
- Post-completion earn-out management

COMMUNICATION STRUCTURE:

- Email and telephone during business hours
- 48-hour response commitment
- Single follow-up consultation included

ASSUMPTIVE CLOSING QUESTIONS:

• "Given the £15M acquisition value and your 60% stake worth £9M+, shall we implement the complete Gold service to maximize your personal wealth and protect the deal?"
• "When should I begin optimizing the tax structure to ensure you keep maximum proceeds from this life-changing transaction?"
• "Shall I commence immediate IP valuation work to ensure your encryption technology achieves full market value?"
• "Should we start employee protection negotiations this week to maintain team stability throughout the acquisition?"

VALUE-BASED QUESTIONS TO ASK:

• "What would an extra £1-2M in final acquisition price mean to your personal financial future?"
• "How much could poor tax structuring cost you personally on a £9M+ stake?"
• "What's the value of your encryption IP if patents are granted versus if they're not?"
• "If key employees leave during acquisition uncertainty, what would that cost the deal value?"
• "What would losing earn-out payments worth potentially millions mean to your long-term wealth?"
• "How much is certainty of deal completion worth when you have a £15M offer on the table?"

VALUE CREATED:

• Wealth Maximization: Optimizes Paul's £9M+ personal proceeds through advanced deal structuring and tax efficiency
• Deal Value Protection: Ensures £15M acquisition achieves maximum possible consideration through expert negotiation
• Tax Efficiency: Minimizes personal tax liability, potentially saving hundreds of thousands in unnecessary charges
• IP Value Extraction: Maximizes encryption technology valuation, ensuring full commercial potential realized
• Employee Retention: Protects team stability, maintaining deal value and operational continuity
• Risk Mitigation: Structures earn-out provisions protecting future income streams worth potentially millions

• Transaction Certainty: Ensures deal completion, preventing loss of life-changing £15M opportunity
• Future Opportunity: Positions Paul optimally for subsequent investment and business ventures

SCENARIO 36: REGULATORY COMPLIANCE

Sophie Taylor, Director of Taylor Financial Services. The FCA (Finance Regulator) has launched an investigation into investment advice practices following a customer complaint. Managing £100M of client funds, 20 advisers' livelihoods at stake. Potential systemic issues in record-keeping have been discovered during an internal review. The company's license is at risk, and they need to manage the investigation, protect clients, and maintain business continuity.

GOLD - COMPLETE REGULATORY DEFENCE & BUSINESS PRESERVATION SERVICE (£££)

• Total FCA Investigation Management: Full regulatory defense strategy protecting license and business continuity
• Client Asset Protection Program: Comprehensive fund management continuity and client communication strategies
• Business Survival Shield: Complete operational continuity planning, ensuring the business remains viable throughout the investigation
• Adviser Protection Strategy: Individual adviser defense coordination and career protection protocols
• Systemic Issue Resolution: Complete record-keeping overhaul and compliance system reconstruction
• Regulatory Relationship Management: Professional FCA liaison maintaining positive regulator relationships
• Crisis Communication: Client retention strategies and stakeholder confidence management
• Future-Proofing Program: Enhanced compliance systems preventing future regulatory issues

ASSUMPTIONS:
• Full access to all client files, investment records, and internal compliance documentation

- Authority to implement immediate operational changes and compliance improvements
- Management team availability for intensive FCA response coordination and strategic planning
- Client communication protocols can be coordinated through existing relationship management systems
- Regulatory investigation scope remains within current complaint parameters

EXCLUSIONS:

- Forensic accounting services for complex fund reconciliation (coordinated but separately charged)
- External compliance consultancy for ongoing system implementation (arranged but separately charged)
- Individual adviser's separate legal representation if conflicts arise
- Client compensation scheme contributions beyond standard regulatory requirements

TECHNICAL DELIVERABLES:

- Comprehensive FCA investigation response strategy and evidence compilation
- Client asset protection protocols and communication framework implementation
- Business continuity plan ensuring operational stability throughout the regulatory process
- Individual adviser protection strategies and regulatory defense coordination
- Complete compliance system overhaul and record-keeping reconstruction program
- Regulatory relationship management and investigation resolution protocols

COMMUNICATION STRUCTURE:

- Immediate: Partner direct access for urgent FCA communications and business decisions (24/7)
- Daily: Morning briefings during active investigation periods with full strategic oversight
- Weekly: Stakeholder management meetings, including client communication and business planning

• FCA meetings: Senior representation with comprehensive preparation and strategic guidance

FOLLOW-UP SERVICES:

• 24-month post-investigation compliance monitoring and regulatory relationship management
• Annual regulatory health checks and compliance system reviews
• Priority access for future regulatory matters across Taylor Financial Services
• Preferred rates for ongoing FCA relationship management and compliance advisory services

SILVER - ENHANCED REGULATORY DEFENCE & COMPLIANCE SERVICE (££)

• FCA Investigation Response: Professional regulatory defense with evidence preparation and submission
• Compliance System Review: Assessment and improvement of record-keeping and advisory processes
• Client Communication Support: Template communications and relationship management guidance
• Business Continuity Guidance: Operational planning ensuring continued trading during the investigation
• Adviser Support: Basic guidance on individual adviser positions and regulatory implications
• Regulatory Liaison: Professional FCA communication and investigation management

ASSUMPTIONS:

• Standard business hours availability with extended support during FCA meetings and submissions
• Sophie manages day-to-day client relationships and operational matters with legal guidance
• Basic compliance improvements are sufficient for regulatory satisfaction
• Investigation resolution achievable through standard response processes

EXCLUSIONS:

• 24/7 availability for regulatory crises

- Comprehensive business continuity planning
- Individual adviser detailed representation
- Extended client retention strategies

COMMUNICATION STRUCTURE:

- Business hours: Direct senior lawyer contact
- Bi-weekly: Progress calls and regulatory strategy updates
- Monthly: Written progress reports and compliance reviews

BRONZE - ESSENTIAL REGULATORY GUIDANCE SERVICE (£)

- Investigation Assessment: Analysis of FCA complaint and available response options
- Compliance Review: Basic guidance on record-keeping improvements and regulatory requirements
- Response Framework: Template FCA submissions and investigation response protocols
- Business Protection: Essential guidance on maintaining operations during regulatory review
- Next Steps Plan: Clear action framework for investigation management and compliance improvement

ASSUMPTIONS:

- Single comprehensive consultation covering regulatory response and compliance basics
- Standard office hours availability only
- Sophie handles FCA communications and internal coordination directly
- Template responses sufficient for initial regulatory requirements

EXCLUSIONS:

- FCA meeting representation and hearing attendance
- Ongoing investigation management
- Complex compliance system overhaul
- Extended business continuity planning

COMMUNICATION STRUCTURE:

- Email and telephone during business hours
- 48-hour response commitment
- Single follow-up consultation included

ASSUMPTIVE CLOSING QUESTIONS:

• "Given that Taylor Financial Services' license and £100M under management are at risk, shall we implement the complete Gold service to preserve your business immediately?"
• "When should I begin coordinating with the FCA to demonstrate your commitment to resolving these compliance issues professionally?"
• "Shall I commence immediate review of your record-keeping systems to address the systemic issues before they escalate?"
• "Should we start implementing client communication strategies this week to maintain confidence and prevent fund withdrawals?"

VALUE-BASED QUESTIONS TO ASK:

• "What would losing your FCA license mean to Taylor Financial Services and the £100M under management?"
• "How much revenue would you lose if clients withdraw funds during this investigation?"
• "What's the real cost of 20 advisers becoming unemployed if the business fails regulatory scrutiny?"
• "If the FCA finds against you, what would rebuilding client trust and business relationships cost?"
• "How long would it take to rebuild a £100M fund management business from scratch?"
• "What would your competitors pay to acquire your client base if Taylor Financial Services loses its license?"

VALUE CREATED:

• Business Preservation: Saves entire financial services operation and £100M fund management business
• License Protection: Maintains FCA authorization enabling continued trading and client service
• Client Retention: Preserves £100M under management through professional crisis communication and confidence maintenance
• Career Protection: Secures employment for 20 financial advisers and their families
• Regulatory Reputation: Maintains positive FCA relationship, enabling future business growth and expansion

• Operational Continuity: Ensures uninterrupted client service and business operations throughout the investigation
• Compliance Excellence: Establishes robust regulatory systems preventing future investigations and penalties
• Market Position: Preserves Taylor Financial Services' reputation and competitive advantage in the financial advisory market

SCENARIO 37: PARTNERSHIP DISSOLUTION

Marcus Thompson, Senior Partner of JTJ Thompson & Partners Architects. A founding partner is retiring from the £1M practice, and there is a dispute over client list valuation and ongoing commission payments. Three major projects are mid-completion. The partner is threatening to contact clients directly, and the office lease is in the retiring partner's name. Need a succession plan and partnership restructuring, while protecting client relationships.

GOLD - COMPLETE PARTNERSHIP TRANSITION & BUSINESS PRESERVATION SERVICE (£££)

• Business Preservation Strategy: Comprehensive partnership dissolution protecting £1M practice value and operational continuity
• Client Relationship Protection Program: Strategic communication plan preventing client defection and maintaining project relationships
• Project Continuity: Complete handover protocols ensuring three major projects proceed without disruption
• Partnership Restructure: Full succession planning and new partnership structure implementation
• Dispute Resolution: Client list valuation and commission dispute resolution, protecting business interests
• Operational Security Program: Lease transfer coordination and premises continuity management
• Stakeholder Management Strategy: Professional client, staff, and supplier communication throughout transition
• Future-Proofing Framework: Enhanced partnership agreements preventing future dissolution disputes

ASSUMPTIONS:

• Full access to partnership agreements, client contracts, and financial records for valuation purposes
• Authority to communicate with clients, staff, and key suppliers during the transition period
• Retiring partner cooperation with structured handover process and client communication protocols
• Access to all project files and client relationship documentation for continuity planning
• Management decisions can be made within reasonable commercial parameters during negotiation

EXCLUSIONS:

• Property valuation services for office premises and partnership assets (coordinated but separately charged)
• Accountancy services for partnership dissolution tax planning (arranged but separately charged)
• Individual partner separate representation if irreconcilable conflicts arise
• Project-specific professional indemnity insurance amendments beyond standard coverage

TECHNICAL DELIVERABLES:

• Comprehensive partnership dissolution agreement with asset and liability allocation
• Client relationship transition strategy and professional communication protocols
• Project handover framework ensuring continuity of the three major commissions
• New partnership structure implementation with enhanced succession planning
• Client list valuation methodology and commission payment resolution framework
• Operational continuity plan, including lease transfer and premises management

COMMUNICATION STRUCTURE:

• Immediate: Partner direct access for urgent client issues and negotiation decisions (24/7)
• Daily: Morning briefings during active dissolution periods and client communication phases

- Weekly: Strategic progress meetings with full business impact assessment and planning
- Client meetings: Senior representation for key relationship preservation discussions

FOLLOW-UP SERVICES:

- 18-month post-dissolution business monitoring and partnership structure support
- Annual partnership agreement reviews and succession planning updates
- Priority access for future partnership matters across JTJ Thompson & Partners
- Preferred rates for ongoing business structure advice and partnership development

---

SILVER - ENHANCED PARTNERSHIP DISSOLUTION & CLIENT PROTECTION SERVICE (££)

- Partnership Dissolution Management: Professional dissolution process with asset valuation and distribution
- Client Communication Strategy: Template communications and relationship management during transition
- Project Handover Support: Basic guidance on maintaining continuity of major architectural projects
- Dispute Resolution: Negotiation support for client list valuation and commission disagreements
- Succession Planning: New partnership structure development and implementation guidance
- Operational Continuity: Lease and premises transition support and coordination

ASSUMPTIONS:

- Standard business hours availability with extended support during critical client communications
- Marcus manages day-to-day client relationships and project coordination with legal guidance
- Basic succession planning is sufficient for partnership restructure requirements
- Dissolution is achievable through standard negotiation and mediation processes

EXCLUSIONS:

- 24/7 availability for partnership crises
- Comprehensive client retention strategies
- Complex project handover management
- Extended business continuity planning

COMMUNICATION STRUCTURE:

- Business hours: Direct senior lawyer contact
- Bi-weekly: Progress calls and dissolution strategy updates
- Monthly: Written progress reports and partnership planning reviews

BRONZE - ESSENTIAL PARTNERSHIP GUIDANCE SERVICE (£)

- Dissolution Assessment: Analysis of partnership agreement and available dissolution options
- Valuation Framework: Basic guidance on client list valuation and asset distribution methods
- Client Protection: Template communications preventing partner interference with client relationships
- Transition Planning: Essential guidance on managing partnership change and business continuity
- Next Steps Plan: Clear action framework for dissolution management and restructure planning

ASSUMPTIONS:

- Single comprehensive consultation covering dissolution basics and transition planning
- Standard office hours availability only
- Marcus handles partner negotiations and client communications directly
- Template agreements sufficient for basic dissolution requirements

EXCLUSIONS:

- Partnership negotiation representation
- Ongoing dissolution management
- Complex succession planning
- Extended client relationship management

COMMUNICATION STRUCTURE:

- Email and telephone during business hours
- 48-hour response commitment
- Single follow-up consultation included

ASSUMPTIVE CLOSING QUESTIONS:

- "Given that JTJ Thompson & Partners' £1M practice value and three major projects are at risk, shall we implement the complete Gold service to preserve your business immediately?"
- "When should I begin coordinating client communications to prevent the retiring partner from damaging these valuable relationships?"
- "Shall I commence immediate negotiation with the retiring partner to resolve the valuation dispute before it escalates further?"
- "Should we start implementing the succession plan this week to ensure business continuity and client confidence?"

VALUE-BASED QUESTIONS TO ASK:

- "What would losing your major clients due to partnership disruption cost JTJ Thompson & Partners in annual revenue?"
- "How much would it cost to rebuild client relationships if the retiring partner damages them through direct contact?"
- "What's the replacement cost of the three major projects if clients withdraw during this partnership dispute?"
- "If the office lease is terminated, what would relocating the practice and rebuilding client confidence cost?"
- "How long would it take to replace a £1M annual practice if key clients are lost during transition?"
- "What would competitors pay to poach your clients during this vulnerable transition period?"

VALUE CREATED:

- Business Preservation: Protects entire £1M architectural practice and ongoing revenue streams
- Client Relationship Security: Maintains a valuable client base, preventing defection during partnership transition
- Project Continuity: Ensures three major architectural projects proceed without disruption or client loss

- Partnership Stability: Creates a robust succession framework, preventing future dissolution disputes
- Operational Continuity: Secures office premises and operational infrastructure throughout transition
- Professional Reputation: Maintains JTJ Thompson & Partners' market standing and architectural industry credibility
- Financial Security: Preserves practice valuation and ensures equitable asset distribution
- Future Growth: Establishes a strengthened partnership structure, enabling continued business development

SCENARIO 38: DATA PROTECTION

Cassy Barker is CEO of KareFirst Medical Services. A private healthcare provider is implementing a £500K patient management system, and there are concerns about cloud storage location and third-party access. The system integrates with National Healthcare records. Five thousand patient records are involved. Need a compliance review before go-live next month. Staff training required. Regulatory approval is essential.

GOLD - COMPLETE DATA PROTECTION COMPLIANCE & SYSTEM CERTIFICATION SERVICE (£££)

- Total GDPR & Healthcare Compliance: Comprehensive data protection strategy ensuring full regulatory compliance for National Healthcare integration
- System Investment Protection: Complete technical and legal review protecting £500K technology investment
- Patient Data Security Excellence: Advanced privacy impact assessment and security protocol implementation
- Regulatory Approval Fast-Track: Accelerated ICO and healthcare regulator approval process management
- National Healthcare integration certification: Specialized compliance ensuring seamless healthcare data sharing protocols
- Staff Training Program: Comprehensive GDPR and healthcare data protection training for the entire workforce
- Cloud Storage Legal Architecture: Complete legal framework for secure cloud storage and third-party access controls

• Ongoing Compliance Shield: 24-month monitoring ensuring continued regulatory compliance and system updates

ASSUMPTIONS:

• Full access to system architecture, cloud storage arrangements, and third-party data processing agreements
• Authority to negotiate contract amendments with technology suppliers and cloud providers
• Management team availability for accelerated compliance implementation and staff training coordination
• Regulatory agencies provide standard response times for approval applications
• Current system design allows for compliance modifications without major architectural changes

EXCLUSIONS:

• Technical system modifications or software development (legal framework provided for implementation)
• External cybersecurity auditing services (coordinated but separately charged)
• Individual staff GDPR certification programs beyond basic compliance training
• Data migration services from legacy systems (legal protocols provided)

TECHNICAL DELIVERABLES:

• Comprehensive privacy impact assessment and GDPR compliance framework
• National Healthcare data sharing agreements and healthcare regulatory compliance protocols
• Cloud storage legal architecture and third-party access control framework
• Complete staff training program with certification and ongoing competency monitoring
• Regulatory approval application management and fast-track processing coordination
• Data breach response protocols and incident management procedures

COMMUNICATION STRUCTURE:

• Immediate: Partner direct access for urgent regulatory and system implementation decisions (24/7)
• Daily: Progress briefings during system implementation and regulatory approval periods
• Weekly: Strategic implementation meetings with full compliance and risk assessment
• Regulatory meetings: Senior representation with comprehensive preparation and submission management

FOLLOW-UP SERVICES:

• 24-month post-implementation compliance monitoring and regulatory relationship management
• Annual data protection health checks and system compliance reviews
• Priority access for future healthcare data protection matters across KareFirst operations
• Preferred rates for ongoing GDPR compliance and healthcare regulatory management

SILVER - ENHANCED GDPR COMPLIANCE & REGULATORY APPROVAL SERVICE (££)

• GDPR Compliance Review: Comprehensive data protection assessment and compliance framework
• Regulatory Approval Support: ICO and healthcare regulator application management and liaison
• Privacy Impact Assessment: Detailed patient data risk analysis and mitigation strategies
• National Healthcare integration guidance: Healthcare data sharing protocols and regulatory compliance advice
• Staff Training Framework: Essential GDPR training program and competency guidelines
• Cloud Storage Compliance: Legal review of data storage arrangements and third-party access controls

ASSUMPTIONS:

• Standard business hours availability with priority support during regulatory submission periods
• Cassy manages day-to-day system implementation with legal compliance guidance

- Basic training program sufficient for staff GDPR competency requirements
- Regulatory approval achieved through standard application processes

EXCLUSIONS:

- 24/7 availability for implementation crises
- Comprehensive ongoing compliance monitoring
- Advanced National Healthcare integration negotiations
- Extended post-implementation support

COMMUNICATION STRUCTURE:

- Business hours: Direct senior lawyer contact
- Bi-weekly: Progress calls and compliance implementation updates
- Monthly: Written compliance reports and regulatory status reviews

---

BRONZE - ESSENTIAL GDPR GUIDANCE SERVICE (£)

- Compliance Assessment: Basic GDPR review identifying key data protection obligations
- Regulatory Guidance: Essential advice on ICO requirements and healthcare data regulations
- Privacy Framework: Template privacy impact assessment and basic compliance protocols
- National Healthcare integration basics: Fundamental guidance on healthcare data sharing requirements
- Training Outline: Basic GDPR training framework and staff competency guidelines

ASSUMPTIONS:

- Single comprehensive consultation covering essential data protection compliance requirements
- Standard office hours availability only
- Cassy handles regulatory submissions and system implementation coordination directly
- Template frameworks are sufficient for basic compliance obligations

EXCLUSIONS:
- Regulatory approval application management
- Detailed privacy impact assessments
- Comprehensive staff training delivery
- Ongoing compliance monitoring

COMMUNICATION STRUCTURE:
- Email and telephone during business hours
- 48-hour response commitment
- Single follow-up consultation included

ASSUMPTIVE CLOSING QUESTIONS:
- "Given the £500K system investment and critical National Healthcare integration deadline, shall we implement the complete Gold service to protect both your investment and regulatory standing?"
- "When should I begin coordinating with the ICO to fast-track your regulatory approvals before next month's go-live?"
- "Shall I commence immediate privacy impact assessment to ensure your 5,000 patient records remain fully protected?"
- "Should we start implementing comprehensive staff training this week to ensure GDPR competency before system launch?"

VALUE-BASED QUESTIONS TO ASK:
- "What would delaying the £500K system go-live cost KareFirst in lost revenue and operational efficiency?"
- "How much would GDPR fines cost if patient data compliance isn't achieved properly?"
- "What's the reputational damage if 5,000 patients lose confidence in KareFirst's data protection?"
- "If National Healthcare integration fails regulatory approval, what would losing healthcare partnership contracts cost annually?"
- "How much would rebuilding patient trust cost if a data breach occurred due to poor compliance?"
- "What would competitors gain if KareFirst couldn't deliver modern, compliant healthcare technology?"

VALUE CREATED:

• Investment Protection: Secures £500K technology investment through comprehensive regulatory compliance
• Business Continuity: Enables on-schedule system implementation without regulatory delays or complications
• Patient Trust: Maintains confidence of 5,000 patients through exemplary data protection standards
• National Healthcare Partnership: Preserves crucial healthcare integration opportunities and partnership revenues
• Regulatory Standing: Establishes KareFirst as a GDPR-compliant healthcare leader with regulatory authorities
• Operational Excellence: Provides competitive advantage through advanced, compliant healthcare technology
• Risk Mitigation: Prevents potentially devastating GDPR fines and regulatory sanctions
• Staff Competency: Creates a skilled, confident workforce capable of managing sensitive healthcare data
• Market Position: Positions KareFirst as a trusted, technology-advanced healthcare provider in a competitive market

SCENARIO 39: COMMERCIAL LEASE

Rohit Gill is the owner of the YumBite Restaurant Chain, with 15 restaurants across the South East. Post-Covid revenue is down 30% and landlords are taking different approaches to rent negotiations. Three sites are loss-making but in the middle of lease terms. Staff redundancies are likely if costs are not reduced. Rohit needs a strategy for lease renegotiation or exits while protecting profitable sites.

GOLD - COMPLETE PORTFOLIO RESTRUCTURING & BUSINESS PRESERVATION SERVICE (£££)

• Total Portfolio Strategy: Comprehensive 15-site lease management protecting profitable operations while restructuring underperforming sites
• Business Survival Program: Strategic cost reduction, achieving viability without compromising operational excellence
• Multi-Landlord Negotiation Management: Professional coordination across all landlord relationships, maximizing negotiation leverage

• Loss-Making Site Resolution: Complete exit strategy for three underperforming sites, minimizing financial exposure
• Staff Protection Strategy: Workforce preservation through lease cost reductions, avoiding redundancy program
• Profitable Site Enhancement: Lease improvements and extensions securing long-term operational stability for successful locations
• Cash Flow Recovery Program: Immediate rent relief negotiations and payment restructuring, improving working capital
• Future-Proofing Strategy: Break clauses and flexibility terms protecting against future market volatility

ASSUMPTIONS:

• Full access to all 15 lease agreements, financial performance data, and landlord correspondence
• Authority to negotiate on behalf of YumBite across all landlord relationships and lease modifications
• Management team availability for intensive portfolio restructuring and strategic decision-making
• Financial information provided enabling evidence-based negotiation with landlords
• Current lease terms allow for meaningful renegotiation or early termination discussions

EXCLUSIONS:

• Property valuation services for lease restructuring (coordinated but separately charged)
• Insolvency advice if business restructuring is insufficient (separate specialist engagement)
• New site acquisition legal services beyond the current portfolio management
• Employment law advice for redundancy processes (coordinated but separately charged)

TECHNICAL DELIVERABLES:

• Comprehensive 15-site portfolio analysis and strategic restructuring plan
• Multi-landlord negotiation strategy maximizing cost reductions across profitable sites

- Complete exit strategy for three loss-making sites with minimal financial exposure
- Cash flow improvement program through rent relief and payment restructuring
- Enhanced lease terms for profitable sites, including break clauses and flexibility provisions
- Business preservation strategy, avoiding staff redundancies through cost management

COMMUNICATION STRUCTURE:

- Immediate: Partner direct access for urgent landlord negotiations and business decisions (24/7)
- Daily: Progress briefings during active negotiation periods with full strategic oversight
- Weekly: Portfolio management meetings, including financial performance and negotiation outcomes
- Landlord meetings: Senior representation with comprehensive preparation and strategic coordination

FOLLOW-UP SERVICES:

- 18-month post-restructuring portfolio monitoring and landlord relationship management
- Annual lease portfolio health checks and market rent reviews
- Priority access for future commercial property matters across YumBite operations
- Preferred rates for ongoing lease management and property advisory services

SILVER - ENHANCED LEASE RESTRUCTURING & NEGOTIATION SERVICE (££)

- Portfolio Assessment: Comprehensive review of 15-site lease portfolio with strategic restructuring recommendations
- Multi-Landlord Negotiation: Professional rent renegotiation across all sites with a coordinated approach
- Loss-Making Site Strategy: Exit planning for three underperforming sites with a cost minimization focus
- Profitable Site Protection: Enhanced lease terms and security for successful restaurant locations
- Cash Flow Improvement: Rent relief negotiations and payment restructuring for immediate cost reduction

- Break Clause Implementation: Future flexibility provisions protecting against market volatility

ASSUMPTIONS:

- Standard business hours availability with priority support during critical negotiation periods
- Rohit manages day-to-day landlord relationships with strategic legal guidance
- Standard negotiation approach sufficient for achieving meaningful cost reductions
- Portfolio restructuring is achievable through conventional lease renegotiation processes

EXCLUSIONS:

- 24/7 availability for negotiation crises
- Comprehensive business preservation strategy
- Detailed employment protection planning
- Extended post-restructuring monitoring

COMMUNICATION STRUCTURE:

- Business hours: Direct senior lawyer contact
- Bi-weekly: Progress calls and negotiation strategy updates
- Monthly: Written portfolio reports and cost reduction analysis

BRONZE - ESSENTIAL LEASE GUIDANCE SERVICE (£)

- Portfolio Review: Basic assessment of 15-site lease obligations and renegotiation opportunities
- Negotiation Framework: Template approaches for landlord discussions and rent reduction requests
- Exit Options Analysis: Fundamental guidance on early termination possibilities for loss-making sites
- Cost Reduction Strategy: Essential advice on lease cost management and cash flow improvement
- Next Steps Plan: Clear action framework for portfolio restructuring and landlord engagement

ASSUMPTIONS:

- Single comprehensive consultation covering portfolio basics and negotiation strategies
- Standard office hours availability only

• Rohit handles landlord negotiations and lease management directly with template guidance
• Basic restructuring advice is sufficient for immediate cost reduction needs

EXCLUSIONS:

• Landlord meeting representation and negotiation management
• Detailed exit strategy implementation
• Comprehensive portfolio monitoring
• Extended business preservation planning

COMMUNICATION STRUCTURE:

• Email and telephone during business hours
• 48-hour response commitment
• Single follow-up consultation included

ASSUMPTIVE CLOSING QUESTIONS:

• "Given that YumBite faces potential staff redundancies without immediate lease cost reductions, shall we implement the complete Gold service to save jobs and preserve your business?"
• "When should I begin coordinating with your 15 landlords to demonstrate YumBite's commitment to restructuring professionally?"
• "Shall I commence immediate negotiations for the three loss-making sites to minimize your financial exposure?"
• "Should we start implementing rent relief strategies this week to improve cash flow before redundancy decisions become necessary?"

VALUE-BASED QUESTIONS TO ASK:

• "What would closing three restaurants cost in lease penalties, fit-out losses, and redundancy payments?"
• "How much annual rent reduction do you need across the 15 sites to avoid staff redundancies?"
• "What's the total cost of redundancy programs if lease costs aren't reduced significantly?"
• "If profitable sites lose their lease security, what would rebuilding YumBite's presence cost?"
• "How much revenue would you lose if forced to close restaurants due to unaffordable lease terms?"

- "What would competitors gain if YumBite had to exit prime restaurant locations?"

VALUE CREATED:

- Business Preservation: Saves YumBite Restaurant Chain through strategic lease cost management and portfolio optimization
- Job Protection: Prevents staff redundancies across 15 restaurants through successful lease cost reductions
- Cash Flow Recovery: Improves working capital through rent relief and payment restructuring arrangements
- Profitable Site Security: Protects successful restaurant locations through enhanced lease terms and operational stability
- Loss Minimization: Achieves clean exits from underperforming sites with minimal financial exposure and penalty costs
- Operational Continuity: Maintains restaurant operations across profitable sites, ensuring continued revenue generation
- Market Position: Preserves YumBite's presence in prime South East locations, maintaining competitive advantage
- Future Flexibility: Establishes break clauses and adaptable terms protecting against future market volatility
- Landlord Relationships: Maintains positive property relationships, enabling future expansion and renegotiation opportunities

SCENARIO 40: TRADEMARK DISPUTE

James Woodcock, Founder of GreenLife Best Foods. GreenLife Best Foods is an organic food brand valued at £1M, and has discovered a competitor using a similar name and nearly identical logo in the European market. Export deals worth £500K are at risk. GreenLife Best Food's trademark is registered in the UK but not the EU. There is evidence of customer confusion on social media, and James needs urgent action to protect the brand before a major trade show next month.

GOLD - COMPLETE BRAND PROTECTION & EUROPEAN MARKET DOMINANCE SERVICE (£££)

• Total Brand Defense Strategy: Comprehensive trademark enforcement protecting £1M brand valuation across European markets
• Export Deal Preservation: Urgent action securing £500K export opportunities and European market expansion
• European Trademark Domination: Fast-track EU trademark registration and international brand protection portfolio
• Competitor Neutralization: Complete enforcement strategy eliminating trademark infringement and brand confusion
• Trade Show Victory: Strategic brand positioning ensuring powerful market presence at a critical industry event
• Social Media Evidence Mastery: Professional documentation and deployment of customer confusion evidence
• International Enforcement Network: Coordinated multi-jurisdictional action across European territories
• Brand Value Protection: Long-term trademark strategy maximizing and protecting £1M brand investment

ASSUMPTIONS:

• Full access to existing UK trademark registrations, brand documentation, and social media evidence
• Authority to initiate urgent trademark applications and enforcement proceedings across European jurisdictions
• James is available for intensive strategy sessions and rapid decision-making during enforcement proceedings
• Competitor responds to enforcement action within standard legal timeframes
• Trade show organizers cooperate with brand protection measures and enforcement actions

EXCLUSIONS:

• Criminal prosecution services for trademark counterfeiting (coordinated but separately charged)
• Private investigation services for extensive competitor intelligence gathering (arranged but separately charged)
• Brand valuation services for insurance or acquisition purposes (legal protection strategies provided)

• Product packaging redesign or brand development consultancy services

TECHNICAL DELIVERABLES:

• Comprehensive trademark enforcement strategy and cease and desist campaign management
• Fast-track European Union trademark applications and international registration portfolio
• Social media evidence compilation and legal documentation for enforcement proceedings
• Trade show brand protection protocols and competitor monitoring systems
• Multi-jurisdictional enforcement coordination across key European markets
• Brand protection agreements and licensing frameworks for international expansion

COMMUNICATION STRUCTURE:

• Immediate: Partner direct access for urgent enforcement decisions and competitor responses (24/7)
• Daily: Enforcement progress briefings during active trademark dispute and application periods
• Weekly: Strategic brand protection meetings with comprehensive market intelligence and legal updates
• Trade show: On-site legal support ensuring brand protection and competitive advantage

FOLLOW-UP SERVICES:

• 24-month post-enforcement monitoring and trademark portfolio management across European markets
• Annual brand protection health checks and competitive landscape reviews
• Priority access for future trademark matters across GreenLife Best Foods operations
• Preferred rates for ongoing international trademark strategy and brand protection services

SILVER - ENHANCED TRADEMARK ENFORCEMENT & PROTECTION SERVICE (££)

- Trademark Enforcement Strategy: Professional competitor action and brand protection campaign
- EU Registration Support: European trademark application management and registration coordination
- Export Deal Protection: Focused action preserving key commercial opportunities and market expansion
- Evidence Compilation: Social media confusion documentation and legal evidence preparation
- Trade Show Preparation: Brand protection advice and competitive strategy for industry event
- Competitor Response Management: Professional handling of trademark dispute and settlement negotiations

ASSUMPTIONS:

- Standard business hours availability with priority support during enforcement and application periods
- James manages day-to-day brand monitoring and commercial negotiations with legal support
- Basic enforcement action sufficient for competitor resolution and brand protection
- Trade show success achieved through standard brand protection measures

EXCLUSIONS:

- 24/7 availability for enforcement crises
- Comprehensive multi-jurisdictional coordination
- On-site trade show legal support
- Extended competitive intelligence gathering

COMMUNICATION STRUCTURE:

- Business hours: Direct senior lawyer contact
- Bi-weekly: Progress calls and enforcement strategy updates
- Monthly: Written reports on trademark applications and competitive landscape

BRONZE - ESSENTIAL TRADEMARK GUIDANCE SERVICE (£)

- Trademark Assessment: Basic analysis of infringement issues and available enforcement options
- EU Application Guidance: Essential advice on European trademark registration requirements and process
- Enforcement Framework: Template cease and desist letters and basic competitor response strategies
- Evidence Review: Guidance on social media documentation and trademark confusion evidence
- Trade Show Advice: Basic brand protection strategies for industry event participation

ASSUMPTIONS:

- Single comprehensive consultation covering essential trademark enforcement and protection basics
- Standard office hours availability only
- James handles competitor communications and trademark applications directly with template guidance
- Basic enforcement measures are sufficient for initial brand protection requirements

EXCLUSIONS:

- Direct competitor enforcement management
- Comprehensive trademark application filing
- Detailed evidence compilation services
- Ongoing dispute resolution support

COMMUNICATION STRUCTURE:

- Email and telephone during business hours
- 48-hour response commitment
- Single follow-up consultation included

ASSUMPTIVE CLOSING QUESTIONS:

- "Given your £1M brand valuation and £500K export deals at risk, shall we implement the complete Gold service to eliminate this competitive threat immediately?"
- "When should I begin fast-track European trademark applications to secure your international expansion before the trade show?"

• "Shall I commence urgent competitor enforcement action to protect your export opportunities and brand reputation?"
• "Should we start comprehensive brand protection strategies this week to ensure trade show dominance next month?"

VALUE-BASED QUESTIONS TO ASK:

• "What would losing £500K in European export deals mean to GreenLife Best Foods' growth strategy?"
• "How much would rebuilding brand recognition cost if customer confusion continues in European markets?"
• "What's the value of trade show success versus arriving with an unprotected, confused brand identity?"
• "If competitors steal your organic food market position, what would regaining leadership cost?"
• "How long would it take to rebuild the £1M brand value if trademark protection fails?"
• "What would your business be worth if European expansion becomes impossible due to trademark conflicts?"

VALUE CREATED:

• Brand Value Protection: Secures £1M brand valuation through comprehensive trademark enforcement and protection
• Export Opportunity Preservation: Maintains £500K European export deals and international expansion potential
• Market Dominance: Establishes GreenLife Best Foods as a protected, dominant organic brand across European territories
• Competitive Advantage: Eliminates competitor confusion, enabling clear market differentiation and premium positioning
• Trade Show Success: Ensures powerful industry presence without brand confusion or competitive undermining
• International Expansion: Creates a secure trademark foundation enabling confident European market development
• Customer Trust: Maintains brand clarity and customer confidence, preventing confusion and loyalty erosion
• Long-term Growth: Establishes a robust intellectual property portfolio supporting future business development and acquisition value
• Legal Certainty: Provides comprehensive trademark protection, enabling confident business decisions and investment attraction

SCENARIO 41: RESTRUCTURING

Elena Kovac, Operations Director at Clifton Manufacturing Solutions Ltd, needs to reorganize a £5M business across three UK sites. Duplicate functions have been identified, and 30 redundancies are likely. A union is involved at the largest site. Key contracts need renegotiating and property leases are complex. Production needs to be maintained whilst restructuring, and customer orders must be protected. A management buyout is a possibility for one division.

GOLD - COMPLETE BUSINESS TRANSFORMATION & CONTINUITY SERVICE (£££)

• Total Restructuring Strategy: Comprehensive business transformation plan preserving £5M enterprise value whilst achieving operational efficiency
• Production Continuity Shield: Complete operational protection ensuring uninterrupted manufacturing and customer order fulfilment
• Union Relations Mastery: Expert collective consultation management, maintaining workforce relationships whilst achieving necessary changes
• Customer Contract Protection: Strategic renegotiation protecting key commercial relationships and revenue streams
• Property Portfolio Optimization: Complex lease restructuring across three sites, maximizing cost savings and operational flexibility
• Management Buyout Facilitation: Complete MBO structuring and negotiation for division divestment opportunity
• Redundancy Program Excellence: Legally compliant and commercially sensitive workforce reduction, minimizing costs and reputational damage
• Business Preservation Framework: 18-month post-restructuring support ensuring sustainable operational success

ASSUMPTIONS:

• Full access to financial records, employment contracts, property leases, and commercial agreements across all three sites

• Authority to negotiate with unions, customers, landlords, and potential MBO participants on behalf of Clifton Manufacturing Solutions
• Management team availability for intensive restructuring coordination and strategic decision-making
• Union representatives engage constructively in collective consultation processes
• Key customer relationships can be maintained through professional contract renegotiation

EXCLUSIONS:

• Financial advisory services for business valuation and MBO structuring (coordinated but separately charged)
• HR consultancy for detailed workforce planning beyond legal requirements (arranged but separately charged)
• Property surveying and lease valuation services (coordinated but separately charged)
• Redundancy payments and pension scheme costs (legal framework provided for calculation)

TECHNICAL DELIVERABLES:

• Comprehensive restructuring plan with legal, commercial, and operational implementation roadmap
• Union consultation strategy and collective redundancy process management
• Customer contract renegotiation program protecting key revenue streams
• Property lease restructuring across three sites with cost optimization strategies
• Management buyout structuring and negotiation for division divestment
• Employment law compliance framework ensuring a legally sound redundancy program
• Business continuity protocols, maintaining production throughout the transformation process

COMMUNICATION STRUCTURE:

• Immediate: Partner direct access for urgent restructuring decisions and crisis management (24/7)
• Daily: Morning briefings during active restructuring phases with full strategic oversight

• Weekly: Stakeholder management meetings including union, customer, and landlord coordination
• Monthly: Board-level reporting on restructuring progress and financial impact assessment

FOLLOW-UP SERVICES:

• 18-month post-restructuring legal support ensuring sustainable business operations
• Quarterly business health checks and employment law compliance reviews
• Priority access for future restructuring matters across Clifton Manufacturing Solutions operations
• Preferred rates for ongoing commercial contract management and employment law advisory

---

SILVER - ENHANCED RESTRUCTURING & EMPLOYMENT COMPLIANCE SERVICE (££)

• Restructuring Framework: Comprehensive business reorganization plan with legal compliance and operational guidance
• Union Consultation Management: Professional collective consultation process ensuring legal compliance and workforce engagement
• Employment Law Compliance: Complete redundancy program management, minimizing legal risks and costs
• Contract Renegotiation Support: Strategic advice on key customer and supplier contract modifications
• Property Lease Guidance: Essential advice on lease obligations and restructuring opportunities across three sites
• MBO Basic Framework: Fundamental legal structure for a potential management buyout transaction

ASSUMPTIONS:

• Standard business hours availability with extended support during critical restructuring phases
• Elena manages day-to-day operational matters with strategic legal guidance
• Union representatives engage professionally in consultation processes

- Basic restructuring approach sufficient for business transformation objectives

EXCLUSIONS:

- 24/7 availability for restructuring crises
- Comprehensive customer relationship management
- Complex property lease negotiations
- Detailed MBO transaction management

COMMUNICATION STRUCTURE:

- Business hours: Direct senior lawyer contact
- Bi-weekly: Progress calls and restructuring strategy updates
- Monthly: Written progress reports and compliance reviews

BRONZE - ESSENTIAL RESTRUCTURING GUIDANCE SERVICE (£)

- Restructuring Assessment: Analysis of legal obligations and available restructuring options
- Redundancy Compliance: Essential guidance on collective consultation and employment law requirements
- Contract Review: Basic advice on key contract obligations and renegotiation strategies
- Property Obligations: Fundamental guidance on lease responsibilities and termination options
- Legal Framework: Template documentation and process guidance for business reorganization

ASSUMPTIONS:

- Single comprehensive consultation covering essential restructuring legal requirements
- Standard office hours availability only
- Elena handles union negotiations and customer communications directly
- Template approaches are sufficient for basic restructuring compliance

EXCLUSIONS:

- Union consultation management and representation
- Customer contract negotiations
- Complex property lease restructuring
- Management buyout transaction support

COMMUNICATION STRUCTURE:

• Email and telephone during business hours
• 48-hour response commitment
• Single follow-up consultation included

ASSUMPTIVE CLOSING QUESTIONS:

• "Given Clifton Manufacturing Solutions' £5M enterprise value and complex three-site restructuring, shall we implement the complete Gold service to preserve your business throughout this transformation?"
• "When should I begin coordinating with your union representatives to ensure smooth collective consultation whilst maintaining production continuity?"
• "Shall I commence immediate customer contract review to protect your revenue streams during the restructuring process?"
• "Should we start structuring the management buyout opportunity this week to maximize division value and strategic options?"

VALUE-BASED QUESTIONS TO ASK:

• "What would losing key customers during restructuring cost Clifton Manufacturing Solutions in annual revenue?"
• "How much would industrial action or union disputes cost in lost production and customer relationships?"
• "What's the financial impact if restructuring delays force you to maintain duplicate functions for additional months?"
• "If employment tribunal claims arise from poor redundancy handling, what would defense costs and settlements total?"
• "How much value could the management buyout generate if structured and negotiated properly?"
• "What would competitors gain if Clifton Manufacturing Solutions' restructuring fails and the business becomes vulnerable?"

VALUE CREATED:

• Business Preservation: Maintains £5M enterprise value through professionally managed transformation, avoiding operational collapse

• Customer Retention: Protects essential revenue streams through strategic contract renegotiation and relationship management
• Production Continuity: Ensures uninterrupted manufacturing capability throughout the restructuring process, maintaining competitive position
• Union Relations: Maintains positive workforce relationships whilst achieving necessary operational changes and cost savings
• Legal Compliance: Prevents costly employment tribunal claims and regulatory penalties through expert redundancy management
• Property Optimization: Maximizes cost savings and operational flexibility through strategic lease restructuring across three sites
• MBO Value: Captures additional enterprise value through professional management buyout structuring and negotiation
• Market Position: Emerges as streamlined, efficient manufacturing operation with enhanced competitiveness and profitability
• Stakeholder Confidence: Maintains confidence of customers, suppliers, and workforce through professional restructuring management

SCENARIO 42: ENVIRONMENTAL COMPLIANCE

William Barnes, Owner of Barnes Printing Ltd. A family printing business, employing 50 staff, faces an Environment Agency investigation into chemical disposal practices, following an anonymous tip from an ex-employee. License renewal is due in three months. Major supermarket contracts require environmental certification. Historical waste management records are incomplete. A £100K equipment upgrade is needed for compliance. Needs to manage the investigation while maintaining operations.

GOLD - COMPLETE ENVIRONMENTAL DEFENCE & BUSINESS PRESERVATION SERVICE (£££)

• Total Environment Agency Investigation Management: Comprehensive regulatory defense strategy protecting business license and operations

• Supermarket Contract Protection: Strategic compliance certification ensuring major contract retention and revenue security
• Business Continuity Shield: Complete operational protection, maintaining printing services throughout the investigation
• Staff Employment Security: Workforce protection strategy securing 50 jobs and the family's business legacy
• Compliance Investment Optimization: Strategic guidance maximizing £100K equipment upgrade effectiveness and regulatory impact
• Historical Records Reconstruction: Professional evidence management addressing incomplete waste disposal documentation
• Regulatory Relationship Excellence: Environment Agency liaison, maintaining positive regulator relationships for future operations
• Environmental Certification Fast-Track: Accelerated certification process ensuring supermarket contract compliance requirements

ASSUMPTIONS:

• Full access to available waste management records, facility operations, and historical disposal practices
• Authority to coordinate with equipment suppliers and environmental consultants for compliance upgrades
• Management team availability for intensive Environment Agency response coordination and strategic planning
• Current printing operations can continue with appropriate environmental monitoring and compliance measures
• Equipment suppliers can deliver a £100K upgrade within investigation timescales

EXCLUSIONS:

• Environmental consultancy services for technical compliance assessment (coordinated but separately charged)
• Equipment installation and technical commissioning services (legal framework provided)
• Forensic waste analysis or site contamination testing (arranged but separately charged)

• Individual staff representation if personal liability issues arise from the investigation

TECHNICAL DELIVERABLES:

• Comprehensive Environment Agency investigation response strategy and evidence compilation
• Business license renewal application management and regulatory compliance certification
• Supermarket contract compliance strategy ensuring environmental certification requirements
• Staff employment protection protocols and business continuity planning
• Equipment upgrade legal framework maximizing compliance and regulatory benefit
• Historical records reconstruction and evidence management for investigation defense

COMMUNICATION STRUCTURE:

• Immediate: Partner direct access for urgent Environment Agency communications and business decisions (24/7)
• Daily: Morning briefings during active investigation periods with full strategic oversight
• Weekly: Stakeholder management meetings, including client retention and operational planning
• EA meetings: Senior representation with comprehensive preparation and strategic guidance

FOLLOW-UP SERVICES:

• 24-month post-investigation environmental compliance monitoring and regulatory relationship management
• Annual environmental health checks and compliance system reviews
• Priority access for future environmental matters across Barnes Printing operations
• Preferred rates for ongoing Environment Agency relationship management and compliance advisory services

SILVER - ENHANCED ENVIRONMENTAL DEFENCE & COMPLIANCE SERVICE (££)

• Environment Agency Response: Professional regulatory defense with evidence preparation and submission management
• License Renewal Support: Strategic application management ensuring continued business operations
• Compliance Assessment: Review of environmental obligations and equipment upgrade requirements
• Contract Protection Guidance: Basic certification support for supermarket environmental requirements
• Business Continuity Advice: Operational planning ensuring continued printing services during the investigation
• Records Management: Guidance on historical documentation and evidence compilation

ASSUMPTIONS:

• Standard business hours availability with extended support during EA meetings and submissions
• William manages day-to-day client relationships and operational matters with legal guidance
• Basic equipment upgrade sufficient for regulatory compliance requirements
• Investigation resolution achievable through standard response processes

EXCLUSIONS:

• 24/7 availability for environmental crises
• Comprehensive business continuity planning
• Advanced supermarket contract certification strategies
• Extended post-investigation monitoring

COMMUNICATION STRUCTURE:

• Business hours: Direct senior lawyer contact
• Bi-weekly: Progress calls and regulatory strategy updates
• Monthly: Written progress reports and compliance reviews

BRONZE - ESSENTIAL ENVIRONMENTAL GUIDANCE SERVICE (£)

• Investigation Assessment: Analysis of Environment Agency complaint and available response options

• Compliance Review: Basic guidance on environmental obligations and equipment upgrade requirements
• Response Framework: Template EA submissions and investigation response protocols
• License Renewal Basics: Essential guidance on renewal application and regulatory requirements
• Next Steps Plan: Clear action framework for investigation management and compliance improvement

ASSUMPTIONS:

• Single comprehensive consultation covering regulatory response and compliance basics
• Standard office hours availability only
• William handles EA communications and operational coordination directly
• Template responses sufficient for initial regulatory requirements

EXCLUSIONS:

• Environment Agency meeting representation and hearing attendance
• Ongoing investigation management
• Complex compliance certification processes
• Extended business continuity planning

COMMUNICATION STRUCTURE:

• Email and telephone during business hours
• 48-hour response commitment
• Single follow-up consultation included

ASSUMPTIVE CLOSING QUESTIONS:

• "Given that Barnes Printing's license renewal and major supermarket contracts are at risk, shall we implement the complete Gold service to preserve your family business immediately?"
• "When should I begin coordinating with the Environment Agency to demonstrate your commitment to environmental compliance?"

• "Shall I commence immediate review of your waste management practices to address the investigation concerns before license renewal?"
• "Should we start protecting your supermarket contracts this week by fast-tracking environmental certification requirements?"

VALUE-BASED QUESTIONS TO ASK:

• "What would losing your Environment Agency license mean to Barnes Printing and your 50 employees?"
• "How much annual revenue would you lose if the major supermarket contracts are terminated due to environmental non-compliance?"
• "What's the real cost of 50 people losing their jobs if the family business fails regulatory scrutiny?"
• "If the Environment Agency finds against you, what would rebuilding client trust and business relationships cost?"
• "How long would it take to rebuild a family printing business from scratch if you lose your operating license?"
• "What would your competitors gain if Barnes Printing loses its major supermarket contracts due to compliance failures?"

VALUE CREATED:

• Business Preservation: Saves the family printing business and maintains operational license, enabling continued trading
• Employment Security: Protects 50 jobs and preserves the family's business legacy for future generations
• Revenue Protection: Maintains major supermarket contracts through environmental certification compliance
• Investment Optimization: Maximizes the effectiveness of the £100K equipment upgrade, ensuring regulatory compliance and business benefit
• Regulatory Reputation: Maintains positive Environment Agency relationship, enabling future business growth and expansion
• Operational Continuity: Ensures uninterrupted printing services and client relationships throughout the investigation
• Compliance Excellence: Establishes robust environmental systems, preventing future investigations and penalties
• Market Position: Preserves Barnes Printing's reputation and competitive advantage in the commercial printing sector

SCENARIO 43: JOINT VENTURE

Karen Cummings, Innovation Director at Caregiver MedTech Solutions, is negotiating a £4M joint venture with a Japanese medical equipment manufacturer. IP sharing is crucial for an artificial intelligence diagnostic tool, and FDA approval is pending. Karen needs to protect the UK research team's rights. Complex regulatory requirements in both jurisdictions. Cultural differences are causing communication issues. Time is critical as a competitor is launching a similar product.

GOLD - COMPLETE INTERNATIONAL JOINT VENTURE & COMPETITIVE ADVANTAGE SERVICE (£££)

• Strategic JV Architecture: Comprehensive £4M joint venture structure maximizing competitive positioning and market opportunity
• AI IP Protection Excellence: Advanced intellectual property framework protecting UK research assets and securing optimal licensing terms
• Dual Regulatory Mastery: Complete UK/Japan regulatory compliance strategy ensuring FDA and Japanese authority approvals
• Cultural Bridge Building: Professional Japanese business culture integration and communication protocol management
• Research Team Protection: Comprehensive employment rights safeguarding and talent retention strategies
• Competitive Time Advantage: Accelerated deal completion, preventing competitor market capture
• Cross-Border Legal Coordination: Seamless UK-Japan legal framework with local counsel management
• Long-Term Partnership Success: Strategic relationship architecture ensuring sustainable joint venture prosperity

ASSUMPTIONS:

• Full access to UK research team IP portfolios, existing Japanese partner negotiations, and competitive intelligence
• Authority to negotiate key commercial terms and coordinate with Japanese legal counsel and regulatory advisors

• Management team availability for intensive cross-cultural negotiation sessions and regulatory coordination
• Japanese partner provides reasonable access to legal and regulatory information for due diligence
• FDA approval timeline remains within the currently projected regulatory framework

EXCLUSIONS:

• Japanese local legal counsel fees (coordinated and managed but separately charged)
• FDA regulatory submission costs and scientific advisory services (legal framework provided)
• Patent filing and prosecution costs in multiple jurisdictions (strategy provided)
• Technical due diligence and AI system validation services (legal structure provided)

TECHNICAL DELIVERABLES:

• Comprehensive joint venture agreement with AI IP sharing and commercialization framework
• UK research team employment protection and retention protocols with equity participation structures
• Dual-jurisdiction regulatory compliance strategy and approval coordination framework
• Japanese business culture integration protocols and cross-cultural communication management
• Competitive positioning strategy and market timing optimization for joint venture launch
• Long-term partnership governance and dispute resolution mechanisms

COMMUNICATION STRUCTURE:

• Immediate: Partner direct access for urgent negotiation and competitive response decisions (24/7)
• Daily: Progress briefings during active negotiation and regulatory approval periods
• Bi-weekly: Strategic partnership meetings with full commercial and legal assessment
• Japanese coordination: Senior representation in cross-cultural negotiations with comprehensive cultural preparation

FOLLOW-UP SERVICES:

• 36-month post-signature partnership management and dispute prevention services
• Annual joint venture health checks and commercial relationship optimization
• Priority access for future Caregiver MedTech international partnership and IP matters
• Preferred rates for ongoing Japanese regulatory and partnership management

SILVER - ENHANCED JOINT VENTURE STRUCTURING & IP PROTECTION SERVICE (££)

• Joint Venture Framework: Professional £4M partnership structure with comprehensive commercial terms
• IP Protection Strategy: AI intellectual property sharing agreements and UK research asset protection
• Regulatory Compliance: UK/Japan regulatory guidance and FDA approval pathway coordination
• Employment Protection: UK research team rights safeguarding and retention framework
• Japanese Partnership: Cross-cultural negotiation support and partnership agreement management
• Competitive Strategy: Market timing optimization and competitive positioning advice

ASSUMPTIONS:

• Standard business hours availability with priority support during critical negotiation periods
• Karen manages day-to-day Japanese partner relationship with legal strategic guidance
• Basic regulatory coordination is sufficient for FDA and Japanese authority requirements
• Joint venture completion is achievable through standard international partnership processes

EXCLUSIONS:

• 24/7 availability for urgent negotiations
• Comprehensive cultural integration management
• Extended post-signature partnership monitoring
• Advanced competitive intelligence coordination

COMMUNICATION STRUCTURE:
- Business hours: Direct senior lawyer contact
- Weekly: Progress calls and negotiation strategy updates
- Bi-weekly: Written progress reports and partnership development reviews

BRONZE - ESSENTIAL JOINT VENTURE GUIDANCE SERVICE (£)

- JV Structure Review: Basic assessment of proposed £4M joint venture terms and risk analysis
- IP Framework: Essential guidance on AI intellectual property protection and sharing arrangements
- Regulatory Overview: Fundamental UK/Japan regulatory requirements and FDA approval considerations
- Employment Basics: Core advice on UK research team rights protection and retention
- Partnership Guidance: Template agreements and negotiation framework for Japanese partnership

ASSUMPTIONS:
- Single comprehensive consultation covering essential joint venture structuring and risk management
- Standard office hours availability only
- Karen handles Japanese negotiations and regulatory coordination directly
- Template frameworks are sufficient for basic partnership protection

EXCLUSIONS:
- Active negotiation participation and management
- Detailed regulatory approval coordination
- Cross-cultural communication facilitation
- Ongoing partnership monitoring

COMMUNICATION STRUCTURE:
- Email and telephone during business hours
- 48-hour response commitment
- Single follow-up consultation included

ASSUMPTIVE CLOSING QUESTIONS:

• "Given the £4M joint venture value and competitive threat, shall we implement the complete Gold service to secure market advantage immediately?"
• "When should I begin coordinating with Japanese counsel to accelerate negotiations and prevent competitor capture?"
• "Shall I commence immediate IP protection strategies to safeguard your UK research team's valuable AI assets?"
• "Should we start implementing cross-cultural negotiation protocols this week to overcome communication barriers?"

VALUE-BASED QUESTIONS TO ASK:

• "What would losing the £4M joint venture opportunity to competitors cost Caregiver MedTech Solutions in market position?"
• "How much revenue would the AI diagnostic tool generate annually with successful FDA approval and Japanese partnership?"
• "What's the replacement cost if your UK research team leaves due to inadequate protection in the joint venture?"
• "If competitors launch their similar product first, what market share would Caregiver MedTech lose permanently?"
• "What would rebuilding AI diagnostic capabilities cost if IP sharing goes wrong?"
• "How much would developing Japanese market access independently cost versus this partnership?"

VALUE CREATED:

• Market Leadership: Secures £4M joint venture enabling competitive advantage in AI medical diagnostics market
• IP Asset Protection: Preserves and optimizes valuable UK research intellectual property worth potentially tens of millions
• Regulatory Success: Ensures FDA and Japanese regulatory pathways protecting investment and market opportunity
• Talent Retention: Protects the UK research team, ensuring continued innovation and competitive capability
• International Expansion: Enables Japanese market entry through a strategic partnership rather than costly independent development

- Competitive Advantage: Prevents competitor market capture through accelerated partnership completion
- Revenue Generation: Unlocks AI diagnostic tool commercialization, potentially worth hundreds of millions in healthcare markets
- Strategic Positioning: Establishes Caregiver MedTech as an international leader in AI medical technology partnerships
- Cultural Integration: Creates a sustainable cross-cultural business relationship, enabling long-term partnership success

SCENARIO 44: SHARE BUYBACK

Victoria Edwards, CEO of Edwards Manufacturing. A minority shareholder (15%) is blocking crucial business decisions and damaging staff morale. The share valuation is disputed, with the shareholder wanting £2M for a stake valued at £800K. The company has cash but needs it for expansion. Other shareholders are supportive of removal. Need a clean exit without damaging the business or banking relationships.

GOLD - COMPLETE SHAREHOLDER RESOLUTION & BUSINESS LIBERATION SERVICE (£££)

- Strategic Shareholder Removal: Comprehensive legal strategy identifying steps to exit a minority shareholder whilst preserving business relationships
- Valuation Victory: Expert negotiation reducing buyback cost from £2M demand to fair market value around £800K
- Business Decision Liberation: Complete removal of shareholder blocking powers, enabling crucial business decisions and growth strategies
- Expansion Capital Protection: Strategic approach preserving maximum cash reserves for planned business expansion
- Banking Relationship Shield: Professional management ensuring banking relationships remain unaffected by shareholder disputes
- Staff Morale Recovery: Rapid resolution, minimizing workplace disruption and management distraction
- Corporate Governance Excellence: Enhanced shareholder agreements preventing future minority shareholder disruption

• Legal Documentation Fortress: Bulletproof legal framework ensuring permanent resolution of shareholder conflicts

ASSUMPTIONS:

• Full access to company accounts, shareholder agreements, and historical business decisions affected by the minority shareholder
• Authority to negotiate directly with minority shareholder and their representatives on behalf of Edwards Manufacturing
• Other shareholders provide unified support and cooperation throughout the resolution process
• Company financial position allows for a fair market value buyback without compromising core operations
• Minority shareholder willing to engage in professional negotiation rather than pursuing destructive litigation

EXCLUSIONS:

• Independent business valuation services (coordinated but separately charged)
• Forensic accounting for complex historical dividend or profit disputes
• Individual director indemnity insurance for past shareholder conflicts
• Corporate restructuring advice beyond immediate shareholder resolution

TECHNICAL DELIVERABLES:

• Comprehensive shareholder exit strategy with negotiated settlement achieving fair market valuation
• Enhanced articles of association and shareholder agreements, preventing future minority disruption
• Complete legal documentation for share buyback, protecting the company and remaining shareholders
• Banking relationship management, ensuring continued financial facility availability
• Corporate governance improvements strengthening management decision-making authority
• Staff communication strategy restoring workplace confidence and operational focus

COMMUNICATION STRUCTURE:

• Immediate: Partner direct access for urgent shareholder negotiations and business decision matters (24/7)
• Daily: Strategic briefings during active negotiation periods with the minority shareholder
• Weekly: Progress meetings with the full shareholder group and management team coordination
• Negotiation meetings: Senior representation with comprehensive preparation and tactical guidance

FOLLOW-UP SERVICES:

• 18-month post-resolution monitoring ensuring shareholder agreement compliance and business stability
• Annual corporate governance reviews and shareholder relationship management
• Priority access for future shareholder and corporate governance matters across Edwards Manufacturing
• Preferred rates for ongoing corporate advisory services and business expansion legal support

---

SILVER - ENHANCED SHAREHOLDER BUYBACK & NEGOTIATION SERVICE (££)

• Shareholder Exit Management: Professional negotiation strategy achieving minority shareholder removal at a reasonable valuation
• Business Protection: Legal framework ensuring continued operations and decision-making authority
• Valuation Negotiation: Strategic approach reducing buyback costs and protecting expansion capital
• Corporate Documentation: Updated shareholder agreements and articles, preventing future disruption
• Banking Liaison: Professional communication ensuring financial relationships remain stable
• Settlement Strategy: Comprehensive approach achieving a clean shareholder exit

ASSUMPTIONS:

• Standard business hours availability with priority support during critical negotiation periods

- Victoria manages day-to-day business operations with legal strategic guidance
- Straightforward negotiation is sufficient for shareholder resolution
- Banking relationships maintained through standard professional communication

EXCLUSIONS:

- 24/7 availability for negotiation crises
- Comprehensive corporate governance overhaul
- Extended banking relationship management
- Detailed staff communication strategies

COMMUNICATION STRUCTURE:

- Business hours: Direct senior lawyer contact
- Bi-weekly: Progress calls and negotiation strategy updates
- Monthly: Written progress reports and settlement discussions

BRONZE - ESSENTIAL SHAREHOLDER BUYBACK GUIDANCE SERVICE (£)

- Buyback Framework: Basic legal guidance on minority shareholder removal options and procedures
- Valuation Guidance: Essential advice on share valuation disputes and negotiation approaches
- Documentation Review: Standard shareholder agreement analysis and basic improvement recommendations
- Settlement Options: Clear framework for negotiating shareholder exit arrangements
- Next Steps Plan: Practical action plan for managing shareholder buyback process

ASSUMPTIONS:

- Single comprehensive consultation covering essential shareholder buyback requirements
- Standard office hours availability only
- Victoria handles shareholder negotiations and business coordination directly
- Template agreements sufficient for basic shareholder exit arrangements

EXCLUSIONS:
- Direct shareholder negotiation representation
- Complex valuation dispute resolution
- Banking relationship management
- Ongoing shareholder agreement monitoring

COMMUNICATION STRUCTURE:
- Email and telephone during business hours
- 48-hour response commitment
- Single follow-up consultation included

ASSUMPTIVE CLOSING QUESTIONS:
- "Given the urgent need to remove this disruptive shareholder and protect your expansion capital, shall we implement the complete Gold service to achieve rapid business liberation?"
- "When should I begin negotiating with the minority shareholder to reduce their £2M demand to fair market value around £800K?"
- "Shall I commence immediate review of your shareholder agreements to prevent future minority disruption?"
- "Should we start protecting your banking relationships this week to ensure expansion funding remains available?"

VALUE-BASED QUESTIONS TO ASK:
- "What's the cost of delayed business decisions whilst this minority shareholder continues blocking crucial strategies?"
- "How much revenue is Edwards Manufacturing losing through staff morale damage and management distraction?"
- "What would paying £2M instead of £800K cost your expansion plans and competitive position?"
- "If this shareholder dispute escalates, what would damaged banking relationships cost in future funding?"
- "How much is management time worth that's currently wasted on shareholder conflicts instead of business growth?"
- "What would competitors gain if Edwards Manufacturing can't make crucial business decisions quickly?"

VALUE CREATED:
- Business Liberation: Removes shareholder blocking power, enabling crucial business decisions and growth strategies

• Capital Protection: Saves up to £1.2M in excessive buyback costs, protecting expansion funding reserves
• Operational Excellence: Restores management focus to business growth rather than shareholder conflicts
• Staff Confidence: Eliminates workplace disruption, improving productivity and employee retention
• Banking Security: Preserves crucial financial relationships, ensuring continued expansion funding availability
• Corporate Governance: Establishes a robust shareholder framework, preventing future minority disruption
• Competitive Advantage: Enables rapid business decision-making crucial for market competitiveness
• Management Freedom: Liberates the leadership team to focus on strategic growth rather than shareholder management
• Stakeholder Harmony: Creates a unified shareholder base supporting business expansion and development plans

SCENARIO 45: DISTRIBUTION AGREEMENT

Mark Stevens, Commercial Director at BigBritishBrands plc. Their European distributor is breaching territory restrictions, selling into the UK through the grey market. Annual revenue impact is £2M. Evidence of trademark infringement. Ten years of previous good relations. The Spanish courts are involved. Need to stop the breaches while preserving the distribution network. Alternative distributors limited.

GOLD - COMPLETE DISTRIBUTION STRATEGY & RELATIONSHIP PRESERVATION SERVICE (£££)

• Revenue Protection Strategy: Comprehensive commercial approach safeguarding £2M annual revenue stream while preserving valuable distribution relationships
• Relationship Rescue Mission: Sophisticated negotiation strategy maintaining a ten-year partnership whilst stopping territorial breaches immediately
• Multi-Jurisdictional Coordination: Expert management of UK and Spanish legal proceedings, ensuring a consistent strategy across territories
• Trademark Protection Program: Complete intellectual property enforcement, preventing further grey market infringement

• Distribution Network Optimization: Strategic review and enhancement of the entire European distribution framework
• Commercial Resolution Focus: Business-first approach prioritizing revenue preservation over litigation warfare
• Alternative Distributor Strategy: Contingency planning and market analysis for potential distribution restructuring
• Long-term Partnership Protection: Ongoing relationship management ensuring sustainable, profitable distribution arrangements

ASSUMPTIONS:

• Full access to distribution agreements, financial records, and evidence of territorial breaches
• Authority to negotiate directly with the European distributor and explore commercial solutions
• BigBritishBrands' management availability for strategic decision-making and commercial negotiations
• Spanish legal proceedings can be coordinated with the UK strategy for a consistent approach
• Current distributor relationship remains salvageable through appropriate commercial incentives

EXCLUSIONS:

• Spanish local counsel fees (coordinated but separately charged through established partnerships)
• Market research for alternative distributors (arranged but separately charged through commercial partners)
• Trademark registration in additional jurisdictions beyond current enforcement needs
• Product rebranding or packaging modifications to address grey market issues

TECHNICAL DELIVERABLES:

• Comprehensive distribution breach analysis and revenue protection strategy implementation
• Multi-jurisdictional legal coordination ensuring consistent UK and Spanish court strategy
• Commercial negotiation framework preserving relationships whilst stopping territorial violations
• Trademark enforcement program preventing further grey market infringement activities

• Distribution agreement restructuring, optimizing territorial protection and performance incentives
• Alternative distributor contingency planning with market analysis and selection criteria

COMMUNICATION STRUCTURE:

• Immediate: Partner direct access for urgent commercial decisions and distributor negotiations (24/7)
• Daily: Progress briefings during active negotiation periods and court proceedings
• Weekly: Strategic commercial meetings balancing legal enforcement with relationship preservation
• Distributor meetings: Senior commercial representation with comprehensive preparation and negotiation leadership

FOLLOW-UP SERVICES:

• 24-month ongoing distribution relationship monitoring and performance management
• Annual distribution agreement reviews, ensuring continued territorial compliance and optimization
• Priority access for future commercial disputes across BigBritishBrands' European operations
• Preferred rates for ongoing distribution strategy and trademark enforcement matters

---

SILVER - ENHANCED DISTRIBUTION DISPUTE & COMMERCIAL RESOLUTION SERVICE (££)

• Commercial Breach Resolution: Professional negotiation strategy stopping territorial violations whilst exploring relationship preservation
• Legal Enforcement Support: Coordinated UK and Spanish legal proceedings with trademark infringement action
• Revenue Protection Guidance: Strategic advice protecting £2M annual revenue through commercial and legal measures
• Distribution Agreement Review: Assessment and improvement of territorial restrictions and performance obligations
• Relationship Management: Balanced approach preserving a valuable ten-year partnership where commercially viable
• Alternative Planning: Basic contingency planning for potential distributor replacement if negotiations fail

ASSUMPTIONS:

• Standard business hours availability with extended support during critical negotiation periods
• Mark manages day-to-day distributor communications with strategic legal guidance and support
• Commercial resolution achievable through standard negotiation and enforcement processes
• Spanish proceedings are manageable through a coordinated but simplified cross-border strategy

EXCLUSIONS:

• 24/7 availability for commercial crises and urgent distributor negotiations
• Comprehensive alternative distributor market analysis and selection
• Advanced trademark portfolio optimization across multiple jurisdictions
• Extended post-resolution relationship monitoring and performance management

COMMUNICATION STRUCTURE:

• Business hours: Direct senior lawyer contact for commercial and legal matters
• Bi-weekly: Progress calls covering negotiation strategy and legal proceedings
• Monthly: Written reports on resolution progress and commercial outcomes

---

BRONZE - ESSENTIAL DISTRIBUTION DISPUTE GUIDANCE SERVICE (£)

• Breach Analysis: Assessment of territorial violations and available legal remedies under the distribution agreement
• Legal Options Review: Basic guidance on UK enforcement rights and Spanish court proceedings coordination
• Commercial Framework: Template negotiation approach balancing enforcement with relationship preservation
• Trademark Advice: Essential guidance on infringement claims and grey market prevention measures
• Resolution Planning: Clear action framework for distributor negotiations and potential legal proceedings

ASSUMPTIONS:

• Single comprehensive consultation covering essential distribution dispute and enforcement options
• Standard office hours availability only with basic follow-up support
• Mark handles distributor negotiations and Spanish court coordination directly with template guidance
• Standard enforcement remedies are sufficient for territorial breach resolution

EXCLUSIONS:

• Direct distributor negotiation and commercial resolution management
• Spanish court proceedings representation and cross-border coordination
• Comprehensive trademark enforcement and grey market prevention
• Alternative distributor analysis and contingency planning

COMMUNICATION STRUCTURE:

• Email and telephone during business hours only
• 48-hour response commitment for standard enquiries
• Single follow-up consultation included for implementation guidance

ASSUMPTIVE CLOSING QUESTIONS:

• "Given the £2M annual revenue at risk and ten years of valuable distribution relationships, shall we implement the complete Gold service to protect both your revenue and partnership immediately?"
• "When should I begin coordinating with your Spanish legal team to ensure a consistent strategy across both jurisdictions?"
• "Shall I commence direct negotiations with your European distributor to resolve these territorial breaches whilst preserving the relationship?"
• "Should we start developing alternative distributor contingency plans this week in case the current relationship cannot be preserved?"

VALUE-BASED QUESTIONS TO ASK:

• "What would losing the entire £2M annual revenue stream cost BigBritishBrands if this distributor relationship completely breaks down?"

• "How much would it cost to replace a ten-year distribution relationship with equivalent market coverage and performance?"

• "What's the real cost of grey market sales undermining your UK pricing strategy and brand positioning?"

• "If trademark infringement continues unchecked, how much brand value and market share could BigBritishBrands lose?"

• "How long would it take to establish an alternative European distribution generating equivalent £2M revenue?"

• "What would competitors gain if BigBritishBrands loses established European market presence through this dispute?"

VALUE CREATED:

• Revenue Preservation: Protects £2M annual revenue stream through strategic commercial resolution rather than destructive litigation

• Relationship Maintenance: Preserves valuable ten-year distribution partnership worth far more than short-term enforcement victories

• Market Position: Maintains established European presence, preventing competitor advantage during distribution disruption

• Brand Protection: Stops trademark infringement and grey market sales undermining UK pricing strategy and brand integrity

• Strategic Flexibility: Provides multiple resolution options, ensuring BigBritishBrands maintains negotiating strength and commercial alternatives

• Cross-Border Efficiency: Coordinates UK and Spanish legal strategies, avoiding conflicting proceedings and wasted legal costs

• Commercial Intelligence: Delivers market insights and alternative distributor options, strengthening future distribution strategy

• Long-term Stability: Creates a sustainable distribution framework, preventing future territorial disputes and maximizing European revenue potential

SCENARIO 46: CORPORATE GOVERNANCE

Sarah Mitchell, Chair of V.CyberTechSecure Ltd. A whistleblower has made allegations about financial irregularities in an Asian subsidiary. Potential £1.5M fraud involving three senior managers. The Audit Committee requires an investigation, and a Stock Market announcement may be needed. Banking covenants are at risk. Need to manage the investigation while protecting the company's value.

GOLD - COMPLETE CORPORATE CRISIS MANAGEMENT & VALUE PROTECTION SERVICE (£££)

• Total Crisis Leadership: Comprehensive corporate governance crisis management protecting company value and market position
• Whistleblower Investigation Excellence: Professional investigation management ensuring regulatory compliance and evidence integrity
• Senior Management Risk Mitigation: Strategic handling of three implicated executives protecting corporate reputation and operational continuity
• Market Confidence Protection: Expert stock market disclosure management, maintaining investor confidence and share price stability
• Banking Relationship Preservation: Proactive covenant management and lender communication, preventing financial facility breaches
• Audit Committee Support: Complete governance framework ensuring proper oversight and regulatory compliance throughout the investigation
• Asian Subsidiary Management: Cross-border investigation coordination, managing jurisdictional complexities and regulatory requirements
• Corporate Reputation Shield: Strategic communications and stakeholder management protecting V.CyberTechSecure's market standing

ASSUMPTIONS:

• Full board authority to implement immediate governance changes and investigation protocols
• Access to all financial records, management information, and Asian subsidiary documentation
• Authority to engage forensic accountants and international investigation specialists as required
• Management team availability for intensive crisis coordination and strategic decision-making
• Regulatory authorities provide standard cooperation and response times for disclosure obligations

EXCLUSIONS:

• Forensic accounting services for detailed financial analysis (coordinated but separately charged)
• International legal representation in Asian jurisdictions (arranged but separately charged)
• Individual executive legal representation if conflicts arise between company and personal interests
• Public relations and crisis communications services (strategic guidance provided but execution separately charged)

TECHNICAL DELIVERABLES:

• Comprehensive whistleblower investigation framework and evidence management protocols
• Senior management risk assessment and strategic response coordination
• Stock market disclosure strategy and regulatory compliance management
• Banking covenant protection plan and lender relationship management
• Audit committee governance framework and oversight protocols
• Cross-border investigation coordination and jurisdictional compliance management

COMMUNICATION STRUCTURE:

• Immediate: Chair direct access for urgent governance decisions and market-sensitive matters (24/7)
• Daily: Morning crisis briefings during active investigation periods with full strategic oversight

• Weekly: Board and audit committee briefings with comprehensive status reports and strategic guidance
• Market/regulatory meetings: Senior representation with expert preparation and disclosure management

FOLLOW-UP SERVICES:

• 18-month post-crisis governance monitoring and compliance oversight
• Annual corporate governance health checks and risk assessment reviews
• Priority access for future governance matters across V.CyberTechSecure group companies
• Preferred rates for ongoing compliance advisory and corporate governance consulting services

SILVER - ENHANCED GOVERNANCE INVESTIGATION & COMPLIANCE SERVICE (££)

• Investigation Management: Professional whistleblower investigation with regulatory compliance framework
• Governance Compliance: Audit committee support and corporate governance best practice implementation
• Market Disclosure Guidance: Stock exchange obligation assessment and disclosure strategy development
• Banking Covenant Review: Financial facility risk assessment and lender communication support
• Senior Management Protocols: Strategic guidance on executive suspension and investigation management
• Regulatory Liaison: Professional communication with relevant authorities and compliance coordination

ASSUMPTIONS:

• Standard business hours availability with extended support during critical investigation phases
• Sarah manages day-to-day crisis coordination with legal strategic guidance and oversight
• Basic investigation framework sufficient for regulatory compliance and evidence gathering
• Standard regulatory and market response processes are adequate for disclosure management

EXCLUSIONS:

• 24/7 crisis availability and immediate response capability
• Comprehensive market confidence and reputation management
• Complex cross-border investigation coordination
• Extended post-crisis monitoring and governance oversight

COMMUNICATION STRUCTURE:

• Business hours: Direct senior lawyer contact for investigation and governance matters
• Bi-weekly: Progress calls and investigation strategy updates with board reporting
• Monthly: Written compliance reports and governance assessment reviews

BRONZE - ESSENTIAL GOVERNANCE GUIDANCE SERVICE (£)

• Investigation Framework: Basic whistleblower investigation protocols and evidence handling guidance
• Compliance Assessment: Essential audit committee obligations and regulatory requirement review
• Disclosure Guidance: Fundamental stock market obligation assessment and basic disclosure protocols
• Banking Review: Initial covenant risk assessment and basic lender communication guidance
• Management Protocols: Essential guidance on executive investigation procedures and governance requirements

ASSUMPTIONS:

• Single comprehensive consultation covering essential investigation and governance compliance requirements

- Standard office hours availability only for guidance and strategic advice
- Sarah handles investigation coordination and regulatory communications directly with template guidance
- Basic frameworks are sufficient for fundamental compliance and investigation obligations

EXCLUSIONS:

- Active investigation management and evidence coordination
- Market disclosure preparation and regulatory liaison
- Banking covenant negotiations and lender relationship management
- Comprehensive governance framework implementation

COMMUNICATION STRUCTURE:

- Email and telephone during business hours for guidance and template support
- 48-hour response commitment for urgent governance questions
- Single follow-up consultation included for implementation support

ASSUMPTIVE CLOSING QUESTIONS:

- "Given the £1.5M fraud allegations and three senior managers involved, shall we implement the complete Gold service to protect V.CyberTechSecure's value and market position immediately?"
- "When should I begin coordinating the investigation to ensure proper evidence gathering and regulatory compliance from day one?"
- "Shall I commence immediate banking covenant review to prevent any facility breaches while the investigation proceeds?"
- "Should we start preparing market disclosure strategies this week to maintain investor confidence and compliance obligations?"

VALUE-BASED QUESTIONS TO ASK:

- "What would V.CyberTechSecure's share price decline cost shareholders if this crisis isn't managed professionally?"

• "How much would banking facility withdrawal cost the company in alternative financing and operational disruption?"
• "What's the cost of losing key customers and contracts if V.CyberTechSecure's reputation suffers permanent damage?"
• "If the three senior managers need to be suspended, what's the operational disruption cost to the business?"
• "How much would regulatory fines and sanctions cost if the investigation isn't conducted properly?"
• "What would competitors gain if V.CyberTechSecure loses market confidence and strategic partnerships?"

VALUE CREATED:

• Company Value Protection: Preserves shareholder value through professional crisis management and market confidence maintenance
• Market Position Security: Maintains V.CyberTechSecure's competitive standing and prevents opportunistic competitor advantage during crisis
• Financial Facility Preservation: Protects banking relationships and prevents costly facility renegotiation or withdrawal
• Regulatory Compliance: Ensures proper investigation conduct, preventing additional regulatory sanctions and penalties
• Operational Continuity: Maintains business operations and customer confidence throughout the investigation process
• Executive Team Stability: Strategic management of senior executive issues, preventing operational chaos and succession crises
• Investor Confidence: Maintains market trust through transparent, professional crisis management and appropriate disclosure
• Corporate Reputation: Protects V.CyberTechSecure's brand value and market reputation, enabling continued business growth post-crisis
• Governance Excellence: Establishes a robust governance framework, preventing future crises and enhancing corporate credibility

SCENARIO 47: SOFTWARE LICENSING

Daniel Wright, CTO of BWright Industries. DecSoftware audit reveals a potential £500K underlicensing across 500 users. The previous IT Manager failed to maintain records, whilst the budget for the entire IT year is only £200K. Cloud migration planned but delayed. Need to negotiate a settlement while ensuring future compliance. Business-critical systems are involved.

GOLD - COMPLETE AUDIT DEFENCE & LICENSING OPTIMISATION SERVICE (£££)

- Total DecSoft Audit Management: Comprehensive audit defense strategy minimizing settlement costs and protecting business operations
- Budget Protection Program: Strategic negotiation reducing £500K exposure to within available £200K budget constraints
- Business Continuity Shield: Ensuring uninterrupted operations of business-critical systems throughout audit resolution
- Licensing Architecture Rebuild: Complete software asset management system, preventing future audit vulnerabilities
- Cloud Migration Legal Framework: Accelerated compliance strategy enabling delayed cloud migration with optimal licensing terms
- Future-Proofing Strategy: Long-term licensing governance preventing repeat audit exposures and cost overruns
- Vendor Relationship Management: Professional DecSoftware relationship building, securing favorable ongoing terms
- Cost Optimization Excellence: Comprehensive licensing review identifying savings opportunities across the entire software estate

ASSUMPTIONS:

- Full access to all IT systems, user records, and available licensing documentation from previous management
- Authority to negotiate directly with DecSoftware and implement immediate licensing compliance measures
- Management team availability for intensive settlement negotiations and system implementation planning
- Business-critical systems can accommodate compliance modifications without operational disruption
- DecSoftware follows standard audit resolution timescales, allowing a structured negotiation process

EXCLUSIONS:

• Technical software implementation or system configuration changes (legal framework provided for technical teams)
• External IT consultancy for cloud migration technical delivery (coordinated but separately charged)
• Replacement software licensing costs (negotiated terms secured, but licensing fees remain the client's responsibility)
• Historical financial audit services for previous IT management decisions

TECHNICAL DELIVERABLES:

• Comprehensive DecSoftware audit response strategy and evidence compilation protecting business interests
• Settlement negotiation achieving maximum cost reduction within available budget parameters
• Complete software asset management system, preventing future compliance vulnerabilities
• Cloud migration legal compliance framework enabling accelerated technology transition
• Licensing governance protocols ensuring ongoing compliance and cost control across 500 users
• Vendor relationship management, securing optimal long-term DecSoftware partnership terms

COMMUNICATION STRUCTURE:

• Immediate: Partner direct access for urgent DecSoftware communications and settlement decisions (24/7)
• Daily: Morning briefings during active audit periods with full strategic oversight and progress updates
• Weekly: Stakeholder management meetings, including budget planning and compliance implementation
• DecSoftware meetings: Senior representation with comprehensive preparation and strategic negotiation leadership

FOLLOW-UP SERVICES:

• 24-month post-settlement compliance monitoring and DecSoftware relationship management
• Annual software licensing health checks and cost optimization reviews across the entire technology estate
• Priority access for future software licensing matters and vendor negotiations

• Preferred rates for ongoing DecSoftware relationship management and licensing advisory services

---

SILVER - ENHANCED AUDIT DEFENCE & COMPLIANCE SERVICE (££)

• DecSoftware Audit Response: Professional audit defense with evidence preparation and settlement negotiation
• Cost Reduction Strategy: Focused negotiation to reduce potential £500K exposure within budget constraints
• Compliance Framework: Basic software asset management and future compliance protocols
• Cloud Migration Guidance: Legal support for delayed cloud migration and licensing transition
• Vendor Negotiation: Direct DecSoftware relationship management and settlement discussions
• Future Prevention: Essential licensing governance preventing repeat audit vulnerabilities

ASSUMPTIONS:

• Standard business hours availability with extended support during DecSoftware negotiations and settlements
• Daniel manages day-to-day IT operations and compliance implementation with legal guidance
• Basic compliance framework sufficient for ongoing DecSoftware relationship management
• Settlement achievable through standard audit resolution processes within reasonable timeframes

EXCLUSIONS:

• 24/7 availability for audit crises and urgent DecSoftware communications
• Comprehensive software estate optimization and cost reduction analysis
• Extended cloud migration legal planning and vendor negotiation support
• Long-term licensing governance beyond basic compliance requirements

COMMUNICATION STRUCTURE:

- Business hours: Direct senior lawyer contact for audit and negotiation matters
- Bi-weekly: Progress calls and settlement negotiation updates with strategic guidance
- Monthly: Written progress reports and compliance implementation reviews

BRONZE - ESSENTIAL AUDIT GUIDANCE SERVICE (£)

- Audit Assessment: Analysis of DecSoftware audit findings and available response options
- Settlement Framework: Basic negotiation guidance and cost reduction strategies within budget constraints
- Compliance Basics: Essential software licensing compliance advice and governance fundamentals
- Cloud Migration Essentials: Basic legal guidance on licensing implications for delayed migration
- Next Steps Plan: Clear action framework for audit resolution and future compliance management

ASSUMPTIONS:

- Single comprehensive consultation covering audit response and basic compliance requirements
- Standard office hours availability only, with no extended audit period support
- Daniel handles DecSoftware communications and settlement negotiations directly with template guidance
- Basic compliance advice is sufficient for immediate audit resolution requirements

EXCLUSIONS:

- DecSoftware meeting representation and direct settlement negotiation
- Ongoing audit management and extended compliance implementation support
- Complex software estate analysis and optimization recommendations
- Extended cloud migration planning and vendor relationship management

COMMUNICATION STRUCTURE:
• Email and telephone during business hours with standard response commitments
• 48-hour response commitment for audit-related queries and guidance requests
• Single follow-up consultation included for settlement implementation support

ASSUMPTIVE CLOSING QUESTIONS:
• "Given the potential £500K DecSoftware exposure against your £200K IT budget, shall we implement the complete Gold service to protect BWright Industries from financial devastation?"
• "When should I begin direct negotiations with DecSoftware to secure settlement terms within your available budget?"
• "Shall I commence immediate audit defense preparation to minimize your licensing exposure and protect business operations?"
• "Should we start implementing comprehensive licensing governance this week to prevent future audit disasters?"

VALUE-BASED QUESTIONS TO ASK:
• "What would a £500K DecSoftware settlement do to BWright Industries' annual budget and business operations?"
• "How much revenue would BWright Industries lose if business-critical systems were disrupted during audit resolution?"
• "What's the cost of delayed cloud migration if licensing compliance issues aren't resolved quickly?"
• "If DecSoftware demands full payment, how would financing £500K impact other critical business investments?"
• "What would competitors gain if BWright Industries faced operational disruption from licensing disputes?"
• "How much would rebuilding software asset management systems cost if this audit exposure isn't properly resolved?"

VALUE CREATED:
• Budget Protection: Saves BWright Industries from devastating £500K licensing exposure exceeding entire annual IT budget
• Business Continuity: Maintains uninterrupted operation of business-critical systems throughout audit resolution

- Cost Optimization: Delivers ongoing software licensing savings across 500 users through strategic governance
- DecSoftware Relationship: Establishes positive vendor partnership securing favorable future licensing terms
- Compliance Excellence: Prevents repeat audit exposure through comprehensive software asset management implementation
- Cloud Migration Enablement: Removes licensing barriers, enabling delayed cloud migration with optimal terms
- Financial Stability: Preserves BWright Industries' financial position and investment capacity for growth initiatives
- Operational Confidence: Provides complete licensing certainty, enabling confident business planning and technology decisions
- Competitive Advantage: Ensures BWright Industries maintains technology capabilities while competitors face similar audit challenges

SCENARIO 48: BUSINESS SUCCESSION

Peter Thomson, Owner of Celtic Thomson Hotels Group. Three hotels valued at £10M. Founder retiring. Two children in business, one of whom wants to sell. Complex pension arrangements, and the property portfolio is in a separate company. Need tax-efficient transfer while maintaining business stability. Staff concerns about future ownership. Bank approval is required for any change.

GOLD - COMPLETE SUCCESSION MASTERY & WEALTH PRESERVATION SERVICE (£££)

- Total Succession Strategy: Comprehensive succession plan preserving £10M business value whilst achieving tax-efficient ownership transfer
- Family Harmony Framework: Professional mediation and conflict resolution, ensuring family relationships survive business transition
- Tax Optimization Excellence: Advanced structuring minimizing inheritance tax, capital gains tax, and maximizing pension benefits
- Business Continuity Guarantee: Seamless operational transition, maintaining hotel performance and staff confidence

- Banking Relationship Management: Complete lender liaison ensuring continued financing and relationship preservation
- Wealth Protection Architecture: Sophisticated estate planning protecting family wealth across multiple generations
- Staff Retention Program: Communication strategy and incentive structures maintaining key personnel through transition
- Multi-Entity Integration: Complete restructuring of hotel operations and property portfolio for optimal tax and operational efficiency

ASSUMPTIONS:

- Full access to all financial records, property valuations, pension arrangements, and banking facilities
- Authority to negotiate with HMRC, pension trustees, and banking partners on behalf of the Thomson family
- Family members participate constructively in mediation and succession planning discussions
- Current hotel performance and property valuations remain stable during succession implementation
- Banking relationships maintained through professional lender communication and compliance

EXCLUSIONS:

- Independent business valuations and property appraisals (coordinated but separately instructed)
- Pension scheme actuarial reviews and trustee services (arranged but separately charged)
- Ongoing hotel management and operational consultancy beyond succession requirements
- Individual family members to have separate legal representation if conflicts cannot be resolved

TECHNICAL DELIVERABLES:

- Comprehensive succession plan with complete tax optimization and family wealth preservation
- Family mediation program resolving ownership conflicts and establishing future governance
- Advanced tax structuring, including inheritance tax planning and capital gains optimization
- Business continuity framework maintaining operational stability and staff confidence

• Banking approval strategy and lender relationship management throughout transition
• Multi-generational wealth protection and estate planning architecture
• Staff communication and retention program ensuring operational continuity

COMMUNICATION STRUCTURE:

• Immediate: Partner direct access for urgent family, tax, and banking decisions (24/7 during critical phases)
• Weekly: Strategic family meetings with mediation support and succession planning progression
• Monthly: Comprehensive progress reviews with tax, legal, and business continuity updates
• Bank meetings: Senior representation with full preparation and relationship management

FOLLOW-UP SERVICES:

• 36-month post-succession monitoring, ensuring plan effectiveness and family harmony
• Annual wealth preservation reviews and tax planning optimization
• Priority access for future Thomson family business and wealth management matters
• Preferred rates for ongoing succession plan maintenance and family governance support

---

SILVER - ENHANCED SUCCESSION PLANNING & TAX EFFICIENCY SERVICE (££)

• Succession Framework: Comprehensive succession plan balancing family interests with tax efficiency
• Tax Planning Strategy: Advanced structuring, minimizing tax liabilities and preserving business value
• Family Mediation Support: Professional guidance resolving ownership conflicts and establishing future governance
• Business Transition Management: Operational continuity planning and staff communication strategies
• Banking Liaison: Lender relationship management and approval process coordination

• Wealth Preservation: Estate planning and multi-generational wealth protection strategies

ASSUMPTIONS:

• Standard business hours availability with extended support during critical succession phases
• Peter coordinates family discussions with professional mediation guidance
• Basic tax planning is sufficient for succession objectives and family requirements
• Succession achieved through standard planning processes without complex restructuring

EXCLUSIONS:

• 24/7 availability for family crises and urgent decisions
• Comprehensive multi-entity restructuring
• Extended staff retention programs
• Ongoing post-succession monitoring

COMMUNICATION STRUCTURE:

• Business hours: Direct senior lawyer contact for succession and tax matters
• Bi-weekly: Progress calls and family mediation updates
• Monthly: Written succession progress reports and tax planning reviews

BRONZE - ESSENTIAL SUCCESSION GUIDANCE SERVICE (£)

• Succession Assessment: Analysis of succession options balancing family interests and tax efficiency
• Tax Planning Basics: Fundamental advice on inheritance tax and capital gains implications
• Family Governance: Essential guidance on resolving ownership conflicts and future management
• Business Continuity: Basic operational transition planning and staff communication advice
• Implementation Framework: Clear action plan for succession execution and professional coordination

ASSUMPTIONS:

- Single comprehensive consultation covering essential succession planning requirements
- Standard office hours availability only
- Peter manages family discussions and banking relationships directly with legal guidance
- Template succession structures are sufficient for basic family and tax objectives

EXCLUSIONS:

- Family mediation services and conflict resolution
- Complex tax structuring and multi-entity planning
- Banking approval process management
- Ongoing succession implementation support

COMMUNICATION STRUCTURE:

- Email and telephone during business hours only
- 48-hour response commitment for succession queries
- Single follow-up consultation included for clarification

ASSUMPTIVE CLOSING QUESTIONS:

- "Given the £10M business value and complex family dynamics, shall we implement the complete Gold service to preserve both wealth and relationships?"
- "When should I begin coordinating with HMRC and your bankers to ensure the succession proceeds smoothly and tax-efficiently?"
- "Shall I commence family mediation immediately to resolve the ownership conflicts before they damage both business and relationships?"
- "Should we start implementing business continuity measures this week to reassure staff and maintain operational performance?"

VALUE-BASED QUESTIONS TO ASK:

- "What would losing the £10M business value to unnecessary tax cost the Thomson family?"
- "How much would family relationships deteriorating over business conflicts cost emotionally and financially?"

- "What's the annual revenue risk if key hotel staff leave due to ownership uncertainty?"
- "If banking facilities were withdrawn during succession, what would refinancing cost?"
- "How much would operational disruption during succession cost in lost bookings and reputation?"
- "What would competitors gain if Celtic Thomson Hotels Group became distressed during succession?"

VALUE CREATED:

- Wealth Preservation: Protects £10M business value through tax-efficient succession planning and optimal structuring
- Family Harmony: Maintains Thomson family relationships whilst achieving fair business succession outcomes
- Tax Efficiency: Minimizes inheritance tax, capital gains tax, and maximizes pension benefits, saving potentially millions
- Business Continuity: Ensures seamless operational transition, maintaining hotel performance and customer confidence
- Staff Retention: Preserves key personnel and operational expertise through professional communication and transition management
- Banking Relationships: Maintains crucial financing facilities and lender confidence throughout the succession process
- Operational Excellence: Provides competitive advantage through stable ownership and professional succession management
- Multi-Generational Planning: Establishes wealth preservation architecture benefiting the Thomson family for generations
- Risk Mitigation: Prevents family conflicts, tax penalties, and business disruption that could destroy decades of hotel industry success

SCENARIO 49: PRODUCT LIABILITY

Lisa Zhang, MD of 21st Century SafePlay Ltd. A safety recall is required for a bestselling toy line as a potential choking hazard has been identified. 50,000 units sold. Social media criticism mounting, and Trading Standards is involved. Supply chain audit needed. Insurance position unclear. Christmas stock is already manufactured. Need to manage the recall while protecting the brand.

GOLD - COMPLETE CRISIS MANAGEMENT & BRAND PROTECTION SERVICE (£££)

• Total Crisis Command: 24/7 crisis management team coordinating all legal, regulatory, and reputational aspects of the recall
• Brand Protection Excellence: Comprehensive reputation management strategy minimizing long-term damage to 21st Century SafePlay brand value
• Regulatory Mastery: Complete Trading Standards liaison and regulatory compliance, ensuring swift resolution and future protection
• Insurance Recovery Maximization: Full insurance claim management and coverage optimization, protecting company finances
• Supply Chain Legal Architecture: Complete audit coordination and supplier liability management across the entire manufacturing chain
• Media & Social Response Strategy: Professional crisis communications and social media damage limitation program
• Christmas Stock Salvage: Advanced legal strategies to minimize Christmas inventory losses and protect seasonal revenue
• Future-Proofing Program: Comprehensive product safety protocols preventing future liability and regulatory issues

ASSUMPTIONS:

• Immediate access to all product records, supply chain documentation, and insurance policies
• Authority to coordinate with Trading Standards, insurers, and supply chain partners on 21st Century SafePlay's behalf
• Management team available for crisis coordination and strategic decision-making throughout the recall process
• Social media and PR teams work collaboratively with legal crisis management strategy
• Supply chain partners cooperate with audit requirements and liability investigations

EXCLUSIONS:

• Physical product testing and safety certification (legal framework provided for coordination)

• Public relations agency services beyond legal crisis strategy (coordinated but separately charged)
• Individual consumer claim settlements beyond the strategic framework (managed but separately costed)
• Product redesign and manufacturing consultancy beyond legal compliance requirements

TECHNICAL DELIVERABLES:

• Immediate crisis management plan with regulatory compliance and brand protection strategy
• Complete Trading Standards liaison and regulatory approval process management
• Comprehensive insurance claim strategy and coverage maximization program
• Supply chain audit coordination and supplier liability assessment framework
• Crisis communications strategy and social media damage limitation protocols
• Christmas stock legal analysis and revenue protection strategies
• Future product safety compliance framework and liability prevention program

COMMUNICATION STRUCTURE:

• Immediate: Partner crisis team available 24/7 for urgent regulatory and media decisions
• Hourly: Crisis updates during peak recall management and media response periods
• Daily: Strategic crisis meetings with comprehensive legal and reputational assessment
• Weekly: Post-crisis review and brand recovery strategy implementation

FOLLOW-UP SERVICES:

• 12-month post-recall monitoring ensuring brand recovery and regulatory compliance
• Priority crisis response for any future product safety issues across the 21st Century SafePlay range
• Annual product liability health checks and compliance reviews
• Preferred rates for ongoing regulatory relationship management and brand protection

SILVER - ENHANCED RECALL MANAGEMENT & REGULATORY COMPLIANCE SERVICE (££)

• Recall Coordination: Comprehensive recall management ensuring regulatory compliance and customer safety
• Trading Standards Management: Professional liaison and compliance strategy with regulatory authorities
• Insurance Claim Support: Insurance coverage analysis and claim strategy coordination
• Supply Chain Assessment: Legal audit framework and supplier liability evaluation
• Crisis Communications Guidance: Legal strategy for media response and reputation protection
• Regulatory Compliance Framework: Future product safety protocols and liability prevention measures

ASSUMPTIONS:

• Standard business hours availability with extended support during critical recall phases
• Lisa coordinates internal crisis management with professional legal guidance
• Basic insurance claim management is sufficient for coverage recovery
• Recall achieved through standard regulatory processes without complex litigation

EXCLUSIONS:

• 24/7 crisis management availability
• Comprehensive social media monitoring and response
• Complex supplier litigation management
• Extended brand recovery programs

COMMUNICATION STRUCTURE:

• Business hours: Direct senior lawyer contact for recall and regulatory matters
• Daily: Progress calls during active recall management phase
• Weekly: Written recall progress reports and regulatory compliance updates

BRONZE - ESSENTIAL RECALL GUIDANCE SERVICE (£)

• Recall Framework: Basic recall process guidance ensuring regulatory compliance and customer notification
• Trading Standards Liaison: Essential advice on regulatory requirements and compliance obligations
• Insurance Review: Fundamental analysis of coverage position and basic claim guidance
• Supply Chain Basics: Template audit framework and essential supplier liability assessment
• Compliance Protocol: Basic product safety guidelines and future liability prevention measures

ASSUMPTIONS:

• Single comprehensive consultation covering essential recall management requirements
• Standard office hours availability only
• Lisa manages recall execution and Trading Standards relationship directly with legal guidance
• Template recall processes are sufficient for basic regulatory compliance

EXCLUSIONS:

• Active Trading Standards representation and negotiation
• Insurance claim management and recovery optimization
• Crisis communications and brand protection services
• Ongoing recall implementation support

COMMUNICATION STRUCTURE:

• Email and telephone during business hours only
• 48-hour response commitment for urgent recall queries
• Single follow-up consultation included for clarification

ASSUMPTIVE CLOSING QUESTIONS:

• "Given the 50,000 units in circulation and mounting social media pressure, shall we implement the complete Gold crisis management service immediately?"
• "When should I begin coordinating with Trading Standards to ensure swift regulatory compliance and brand protection?"

• "Shall I commence insurance recovery procedures immediately to protect 21st Century SafePlay's financial position during this crisis?"
• "Should we start implementing supply chain audit protocols today to identify and manage all liability exposures?"

VALUE-BASED QUESTIONS TO ASK:

• "What would losing 21st Century SafePlay's brand reputation cost in future sales and market position?"
• "How much would Trading Standards penalties and enforcement action cost the business?"
• "What's the potential Christmas trading loss if the recall isn't managed professionally?"
• "If insurance claims aren't optimized, what would the financial exposure cost 21st Century SafePlay?"
• "How much would competitors gain if 21st Century SafePlay's brand became associated with unsafe products?"
• "What would rebuilding consumer trust after poor crisis management cost in marketing and time?"

VALUE CREATED:

• Brand Preservation: Protects 21st Century SafePlay's reputation and market position through professional crisis management and strategic recall coordination
• Regulatory Compliance: Ensures swift Trading Standards compliance, avoiding penalties and enforcement action
• Financial Protection: Maximizes insurance recovery and minimizes recall costs, protecting company cash flow and profitability
• Crisis Resolution: Provides expert crisis management, preventing escalation and long-term reputational damage
• Supply Chain Security: Establishes a comprehensive supplier liability framework protecting against future exposures
• Market Position: Maintains competitive advantage through professional crisis response and brand protection
• Consumer Confidence: Rebuilds customer trust through transparent, professional recall management, demonstrating 21st Century SafePlay's commitment to safety

• Future Protection: Implements robust product safety protocols, preventing future liability issues and regulatory problems
• Christmas Trading: Protects crucial seasonal revenue through strategic legal intervention and brand damage limitation

SCENARIO 50: COMPETITION LAW

Robert McKay, CEO of Packaging GB. Industry-wide price increases are attracting the Competition and Markets Authority attention. Suspicion of cartel activity following trade association meetings and dawn raids are expected. Five major companies are involved, and there is a need to protect the company's position while maintaining its industry leadership role. Potential fines could exceed £10M.

GOLD - COMPLETE COMPETITION LAW DEFENCE & CRISIS MANAGEMENT SERVICE (£££)

• Total CMA Defense Strategy: Comprehensive competition law protection, minimizing investigation impact and potential £10M+ fines
• Dawn Raid Response: Immediate 24/7 crisis team deployment ensuring proper legal protection during regulatory raids
• Industry Leadership Preservation: Strategic advice maintaining Packaging GB position whilst protecting company interests
• Multi-Company Coordination: Expert management of the five-company investigation, ensuring optimal defense coordination without further competition law breaches
• Regulatory Relationship Management: Professional CMA liaison maximizing cooperation benefits whilst protecting company position
• Reputation Protection Program: Crisis communication strategy preserving business relationships and market position
• Compliance Architecture: Complete competition law compliance system preventing future regulatory exposure
• Commercial Strategy Integration: Business advice ensuring continued operations and competitive advantage throughout the investigation

ASSUMPTIONS:

• Full access to all company records, trade association documents, and executive communications
• Authority to coordinate with other companies' legal teams without creating further competition law risks
• Management team availability for immediate crisis response and ongoing investigation cooperation
• CMA follows standard investigation procedures and timelines
• Company records and communications are comprehensive and retrievable for regulatory review

EXCLUSIONS:

• Economic expert witness services and market analysis (coordinated but separately instructed)
• Public relations consultancy beyond legal crisis communication advice
• Individual director personal legal representation if separate interests arise
• Settlement negotiations requiring separate economic and financial advisory services

TECHNICAL DELIVERABLES:

• Comprehensive dawn raid response protocol with immediate deployment capability
• Complete CMA investigation defense strategy, minimizing fine exposure and reputational damage
• Industry coordination framework ensuring optimal multi-company defense without further breaches
• Advanced compliance program preventing future competition law exposure
• Crisis communication strategy protecting business relationships and market position
• Regulatory cooperation strategy maximizing investigation benefits whilst protecting company interests

COMMUNICATION STRUCTURE:

• Immediate: Partner direct access for urgent CMA and crisis decisions (24/7 during investigation phases)
• Daily: Investigation progress briefings and strategic decision coordination during active phases

• Weekly: Comprehensive strategy reviews with risk assessment and business impact analysis
• CMA meetings: Senior KC representation with full preparation and strategic coordination

FOLLOW-UP SERVICES:

• 24-month post-investigation monitoring, ensuring continued compliance and regulatory relationship management
• Annual competition law health checks and compliance system reviews
• Priority access for future competition law matters across Packaging GB operations
• Preferred rates for ongoing compliance advice and regulatory relationship management

SILVER - ENHANCED COMPETITION LAW DEFENCE & COMPLIANCE SERVICE (££)

• CMA Investigation Defense: Comprehensive competition law protection and fine mitigation strategy
• Dawn Raid Preparedness: Crisis response planning and immediate legal protection during regulatory visits
• Industry Coordination: Professional management of multi-company defense coordination
• Regulatory Compliance: Competition law compliance program and ongoing regulatory relationship management
• Business Continuity: Strategic advice for maintaining operations and competitive position throughout the investigation
• Crisis Communication: Legal communication strategy protecting reputation and business relationships

ASSUMPTIONS:

• Standard business hours availability with emergency support during dawn raids and critical investigation phases
• Robert coordinates industry relationships with legal compliance guidance
• Basic compliance program sufficient for ongoing competition law requirements
• Investigation managed through standard regulatory cooperation processes

- 24/7 availability throughout the entire investigation period
- Comprehensive industry leadership preservation strategies
- Advanced crisis communication and reputation management
- Extended post-investigation compliance monitoring

COMMUNICATION STRUCTURE:
- Business hours: Direct competition law specialist contact with emergency dawn raid response
- Bi-weekly: Investigation progress calls and compliance implementation updates
- Monthly: Written investigation reports and regulatory strategy reviews

BRONZE - ESSENTIAL COMPETITION LAW GUIDANCE SERVICE (£)

- Investigation Assessment: Analysis of CMA investigation risks and potential fine exposure
- Dawn Raid Basics: Essential guidance on regulatory visit procedures and legal protection requirements
- Compliance Framework: Fundamental competition law compliance advice and policy templates
- Regulatory Cooperation: Basic advice on CMA cooperation strategies and investigation processes
- Risk Mitigation: Essential guidance on minimizing competition law exposure and fine liability

ASSUMPTIONS:
- Single comprehensive consultation covering essential competition law defense requirements
- Standard office hours availability only
- Robert manages CMA relationships and industry coordination directly with legal guidance
- Template compliance frameworks are sufficient for basic competition law obligations

EXCLUSIONS:
- Dawn raid attendance and crisis response services
- Multi-company coordination and industry relationship management

- Ongoing investigation management and regulatory liaison
- Comprehensive compliance program implementation

COMMUNICATION STRUCTURE:

- Email and telephone during business hours only
- 48-hour response commitment for competition law queries
- Single follow-up consultation included for investigation clarification

ASSUMPTIVE CLOSING QUESTIONS:

- "Given the £10M+ potential fines and imminent dawn raids, shall we implement the complete Gold service to protect both your company and industry position?"
- "When should I deploy our dawn raid response team to ensure your legal position is fully protected during CMA visits?"
- "Shall I begin coordinating with the other companies' legal teams immediately to establish an optimal defense strategy without creating further competition law risks?"
- "Should we start implementing comprehensive compliance measures this week to demonstrate cooperation and minimize potential fines?"

VALUE-BASED QUESTIONS TO ASK:

- "What would £10M+ in competition law fines cost the company in terms of profitability and future investment capability?"
- "How much would losing your industry leadership position cost in terms of business influence and competitive advantage?"
- "What's the reputational damage cost if customers and suppliers lose confidence due to cartel allegations?"
- "If dawn raids are handled poorly, what would the increased investigation intensity and fine exposure cost?"
- "How much would losing key business relationships cost if the company is seen as non-compliant with competition law?"
- "What would competitors gain if the Packaging GB were weakened through regulatory action?"

VALUE CREATED:

- Fine Mitigation: Protects company from potentially devastating £10M+ competition law fines through expert legal defense

- Crisis Management: Ensures professional dawn raid response, protecting legal position and minimizing investigation impact
- Industry Leadership: Preserves valuable Packaging GB position whilst protecting company commercial interests
- Business Continuity: Maintains operational effectiveness and competitive advantage throughout regulatory investigation
- Reputation Protection: Safeguards business relationships and market position during competition law investigation
- Regulatory Relationship: Establishes professional CMA relationship, maximizing cooperation benefits whilst protecting the company's position
- Compliance Excellence: Creates a robust competition law compliance system, preventing future regulatory exposure and potential fines
- Commercial Strategy: Integrates legal defense with business strategy, ensuring continued market success and competitive advantage
- Risk Mitigation: Prevents company-ending regulatory action whilst maintaining industry influence and commercial relationships

PART 3 – WORDS FROM THE WISE

A heartfelt salute to the brilliant minds who've shared their wisdom here.

To every generous contributor in this section – practitioners who've been in the trenches, strategists who've mapped the territory, data wizards who've crunched the numbers, marketers who've crafted the conversations, and reformers who've challenged the status quo – thank you. Your insights don't just support this book's central premise; they prove it in living color. Clients don't buy hours, they buy outcomes, confidence, and progress. You've walked the walk, and now you're sharing the map with everyone brave enough to follow.

What awaits you in these pages is pure gold dust.

You'll hear from voices spanning continents and specialties, each offering battle-tested experience about the journey from selling time to creating options that marry price with value. Their counsel runs the full spectrum: pragmatic wisdom (run pilots, build pricing councils, divorce pricing from profitability), cultural insights (build trust, master better conversations, empower your teams), and technological clarity (use AI as your thinking partner, not your crutch). These contributions aren't just generous – they're transformational.

Watch for the patterns that emerge like a perfectly choreographed penguin parade.

You'll read stories of procurement departments still demanding hourly rates – and learn exactly how to hold firm on outcomes instead. You'll encounter stark warnings about disguising fixed fees as "hours x rates in fancy dress," plus compelling arguments for keeping time data for internal insights, while never making it the foundation of client conversations. You'll see why forward-thinking firms are pairing value-based pricing with service guarantees and crystal-clear scoping. You'll learn how others are building pricing buddies and councils to boost confidence, and discover how AI can elevate your value conversations rather than mechanically spitting out numbers. Different paths, same destination.

Here's your roadmap for maximum impact:

Read with a pencil in hand and fire in your belly! After each contribution, challenge yourself with five game-changing questions: *What would this mean for our clients? What option could we launch next week? What risk could we eliminate or transfer? What data would give us unshakeable conviction? What language should we revolutionize in our proposals?* Then – and this is crucial – pick ONE idea and test it within a fortnight: craft a three-option proposal instead of a single price; write a crisp scope with assumptions and exclusions; make a service promise you'll stake your reputation on; hold a pricing huddle before your next major quote; or simply grab coffee with a client to understand "what success looks like" in their own words. Small experiments, repeated consistently, become transformational habits.

Finally, a personal invitation that could change everything.

Treat these contributions as intimate conversations with seasoned guides who've already navigated the terrain you're exploring. Steal their language shamelessly. Stress-test their ideas against your unique reality. Keep what fits, adapt everything else, and – most importantly – weave the wisdom you absorb from these brilliant minds into the very fabric of your business. If this section helps you design even one clearer option, conduct one more compelling value conversation, or feel one degree braver about ditching the tyranny of time, then it has fulfilled its destiny.

The future of legal pricing is being written by pioneers exactly like these. Now it's your turn to add your chapter. On we waddle!

John Chisholm
John Chisholm Consulting
Melbourne, Australia

An Australian Perspective

At the risk of upsetting *Oldlaw* (those still clinging to the people x time x hourly rate formula), the Australian legal profession has long been at the forefront of innovation. In recent years, that has included a growing interest in new business and pricing models. While we're still some way from a full-scale shift, the momentum toward outcome and value-based models is unmistakable, particularly in small to mid-sized firms.

Much of this change is being accelerated by AI. Even before the current explosion of AI tools, the logic was clear: why would firms invest in legal tech designed to save time when their entire business model relies on selling it? AI has now made that tension impossible to ignore. For firms still wedded to billing by the unit, the question isn't *if* AI will disrupt them, but *when*. In reality, firms will soon have no choice. Market, peer, and client pressure, coupled with the relentless advancement of AI, will force adoption. It's adopt or die.

Some firms are responding with financial gymnastics: trying to retrofit AI into their hourly billing model while extending fixed-fee offerings only in commoditized areas. But measuring success in six-minute units is increasingly unsustainable. By contrast, a small but growing vanguard of courageous firms are showing the way. These lawyers have moved beyond billing by time, embracing value-based pricing and subscription models. They've seen, first-hand, how sustainable the results can be both financially and culturally.

For firms beginning this journey, I advocate a "First Steps" approach:

- **Educate deeply.** Read widely and learn from the trailblazers.

- **Communicate, communicate, communicate.** A value-based model requires buy-in from the whole firm; lead with strength.

- **Start small.** Look for low hanging fruit. Expand fixed prices to include options, or turn retainers into subscriptions.

- **Run a pilot program.** Try value pricing on for size in a selected area of your practice.

- **Don't price alone.** Price collaboratively using pricing buddies or councils. Build team pricing skills and confidence.

- **Get better at "no".** Not every client is right for your firm.

- **Learn through mistakes.** Pricing missteps are inevitable, but invaluable.

- **Consider a service guarantee.** Inviting clients to hold you to your agreed standards of quality is both powerful and differentiating.

AI is the catalyst, but the bigger story is cultural. Value-based firms understand that clients don't buy hours, they buy outcomes, certainty, and trust. Those who recognize this and act decisively will not only survive the disruption ahead but thrive because of it.

Thomas L. Bowden,
Timeless Counsel, PLC
Virginia USA

I've tried most AI-assisted legal drafting and contract review programs. They're promising, but the signal-to-noise ratio is still high. Submit a contract for review and you'll usually get one or two meaningful insights along with a slew of others you have to wade through and discard. I really don't need a $300-a-month platform to tell me that 7% interest is more favorable to my client than 8%.

I've cancelled all those subscriptions for now, preferring direct give-and-take with the chatbot rather than working through a structured interface. I find it easier to zero in on issues where I most want support than to drop a contract into a pretty, one-size-fits-all interface. This will probably change in time, but for now I like the flexibility of direct conversation.

What's Coming Next

As for the future, I have no doubt there will soon be multiple subscription platforms promising to do value-based pricing for you. It's easy to imagine firms feeding their historical billing information to train an LLM. The risk is that if your previous pricing was all hourly-based, you're just perpetuating a non-optimal strategy. Ideally, you'd start with only value-based pricing examples in the database.

But while it may seem you'd need huge volumes of data, it's evident that even with no training, chatbot interactions can yield valuable pricing insights. As a statistical analyst friend and former client pointed out, you really don't need that much data to start extrapolating. He's quite successful, so I'm pretty sure he knows what he's talking about.

So, if I don't do it myself, someone will create a platform promising seamless, friction-free value-based pricing. Be skeptical. Don't let anyone tell you that value-based pricing is easy or that someone else – let alone an AI – can just do it for you. AI's value in pricing won't be mechanically grinding out price quotes, but serving as an informed expert sounding board.

The Real Transformation

A few things are obvious. First, AI is here to stay and will become integral to the pricing process. Just as attorneys today cannot imagine practicing without word processors, email, and online research, future pricing will be AI-supported, if not AI-dominated. AI's ability to assimilate vast information and synthesize meaningful answers with justification is miraculous.

And that's what pricing is about – getting as much information into the price as possible.

No simple formula, database, or rule of thumb can solve the problem of getting the right price for each client. That's the essence of profit maximization. Traditional supply and demand analysis assumes you must pick one price for a service – hourly rates being one example. But that leaves money on the table from customers willing to pay more while excluding those who won't pay your standard rate.

There's no reason to assume there must be only one price, whether hourly or flat fee. Each customer is unique. If we can charge each the maximum they're willing to pay, we maximize the value of our efforts. And there's nothing wrong with that.

Second point, equally obvious: firms that aggressively adopt AI for value-based pricing will transition faster than those that don't. Hourly-billing firms remain stuck with their security blanket of time-tracking systems, hemmed in by the thinking those systems promote and reinforce. That's still the biggest obstacle to implementing value-based pricing in law firms.

But if a firm decides to transition to value-based pricing, AI can catalyze the process by removing fear, uncertainty, and doubt. After all, hourly billing, for all its faults, is at least predictable. An attorney who has spent decades incorporating their billable rate into their psyche can be forgiven for recoiling when faced with pricing a new matter – looking into that dark abyss without so much as a candle to show the way to an actual price.

That's where AI plays a critical role. It's not a laser pointer that pinpoints the perfect price, but it provides enough illumination to move forward with confidence. With each successful pricing engagement, confidence grows, and the firm's experience gets reflected in its own AI interactions – and eventually, perhaps, in its own specialized LLM.

In conclusion, I predict that in the very near future, AI will affect law firms more by its application to the value-pricing problem than by eliminating associates or drafting agreements or pleadings. In fact, the more successful AI is in performing everyday legal tasks, the more its integration into the pricing process will become its dominant contribution.

Matthew Burgess
View Legal
Brisbane, Australia

The seemingly unstoppable role of machine learning and AI in the legal arena has, it would seem, not yet had a material impact on the prevalence of time recording and the billable hour.

Extraordinarily coherent and compelling arguments for a model based on customer outcomes, rather than lawyer inputs, have existed for decades. It is, therefore, perhaps to be expected that the resistance to change would (at least initially) withstand technology that at its core obliterates the entire logic of time billing.

Anecdotally, the main responses to AI from time billing lawyers all seem to fall within the ambit of the John Kenneth Galbraith observation that when "faced with the choice between changing one's mind and proving that there is no need to do so, almost everyone gets busy on the proof."

Some examples View has seen recently:

1. proponents suggesting that, for the immediate future, time recording should go up due to AI as it takes longer to check all the potential 'AI hallucinations'.

2. the ubiquitous annual uplift of hourly rates via the dual strategy of CPI increases and 'bracket jumping' (i.e., promotions).

3. firms offering the price point of free if the work can be done by AI (assumingly to encourage the more complex work to be then sent in for time recording to commence).

For View, we have continued to invest in systems and processes that focus on the value created for the customer. AI, to date, has been simply another enabler. However, its – overwhelmingly positive – impact seems to improve markedly every other month; and, at times, even more rapidly.

For law firms wanting to grow, one challenge we have faced that may only change with talent from outside the industry is the fact that virtually the entire legal industry, for generations, is populated by those who excel with billable hour recording.

By definition, those that do so, therefore, often struggle most in a value-based environment; they're wired solely for time spent, not impact created.

The end of time billing? Not happening yet; however, we might just be on the trajectory summarized by another leading thinker from days gone by, Ernest Hemingway, (in 'The Sun Also Rises'), with the exchange:

"How did you go bankrupt?" Bill asked. "Two ways," Mike said. "Gradually and then suddenly."

Katharina Bisset
Attorney. Cohost of Nerds Of Law Podcast
Vienna, Austria

I wanted to come up with a very practical example, but then a real-life story came up.

A client asked for a template contract but with extended rights (compared to what I'd usually give in my T&C). Obviously, I gave them a fixed price. Their procurement department called to ask for my hourly rate so that they can figure out if my price is competitive. I want to share what I had to explain to them:

1. Coming up with an hourly rate I think they might want to hear would not be genuine.

2. If they compare my hourly rate with that of another attorney, it will tell them nothing about the price. I told them they can ask another attorney about their duration and hourly rate and then have an actual sum (still not really comparable because his will be an estimate, but whatever ;)).

3. Telling them how long I will think it will take me wasn't going to help either because:

- I haven't tracked my time for an individual task in... forever.
- A big part was the extended rights which has a value on its own.
- I could have my associate do it, who would take much longer.
- What I didn't add: we have so many templates, it would be crazy to count time.

4. Comparing similar contracts would not work because of the extended rights but, even more, value pricing takes things like risk, company size, urgency, etc. into account, so their case was not comparable.

5. That – plainly and simply – I was not going to do it because I don't have an hourly rate and I haven't for years and wouldn't fake a number.

Dan Hodges,
Head of Account Management at Conscious Solutions UK

In the legal sector, value-based pricing (VBP) has been talked about for years. But in 2025, it's clear that the firms moving fastest toward VBP are the ones strengthening client relationships, improving profitability, and future-proofing their businesses. The transition isn't just about changing what clients see on an invoice, it's a cultural shift inside firms, one that requires vision, empowerment, and consistency.

How Client Expectations Have Changed Since 2022

Over the past three years, client expectations have evolved dramatically. We've seen increased transparency and a decrease in tolerance for "mystery bills". Corporate legal departments and private clients alike want clarity before a matter begins.

Technology is raising the bar. With AI-driven tools in play, clients assume that efficiency should translate into either lower cost or greater value. The perception is: if software is doing the heavy lifting, why should they pay the same hourly rate?

Client journeys must be digital-first. COVID exposed how outdated manual onboarding processes were. Yet many firms still underinvest in client experience. A slick digital intake, clear pricing agreements, and touchpoints that reinforce value are now expected, not optional.

Embedding VBP: An Internal Cultural Shift

Too often, firms treat pricing as a communications exercise. In reality, implementing VBP is an internal cultural project first. Teams need to understand what value means, how to express it, and how it connects to firmwide values.

This requires empowerment in pricing decisions. Staff should feel confident quoting smaller matters, while leadership reviews major projects. This balance fosters accountability and accelerates response times.

In addition, celebrating short-term wins is important. Case studies, success stories, and examples of re-framed quotes help teams, and clients, see VBP in action. Marketing teams can play a powerful role here, turning wins into learning moments.

Leveraging AI as a Pricing Advantage

Forward-looking firms are recognizing that AI isn't just about cutting costs, it's a chance to increase the value narrative.

Just as marketing audits that once took days can now be completed in hours, law firms can use AI to streamline research, drafting, and admin. The price point may remain the same, but clients receive more in terms of speed, personalization, and communication.

In addition, AI allows for more touchpoints and less lawyer time. AI allows firms to create more client updates, personalized documents, and proactive outreach without adding to the lawyer's workload. This strengthens perceived value and reinforces the logic of VBP.

It's important to use everyone in your firm in the embedding process of VBP. Instead of "AI makes it cheaper," the message becomes: "AI lets us spend more time on high-value strategic advice, while automating the admin." That repositioning is critical to counter the client perception that technology should automatically mean lower fees.

Emerging Risks and How to Manage Them

As mentioned, some clients assume AI means less lawyer effort, and therefore less justification for fees, but firms must counter this by articulating how AI enhances outcomes.

Another risk we've seen in law firms is implementing VBP without clear processes; AI efficiencies may lead to inconsistent fee quotes across teams. Standardized templates, decision frameworks, and leadership oversight help avoid this.

But one of the biggest risks with law firms is cultural inertia, which is the most significant barrier. Training, vision, and role modelling from leadership remain essential to embedding new ways of working. That's why it's essential first to get the internal messaging right before moving to external messaging.

Looking Ahead: Opportunities and Challenges

Over the next two to three years, the most pressing challenges and opportunities around pricing will be:

- Deepening client conversations. Lawyers must learn to ask better questions about client sensitivity to price, appetite for investment, and definition of value. Observing how clients frame their own spend helps tailor the narrative.

- Balancing efficiency and value. AI and automation will keep reducing the time tasks take. The firms who thrive will be those who translate those efficiency gains into stronger value stories, not discounts.

- Making pricing a strategic tool. Rather than leaving pricing decisions to chance, firms will increasingly use pricing directors, data tools, and project management insights to shape profitability.

In 2025, value-based pricing is no longer just an experiment for progressive firms, it is the expected direction of travel for the entire legal sector. Clients want clarity, fairness, and alignment with outcomes. Law firms that embed VBP into their culture, empower teams to make pricing decisions, leverage AI for added value, and communicate that story clearly will not only meet expectations but also stand out in an increasingly competitive market.

Bernard Savage
Director, Size 10½ Boots
UK

Stop Selling Time: Start Drinking Coffee

If you want clients to see the value in what you do, stop selling hours and start building relationships. At *Tenandahalf*, we've seen it time and again: when lawyers invest time up front to sit with clients, ask good questions, and really understand what outcomes matter most, the pricing conversation changes completely.

It's no longer about "how long will this take?" but "what's it worth to get this solved, in the way only you can deliver?" That shift means clients are far happier to pay a fair price. They're not buying units of time; they're buying your judgement, your experience, and the confidence that you'll deliver the result.

Of course, this requires effort. You can't shortcut building trust. You need to have the coffee, learn about their business, and show that you understand the pressures they're under. But the payoff is enormous: stronger connections, stickier relationships, and pricing that reflects real value rather than a race to the bottom.

AI has made this even more apparent. If technology can automate routine tasks, billing by the hour makes no sense. But if you've invested in a genuine relationship, clients won't care how long it takes. They'll care that you get them the outcome they want – and that's something they'll happily pay for.

Graham Moore
Managing Director, Katchr
UK

For many firms exploring value-based pricing, there is a temptation to view time recording as redundant. If the client is paying for outcomes rather than hours, why bother measuring time? Yet this thinking misses an important distinction between *pricing* and *profitability*. Time recording may be less relevant as the basis for the client conversation, but it remains vital as a tool for the firm to understand cost, efficiency, and ultimately margin. Value-based pricing does not remove the need to know what it costs you to deliver the work.

The challenge is that most firms still approach pricing with the billable hour as their default lens. They may label a fixed fee as "value based" but in practice it is often just a calculated estimate of hours times rates. True value-based pricing requires shifting the conversation to the client's perception of value – speed, certainty, expertise, risk transfer – rather than the mechanics of how the firm expends effort. That shift requires confidence: confidence in the quality of data about past performance, and confidence that margins will remain healthy even when fees are decoupled from hours worked.

This is where time recording retains its place. Capturing time does not mean you must charge by the hour. It simply provides the raw information for profitability analysis: which matters, clients, and practice areas deliver the best return relative to the resources invested. Without that data, firms are left guessing whether their value-based pricing strategy is sustainable. The firms that succeed at this are those who combine client-centric pricing discussions with rigorous internal analytics – turning time data into insights rather than invoices.

The opportunity for firms is to reframe time recording not as a straitjacket on innovation, but as one of the inputs into smarter decision-making. By separating the disciplines of pricing and profitability, firms can move beyond the billable hour while still maintaining the financial visibility they need to scale and compete. Those that master this balance will be the ones to demonstrate that value-based pricing is not just a marketing badge, but a sustainable and profitable business model.

Heather Suttie
Legal Market Strategy and Management Consultancy
Toronto, Canada

The internet changed the world. AI is flattening it. Therefore, it's fair to expect disintegration of the traditional law firm pyramid structure as a result of a three-pronged juggernaut: AI, pricing, and transience of the legal sector's workforce.

In my experience, pricing is entirely within one's control. For example, value-based pricing (VBP) is the cost placed on a tightly scoped deliverable and its outcome, both of which are predicated on how this work will affect a client's business now and in the future.

Enabling VBP means fully understanding the client's business objectives and strategies from their point of view, not how your role and work impact it.

Therefore, the VBP process pertains to pricing the work according to the needs of each specific client. It's not about asking a client what they want to pay. Neither is VBP about billing or how it converts to billing by time. There's no correlation between the two, much as lawyers may try to make the math work.

To enable VBP, lawyers and law firms must have the intestinal fortitude to do only work that they do better and with a distinctive difference than any other in the market – and be able to prove it.

This is when – regardless of other business conditions – a one of one distinction enables a go-to legal market position that enables trust, builds brand, and results in referral business

Will Whawell
T3PS Legal Dynamics
UK

AI hasn't become the game changer that it has the potential to be and save for the firms who can afford to invest in their own models and/or the monthly charge that many models demand, there is a very disjointed view of what it can do. This is, in my view, because of the inability for many whose sole focus is litigation then the billable hour is still seen to be the measure.

The ongoing view that only a fee earner brings value, that non-lawyers don't understand law firm business models, and I believe that business still isn't taught at law school and the frankly dire way in which after 12 years budgets are still seen as some form of evil Excel spreadsheet, the ability that AI can provide value to outcomes is still not seen as value to many lawyers.

In my own area of work, which has become far more strategic assessment and analysis focused, and far less costs focused, what is still very visible is a lack of vision for a way to improve how work is done and a lingering obsession that the only way to measure value is by units billed, regardless of outcome.

The rise, however, of and extension to Fixed Recoverable Costs and more budgeting will only lead to a need for more VBP and the outcomes that customers need and demand.

Leaving aside the competition and wider consumer litigation, the real change in pricing will be driven by the demand of business customers, be they individual business and in-house legal teams.

They demand outcomes that aren't always driven by price. They certainly don't like to be taken for mugs by lawyers. In my work as an ISO consultant, I do regularly come into contact with organizations with in-house legal teams and a large legal spend and a feature of those chats is always, as many know I work as a LPM, how can we reduce our legal spend, why is the fee so high for a simple outcome, why can't an estimate be kept to.

Often, lawyers are seen as too expensive, too inflexible and not value, and cannot see any other way of charging than by reference to what is billed per hour.

Moving ahead, firms all need to have both a pricing champion and an AI champion who can analyze legal spend and tech use and move the firm forward with AI-driven outcomes, where the skill and knowledge of the lawyer is what is paid for, based on an agreed outcome.

Firms need to adapt models that are fit for purpose for the work they do, but we need to stress this is not a race to the bottom.

Any form of pricing change shouldn't be let's look on the web, see what our nearest rival is charging, and lower the price.

Rather, law firms need to be able to look at a range of pricing models that fit their work type and allow a profit to be made.

Embracing and using all forms of pricing needs to be considered.

Providing some services free, may well be the way to go. For discovery, this makes sense; allow the machine to do the work and the lawyer's brain to provide the outcome. Why have 30 paralegals shift through thousands of e-mails when R2D2 and C3PO can do it for you.

Lawyers do need to look at other trades and professions. Accountants provide a fixed fee for much of their work; ISO auditors do so too, as do many consultants. In my analysis work (audits), I must provide the fee well in advance of doing the work and there is no way to suddenly say I have made a mistake. Plumbers will charge a fee for coming out at 3am to fix the burst pipe and they know what that will be. So why can't a law firm have a matrix ready, based on the needed outcome and the complexity and urgency? It can be done.

AI will change how tasks are undertaken, but customers will still pay for outcomes. AI costs will not necessarily come down in price. While there may well be a period of enticement, the investment and ongoing need to feed the LLMs with more data will mean that the costs of these will need to be built into the overhead costs or billed to the client within the overall price.

Perhaps VBP is the wrong term. Should it be Outcome Focused Pricing, Results Based Pricing?

In my own work, again, I see the frailty of legal software systems that are years behind what many CRM/CMS systems and tools such as 365 and Workspace can do. There is an unwillingness to pay for team members to be upskilled and invest in hardware and software that will aid productivity and allow the benefits of AI to be felt.

This is very much driven by the 'but why train we cannot bill' approach and the lack of any vision of how to build into overhead costs, and indeed client billing, the investment that hardware/software and training will bring.

As AI becomes more common, though not necessarily cheaper, no matter how hard some firms try to entice, the firms who invest in this along with those who change the approach to pricing will move ahead of firms who don't embrace change.

Alistair Marshall
Professional Services BD
Sydney, Australia

Example 1: The Psychology of Premium Pricing

A boutique firm launched by two former Clayton Utz partners provides a masterclass in pricing psychology. At their previous firm, they'd been charging clients around $800 per hour with confidence and success. Yet when striking out on their own, fear crept in – they dropped their rates to just $550 per hour, convinced they needed to be "more affordable" to attract clients.

I explained the brutal reality: existing clients who'd happily paid $800 for their expertise would now be scratching their heads, wondering either whether they'd been ripped off previously, or whether these lawyers had somehow lost their mojo. Premium clients often equate low prices with low quality – it's counterintuitive but true.

My advice? Become competitive, not cheap. They repositioned at $700 per hour—a meaningful but not dramatic reduction from their previous rate. The result? They're now "smashing it out of the park" and hiring multiple new staff members to cope with surging demand. Sometimes the bravest pricing decision is charging what you're actually worth.

Example 2: AI Reshapes the Legal Landscape

Here's a glimpse into the future, courtesy of a friend who's a major legal services buyer for a UK government agency. Last year, his department spent millions with an international firm, deploying a team of up to 40 lawyers on their contract.

This year's re-pitch told a dramatically different story. The same firm returned with an AI-enhanced approach using just 12 lawyers and offered a 20% discount on the previous year's fees. They're delivering the same quality outcomes with radical efficiency improvements, passing genuine savings to the client while protecting their own margins.

This is our future arriving at breakneck speed. Firms that embrace AI as a force multiplier will thrive. Those clinging to the "more hours = more profit" model will find themselves pricing their way out of the market. The smart money is on value creation through technology, not time multiplication through inefficiency.

The lesson from both examples? Whether you're pricing premium expertise or leveraging cutting-edge technology, value-based pricing puts you in control of your destiny rather than at the mercy of hourly rate wars.

Dr Jaqui Rigby
Rigby Pollitt and Associates
UK

Confidence and Fear in Pricing

One of the key factors holding back business growth in any service sector is confidence in pricing. I see it time and again when working with SMEs on their growth plans. A fear of 'overcharging'. A misguided comfort that if you are 'one of the cheapest', you will get business. A lack of recognition of the value they bring to their clients.

For business leaders to define their value proposition, start with two questions…

1. 'What happens to your customer's business when you deliver your service? What are the tangible benefits in financial and non-financial terms?'

2. 'What happens to your customer's business if they *don't* employ your services? What are the tangible *negative* impacts in financial and non-financial terms?'

Working with business leaders, we talk about revenue, profit, customer retention. We talk cost avoidance and time saving. We talk about reputational damage and adherence to regulations.

Now, business leaders can switch the conversation from one about price, to one about the VALUE the business brings. In hard facts.

Two examples:

'White': A white labelled outsourced sales business priced on the basis of the cost of the equivalent sales person in-house. However, 'White' sales were consistently 30% above that achieved by the internal sales person. 'White' adjusted their price and sales conversation. At the first time of presenting the value proposition, they won a contract extension at the higher price.

'Green': A specialist in asset management sells services based on timesheets. 'Green' were being pushed down on price in every pitch. We defined the value to their clients. The value in preventing equipment/plant downtime and in avoiding regulatory issues and fines. 'Green' company now focus on promoting value and tangible outcomes for their clients. The result is a reduction in margin erosion on contract price.

Chantal McNaught
Consultant, Fully Automated Luxury Lawyering
Auckland, New Zealand

In this part of the world, as I suspect in others, there has been a sharp uptick in billing disputes between clients and lawyers. The threat and fear of facing the accusation of overcharging has been a strong motivator for firms to implement value-based pricing models. Just as it has been said of technology by the sci-fi novelist William Gibson, "the [value-based billing] future is here, it just isn't evenly distributed." Two Australian firms recently shared with me that since they completely implemented value-based pricing into their firms' processes, they have not had a single billing complaint. One of these firms was a traditional firm that had to transition from a time-based model, whereas the other had value-based pricing from the beginning.

Successful implementation requires more than the decision to change. Effective change management is key. Unfortunately, firm leadership which fails to adequately resource the change process risk their credibility with their staff. Staff that are not brought along on the journey and are not convinced of the benefits of value-based pricing will not be helpful in the implementation process. These kinds of staff are also quick to point and shout, "See! I knew it wouldn't work all along" when it "inevitably" fails due to a poor change management process. I have seen this in at least three firms here in New Zealand, who have admitted to me that they "experimented with" value-based pricing. But it became obvious what the issue was after a short conversation. Leadership did not come with a plan for the change and did not have the wherewithal to see it through the natural friction.

Because change management is the hardest piece of a value-based pricing transformation in firms, most firms in both Australia and New Zealand operating with those pricing strategies began with them from the beginning. Far fewer established and traditional Australian and New Zealand firms have successfully implemented value-based pricing strategies, or they are sporadic and are limited to a handful of practice areas (property and wills, for example). What this indicates is that the transition to value-based pricing is generational. Firm leaders who do not transition to value-based pricing doom their firms to repeat the sins of the past with time-based billing models, paying the price through additional administrative overheads to deal with the complexity of narrating time-based bills and the inevitable billing dispute. More recently established firm leaders have greater drawings and spend less time in the office. I suspect their billing-related stress would be lower, too.

Law firms operating with value-based pricing strategies are not living in a world full of sunshine and rainbows, however. One limitation observed in several of these is that firm leaders have done away with timesheets altogether. I think that's a mistake. Especially with the continued advancement of artificial intelligence technologies, timesheets are an easy measurement of other transformation success. Time recordings are also still useful in jurisdictions where court scales require time to enforce costs. This is possibly the biggest challenge newer firms have, that without the incentivized pressure to record time, these firms are lacking the consistent data to be informed of the success of other initiatives. I predict this will ease a bit as more automated timekeeping options become affordable on the market. This way, staff can have their time captured when delivering legal services so that leadership has the data to assess whether a process or technological change has been successfully implemented.

Tim Williams
Founding Partner, Ignition Consulting Group, Inc.
USA & UK

How AI is Flattening the Professional Services Business Model

A future in which law firms, advertising agencies, and accountancy practices consist of a founder and zero employees isn't a theoretical construct; it's already here.

No doubt a "law firm of one" is an extreme example of an AI-optimized professional services firm, but it's a more practical business model than most of us would have ever imagined.

Already, business schools are helping entrepreneurs build zero-employee models for start-up businesses. Karim Lakhani of Harvard Business School offers a leadership course for executives in which they use generative AI to build a food company in 90 minutes, using AI tools to execute consumer research, create recipes, locate suppliers and design packaging for the brand. The Economist, which reported this story, calls this the rise of the "solopreneur" – an entrepreneurial business executive that relies not on human capital, but rather intellectual capital supplied by machines.

Value chains are being reconfigured

Thanks to new emerging technologies, we are witnessing a massively disruptive reconfiguration of value chains. A single individual can now employ armies of specialist resources to deliver the kind of value previously available only from large integrated companies.

Legacy business models typically require a fairly large infrastructure in order to fulfil the needs of customers seeking a "one-stop" solution to business problems. To provide integrated, multi-channel marketing campaigns, advertising agencies have built business models consisting of many different departments and disciplines. These are labor-intensive structures requiring constant collaboration and coordination.

But now, technology platforms are providing these same solutions at a fraction of the cost in a fraction of the time, with a fraction of the people. This model can work just as well for high-touch businesses as high-tech. A restaurant can now consist of just a brand, recipes, and a menu. As Harvard Business School professor Antonio Moreno observes, everything else in this restaurant can be outsourced to a network of "cloud kitchens," which manage everything from procurement and staffing to cooking and coordinating with food delivery platforms. We can now imagine not only a restaurant that relies upon this kind of model (powered by Kitopi), but also a shipping business (ShipBob), and yes, even an advertising agency (Product).

"Solopreneurs" are leveraging hyperspecialized providers

The new breed of "solopreneurs" are essentially orchestrators who bring together end-to-end solutions delivered by a network of hyperspecialized, technology-enabled platforms and providers.

And now with the help of agentic AI, these new businesses will benefit from the ability of autonomous agent systems to learn, adapt, and make decisions independently. As Moreno notes, AI agents can be embedded into workflows so they can manage and improve processes without human involvement. They can integrate data from a variety of sources and respond dynamically to changes, automatically adjusting production schedules, resource levels, and other critical logistics. Moreno points to numerous companies — from FedEx to Amazon — who are already working this way.

Organizational structures are being reimagined

The professional services business is no exception. In England, the Solicitors Regulation Authority has already authorized the first law firm providing a legal service through large language model artificial intelligence – Garfield Law. As at June 2025, over 630 law firm case management providers have built AI into their platforms to provide integrated solutions to clients faster, cheaper, and arguably better. End-to-end AI-powered platforms like Multiply are helping advertising agencies do the same.

To describe the resulting business model as a "flattened" structure is a gross understatement. It is, in fact, a complete reimagining of organizational structure, requiring fewer people doing very different jobs. Job descriptions are being thoroughly redescribed and rewritten, carrying a new set of job titles that didn't exist just a few short months ago. For example, advertising agencies now require positions like:

AI Content Orchestrators

- Manages AI content generation tools
- Ensures brand consistency across AI-generated content

- Trains teams on prompt engineering
- Quality control for AI outputs

AI Project Orchestrators

- Replaces traditional project managers
- Designs automated workflow systems
- Identifies AI optimization opportunities
- Manages human-AI collaboration workflows

Prompt Engineering Specialists

- Develops and maintains prompt libraries
- Trains creative teams on AI tools
- Optimizes AI outputs for specific brand voices

AI Ethics & Compliance Officer

- Ensures responsible AI use
- Manages copyright and attribution issues
- Develops AI usage policies

Hybrid Creators

- Traditional creative skills plus AI proficiency
- Can work across copy, design, and content
- Focus on ideation and AI output refinement

The professional services firm of the future is an AI-powered platform that draws upon a large army of specialist cloud-based platforms and technologies managed by a much smaller army of human orchestrators. And, based on hundreds of emerging use cases, it appears that the future is now. And guess what? The professional services firms of the future are certainly not charging by time!

EPILOGUE

So, now you have seen a glimpse of the future. Is charging by the hour still viable? You have seen that choices can be created and which client wouldn't want choice? Where to go from here?

1. If you want to implement VBP across an organization, check out *Ditch The Billable Hour!* which covers all the detail required to plan and start your journey.

2. Check out "Declan AI" (the world's first VBP-powered pricing assistant) and the comprehensive Value Voyage™ online training platform, which are both coming onstream now. Details at www.bigyellowpenguin.co.uk

3. Do something... please!

WHAT IF IT WORKS?

That's the question that should keep you awake at night – not "What if it fails?"

- What if that next client conversation goes brilliantly when you present three options, instead of one take-it-or-leave-it quote?

- What if they choose the Gold service and thank you for giving them the choice?

- What if your profit margins improve by 30% whilst your clients become happier?

- What if you stop apologizing for your fees and start confidently explaining your value?

- What if you finally escape the race to the bottom that's been crushing your spirit and your bank balance?

- What if those sleepless nights, worrying about cash flow, become a distant memory?

- What if your team actually enjoys talking to clients about pricing because they're offering solutions not just bills?

- What if the worst-case scenario isn't failure at all, but staying exactly where you are right now?

The truth is, most lawyers never find out because they never try. They spend years wondering "What if?" whilst their competitors quietly implement VBP and steal their market share.

Here's the thing: you don't need to transform your entire practice overnight. Start with one client, one matter, one conversation. Test it. Learn from it. Adjust it.

Because the most dangerous four words in business aren't "What if it fails?" – they're "What if it works… and I missed it?"

Stop wondering. Start testing.

What if it works?

Other Books from the Publisher

DITCH THE
BILLABLE
HOUR!

Implementing Value-Based
Pricing in a Law Firm

Shaun Jardine

Ditch The Billable Hour! Implementing Value-Based Pricing in a Law Firm

Is the billable hour on its way out? Does *any* client like paying for legal services by the hour?

With generative artificial intelligence soon to create tidal waves in the legal industry – helping lawyers to create legal documents in mere seconds – the time-honoured billable hour is under threat more than ever. But what is the alternative?

In *Ditch The Billable Hour!*, Shaun Jardine explains how lawyers should move away from *time* as the driving element of pricing, and focus on the results that clients want to achieve. In doing so, he shows why legal firms need to adopt Value-Based Pricing (VBP), and how to do so.

Ditch The Billable Hour! is the extensive and practical new book, from a former law firm CEO, that is filled with real-world expertise, advice, and perspectives, and which digs deep into all aspects of VBP for the legal industry.

In the book, you will discover

> What clients truly value, and how to have conversations to establish the value that lawyers create.

> How to price and capture a share of that value, and how to create pricing options which give clients choice.

> How to lead and implement the change to make Value-Based Pricing a reality.

> Includes more than 20 interviews with lawyers and other professionals who have views on VBP.

> Includes additional learning resources, hints, tips, and practical exercises, plus a RACI checklist.

From the author of
THE PERFECT LEGAL BUSINESS
and *THE PERFECT PARTNER*

THE PERFECT
LAWYER

Simon McCrum

The Perfect Lawyer

What makes a perfect lawyer? To start answering this question, we need to use a classic lawyer approach - it depends!

In *The Perfect Lawyer*, Simon deep dives into what makes a perfect lawyer in a perfect legal business. It is someone who does a great job from the client's perspective but also does a great job from their law firm's – and they are very different things. When combined effectively, such lawyers not only change their clients' lives, but also the destiny of the legal business they work in, and the lives of themselves and their colleagues.

Whether you are part of a large legal firm or a small one, the themes explored in *The Perfect Lawyer* examine the symbiosis between a law firm's team members and the organisation, as they both evolve into higher-earning and more effective entities.

Note: *The Perfect Lawyer* is the sister book to *The Perfect Legal Business* in that it looks at many of the same themes, but from the viewpoint of the individual lawyer. As such, it contains material that crosses both titles. If you already have a copy of *The Perfect Legal Business*, you won't need *The Perfect Lawyer*.

The Perfect Partner

From the author of
THE PERFECT LAWYER
and THE PERFECT LEGAL BUSINESS

THE PERFECT PARTNER

Simon McCrum

If you've made it to Partner, or you're determined to become one, what are the key qualities and strengths required of a Partner in a modern-day law firm?

In *The Perfect Partner*, Simon examines what makes a Perfect Partner from the viewpoint of numerous key stakeholders, including clients, colleagues, and the business itself. Detailing the characteristics and behaviours that a Partner needs, the book digs deep into a Partner's commercial contribution to the business, their relationships with staff and other Partners, business development, accountability, compliance, and much more. And all under the central umbrella of making a profit and growing a business.

Working through the layers of value (or destruction) that a Partner can bring, Simon arrives at a surprising conclusion. Measurable things count, but other more human things *count more*. If that law firm rocket is going to take off, and prove able to shoot for the stars, each Partner – and all the Partners together – need to focus unequivocally on a 'magic ingredient' to make the firm unstoppable.

Have you got what it takes to be a Perfect Partner? And, just as importantly, have your Partners got the right stuff, too?

The Perfect Legal Business

From the author of
THE PERFECT LAWYER and THE PERFECT PARTNER

THE PERFECT
LEGAL
BUSINESS

Simon McCrum

What if a law firm's sustained success isn't about billing more and more hours, but shaping its structure, approach, and attitude differently?

In *The Perfect Legal Business*, Simon unlocks a fresh framework for the modern legal firm, built around a number of key pillars including: intelligent client selection, proactive client care, purposeful senior and middle management, higher pricing for a higher level of service, lawyer inputs (not outputs), and the importance of cash to the business – all brought together into a powerful force by the glue that is leadership.

This book invites you to dig deep into law firm management as a constant and fluid problem-solving enterprise – one driven by lawyers at all levels – that seeks to change the fortunes and destinies of law firms, their owners, their people, and their clients.

Note: *The Perfect Legal Business* is the sister book to *The Perfect Lawyer* in that it looks at many of the same themes, but from the viewpoint of the business. As such, it contains material that crosses both titles. If you already have a copy of *The Perfect Lawyer*, you won't need *The Perfect Legal Business*.

Delegate Now to Supercharge Your Profits

How can law firm owners bill fewer hours but make bigger profits? How can they grow their businesses with reliable team members and take well-earned breaks without worrying their firm will fall apart? The answer is effective and profitable delegation.

Delegation drives profitability more than anything else, yet few fully understand its power. It is self-evident that ten team members billing per hour is more profitable than a law firm owner billing an hour on their own, yet most law firm owners are trapped in heavy billable workloads and unknowingly greatly limit their profits. This is because – for most – at no stage has anyone shown them how to run their law firms effectively!

In *Delegate Now to Supercharge Your Profits*, law firm growth consultant Dan Warburton shows how skilful delegation multiplies profits for law firm owners and frees them up to do the work they enjoy. He then shows you – practically and effectively – how to build a firm that doesn't constantly rely on you as it becomes more profitable than ever.

The Secret Magistrate

Every criminal case starts in a magistrates' court, and most end there. Last year, the 14,000 magistrates of England & Wales dealt with almost 1.4 million cases.

But what exactly does a magistrate do, who are they, and how are they recruited and trained? Are they out-of-touch and unrepresentative, or still fit for purpose with a role to play in today's increasingly sophisticated and complex judicial system?

The Secret Magistrate takes the reader on an eye-opening, behind-the-scenes tour of a year in the life of an inner-city magistrate. Chapters cover a variety of cases, including the disqualified driver who drove away from court, the Sunbed Pervert, and Fifi the Attack Chihuahua.

www.ingramcontent.com/pod-product-compliance
Lightning Source LLC
Chambersburg PA
CBHW041143230326
41599CB00039BA/7152

* 9 7 8 1 9 1 5 8 5 5 4 2 8 *